LIVE OR DIE TRYIN'

Live or Die Tryin'

A True Story

Yahkhahnahn Ammi

PDG

PUBLISHING COMPANY LLC

A VOICE OF NECESSITY
READ, SPEAK AND GROW RICH

First Published by PDG PUBLISHING COMPANY LLC

pdgpublishingcompany.com

Live or Die Tryin'

First Edition

Includes index.

ISBN: 9780983081555 (Print) 9780983081531 (E-book)
9780983081548 (Hardback)

Cover Design by Perrie Daniell Gibson

DEDICATION

This book is dedicated to my mother for her endless love and my dear children; may you always know the truth, and that I will always love you. To victims of sex and human trafficking—may justice find you. To those lost to suicide due to abuse—you are not forgotten. To survivors of assault—keep fighting, you matter. Parents, love your children by listening and supporting them. To those who doubted or supported me, you've shaped me. This is for all of us—a testament to resilience.

EPIGRAPH

"The ultimate measure of a man is not where he stands in moments of convenience and comfort, but where he stands at times of challenge and controversy."

-Dr. Martin Luther King Jr.

Contents

FOREWORD

It is with great pleasure that I introduce *"Live or Die Tryin'"* Book III, by Yahkhahnahn Ammi. In this compelling memoir, Yahkhahnahn takes us on a deeply personal journey through his life, highlighting his passion for social justice, community leadership, literacy advocacy among youth, and raising awareness for mental health.

As a dedicated activist, Yahkhahnahn hosts several podcasts and online radio shows focused on healing from childhood and relationship trauma, as well as the importance of mental health awareness. Through his writing, he shares the importance of seeking professional counselors or therapists to address mental health concerns, encouraging others to prioritize their well-being.

"Live or Die Tryin'" Book III is more than just a memoir; it is a call to action. Yahkhahnahn's words inspire us to confront our own challenges, seek help when needed, and advocate for mental health awareness in our communities. His message of compassion, understanding, and perseverance is a beacon of hope for all who have struggled with mental health issues.

I am confident that this book will resonate with readers from all walks of life. Yahkhahnahn's message is a powerful reminder of the importance of taking care of our mental health and supporting others in their journey to wellness. May his words inspire you to join him in his mission to create a more compassionate and understanding world for all.

This is a pivotal time of change in the world, and life as we know it is being threatened from all sides. We are forced to reassess our values and decide whether to succumb to the darkness or live in the light. We must focus on healing, not just treatment. Yahkhahnahn offers a world of healing and makes wellness the foundation of our lives. Mentally, physically, and socially, we need to heal. His memoir is an offering that should not be ignored.

-Abiodun Oyewole The Last Poets

PREFACE

About the Name

In this book, you'll notice that I refer to myself as "Yahkhahnahn Ammi"—which means *'God is compassionate and merciful'* in Hebrew. This name holds deep spiritual significance, not an alias. This name, bestowed upon me by my spiritual leader at that time, Rahbee Ben Ammi, symbolizes a profound journey of transformation and reclamation of identity. Born as Perrie (Par-ree) Daniell Gibson, I was given what many individuals of African descent recognize as a slave name. At the age of 18, I made a conscious decision to embrace the Hebrew or Judaic way of life, shedding my birth name publicly and fully embodying the spiritual path laid before me. Yet, within the privacy of my family and loved ones, I remained known as and called by my birth name.

The names of others in this book have been changed to protect the identities of both the guilty and the innocent. However, the name I carry now stands as a testament to my rebirth—a symbolic act of defiance against the traumas inflicted upon me by abusers and conspirators. It was a crucial step in my healing—a way to rise from the fire and ashes of my past and recreate myself with purpose and power.

In a community that honored every man of African descent as "King" and every woman as "Queen," I adopted the name Kingya (King Yah), a fusion of my initials Y and A, signifying Yah and

Ammi. (Kingya: *A soul destined to rise, embodying the divine strength and resilience to overcome life's trials and ascend after every fall).*

This name is not merely a title; it is an affirmation of my identity, resilience, and spiritual journey. As you continue reading, you'll come to understand the depth of this transformation and why embracing a new identity was not just a choice, but a vital act of survival and empowerment.

Trigger Warning

This book contains sensitive material relating to:

Trauma

Grief

Rape

Race Relations

Human Rights

Social Justice

Black Nationalism

Characters

The individuals depicted in the story are actual people, though their names and personal information have been excluded. Fictitious information has been inserted for privacy, but this is my truth. As an American revolutionary, my identity as a melanated nationalist has always been more than just a political stance—it is a calling, a mission, rooted in the liberation of oppressed melanated people. My belief in the principles of human rights and Black Nationalism, or as I prefer to call it, Melanated Nationalism, has been the guiding force behind my life's work.

ACKNOWLEDGMENTS

Writing this memoir has been a journey of reflection, healing, and growth, and I could not have completed it without the love, support, and encouragement of many.

First, to my mother, whose unconditional love and strength have been my guiding light. You have shown me what it means to be resilient in the face of adversity, and for that, I am forever grateful. Your belief in me, even when I doubted myself, gave me the courage to share my truth.

To my children, who inspire me daily to be the best version of myself. You are my greatest joys and my deepest motivations. This story is as much for you as it is for me. May it remind you always to seek truth, stand in your own light, and know that you are loved beyond measure.

In loving memory of my late grandmother, Jacqueline E. Mitchell ("Mama Jackie"), whose wisdom, kindness, and love continue to guide me even though she is no longer physically here. "Mama", you were my anchor, and I miss you every day. It has been two years since I lost you, but your spirit lives on in every word of this book. This memoir is a testament to the strength and grace you embodied.

To my late sister, April L. Riley, who was taken from us far too soon at the tender age of 35 by stage four pancreatic cancer. April, you were a beacon of light and love, and not a day goes by that I don't think of you. You didn't get the chance to see the publication of this book, but your strength and courage are woven into its pages. This work is a tribute to your life, your fight, and the love we shared. I miss you more than words can express.

As a youth advocate promoting literacy and education through the Read, Speak, and Grow Rich program, I am deeply grateful to those who inspire and support this mission. **To Amanda S. C. Gorman**, an American poet, activist, and model, thank you for your unwavering commitment to our youth. Your voice and dedication have brought hope and empowerment to the next generation.

To the victims and survivors of sex and human trafficking, this book is a testament to your courage. May your voices be heard and your stories recognized. You are warriors, and I dedicate this work in part to you, in the hope that justice and healing find their way into your lives.

To those who have been lost to suicide as a result of abuse, you are not forgotten. Your pain, though silent now, is not erased. I hold you in my heart, and this book honors the battles you fought in silence.

To survivors of abuse, both mental and physical, who continue to fight daily battles, your strength is extraordinary. You are loved, you matter, and your fight is a testament to the human spirit's resilience.

I also want to acknowledge those who have been falsely accused of sexual assault or rape. The weight of such accusations can be devastating, and your struggle is a reminder that justice and truth must be sought for all. My thoughts are with you as you navigate this difficult path.

To my friends and family, who have stood by me through this process, thank you for your patience, your love, and your unwavering support. Whether you cheered me on or provided a listening ear, I owe you my deepest gratitude.

To those who doubted me or prayed for my failure, your doubts fueled my determination to rise above. You too have played a role in shaping the person I am today, and for that, I thank you.

Finally, to the women and men who have lifted me up, shared their wisdom, and believed in me when it felt like no one else did—this book exists because of you. Your inspiration has given me the strength to turn pain into purpose, and I will carry your influence with me always.

This memoir by spiritual incidence is a tribute to resilience, survival, and the power of the human spirit. To everyone who has walked with me on this journey, whether through support or challenge—this is for all of us.

With love and gratitude,

Yahkhahnahn Ammi

PROLOGUE

An Ode to Ending Parental Alienation

To parents, I call, both gentle and grand,
Our children seek the warmth of your hand.
In love and understanding, let them stand,
Nurtured by heart, in this vast land.
To the women and men in my life's story,
Your doubts and support, both shadow and glory,
Have shaped me, in all my complexity,
Guided by your presence, through life's tapestry.
This verse unfolds as a declaration,
A plea for unity, an end to separation.
For in resilience, we find our liberation,
And celebrate the spirit's dedication.
Parental love, let it not be divided,
For in its fullness, children are guided.
End the alienation, the silent wall,
For together, we rise and stand tall.
Together, we embrace this shared journey,
Inscribed in this ode, a pledge to harmony.
Let no rift rob a child of their grace,
No bitterness clouds their tender face.
In unity, may families heal and grow,
In the light of love, let true bonds show.
So here's to us, in unity and clarity,
Crafted by trials, with sincerity.

INTRODUCTION

This struggle for freedom, equity, dignity, and equality is not just a distant ideal; it is a personal battle, fought every day in the face of systemic oppression and deep-seated racism. From the moment I embraced this cause, I knew the path would be fraught with challenges. But my commitment has never wavered. Each act of resistance, each effort to uplift my community, is driven by an unwavering belief in our right to self-determination. The fight for our freedom is not just a political struggle—it is a fight for our very existence, for our right to live with dignity, free from the chains of oppression.

Being at the forefront of this struggle means carrying the weight of generations of pain and resilience. It means standing firm in the face of adversity, knowing that the liberation of our people is both a personal responsibility and a collective mission. The stakes are high, but so is the reward: a future where melanated people can live freely, without fear, in a society that truly values our contributions and humanity.

In this battle, I have found my purpose—a purpose that transcends the political and touches the very core of who I am. It is a purpose that drives me to continue the fight, to inspire others to rise up, and to never, ever, surrender to the forces that seek to keep us down.

But with this commitment comes a heavy price—one that I've paid through the constant and calculated efforts of those who seek to silence, discredit, and ultimately destroy me. In the words of Bryan Allen, I have faced the "Four D's" head on: Dismiss, Discredit, Demonize, and Destroy. I emphasize Cancel Culture.

1. Dismissed: The Politics of Cancel Culture

The first attack I encountered was the tactic of dismissal, a tool sharpened by the blade of cancel culture. The moment I began to speak out against the systemic oppression of Black people, those in power—and even some within our own community—sought to silence me. They labeled my ideas as "radical" "anti-police" or "extreme," attempting to paint me as an outlier, someone whose views were too dangerous to be taken seriously. The more I spoke the truth, the more they worked to cancel my voice, erasing my contributions from the conversation, Ferguson Unrest history, and diminishing the impact of my work.

In many ways, this dismissal was the easiest for them to achieve. By casting me as a fringe element, they hoped to marginalize my influence and make my message disappear. But I refused to be silenced, and I continued to push forward, even as the doors of opportunity were shut in my face, and my voice was systematically excluded from the platforms where it was needed most.

2. Discredit: Undermining the Messenger

As my voice grew louder, so did the efforts to discredit me. The second tactic they employed was to attack my credibility, to paint me as a hypocrite, a rapist, a murderer and a fraud. They dredged up every mistake I had ever made, twisting my past felony conviction as a minor to fit their narrative. They questioned my integrity, my motives, and even my sanity, all in an effort to make me seem less trustworthy in the eyes of the people I was trying to reach.

The media played a significant role in this, running stories that were skewed and biased, labeling me a rapist, a felon, a woman beater all designed to cast doubt on my character. They interviewed people who barely knew me, who were more than willing to speak ill of me for their own gain. They turned my personal struggles into public spectacles, all to convince the world that I wasn't the leader or the activist I claimed to be. Despite these attacks, I remained steadfast, knowing that the truth would eventually prevail.

3. Demonize: Turning the Activist into the Enemy

When discrediting me wasn't enough to halt my momentum, the next step was to demonize me. They began to portray me as the enemy, someone who was not just wrong, but a dangerous felon. My words were twisted, my intentions distorted, until I was no longer seen as a voice for justice, but as a threat to society. They called me a "felon," a "militant," even a "rapist"—labels meant to instill fear in those who might otherwise have supported me.

This demonization was perhaps the most painful to endure because it targeted not just my message, but my very identity. It sought to turn the people I was fighting for against me, to make them believe that I was the problem rather than the solution. But even as they painted me as a villain, I knew that my fight was just, and I refused to let their lies define me.

4. Destroy: Attempts to End It All

Finally, when all else failed, they sought to destroy me. The ultimate goal of those who oppose revolutionary change is to eliminate the threat entirely, and they were willing to go to any lengths to make that happen. I faced threats to my life, attempts to ruin my livelihood, and efforts to break my spirit. The weight of these attacks was heavy, and there were moments when I wondered if I could continue.

But I also knew that these attempts to destroy me were proof that I was on the right path. The more they tried to kill my spirit, the more determined I became to fight back. I knew that if they succeeded in silencing me, it would only embolden them to do the same to others. So I stood tall, even when the world seemed to be crumbling around me, because I knew that the struggle for liberation is worth any price.

The Struggle Continues

The "Four D's" may have been their strategy, but they were also the measure of my resolve. Every time they tried to dismiss, discredit, demonize, destroy or cancel me, I found within me a deeper well of strength and determination. My journey has been one of relentless perseverance, and I share this not as a tale of victimhood, but as a testament to the power of resistance. I am still here, still fighting, because I fear no one but God. I am an unbreakable spirit and the cause of so-called Black or Melanated liberation is too important to abandon.

For those who seek justice, who fight for the oppressed, know that these tactics will be used against you too. But also know that you are not alone. We stand together, and as long as we do, we cannot be defeated. The struggle continues, and so does the fight for our freedom.

I never thought I would make it to live this long. It is only by the grace and mercy of God. My spiritual name is Yahkhahnahn Ammi. I am the author of a three-book series entitled *Live or Die Tryin' Book Three.* I was reborn in Statesville prison. In isolation confinement to be exact, or what fellow prisoners call, "The Hole," for three years. Sentenced to serve a 16-year prison sentence. I was transferred to this maximum prison for breaking the prison rules at a prior prison, and I was sent there for my eighteenth birthday out of retaliation to the Illinois Department of Corrections at the Statesville Correctional Center in 1999 located in Joliet, Illinois.

Over the past 30 years, I've lived a life marked by profound challenges, indomitable resilience, and an unwavering quest for justice. This memoir, Live or Die Tryin' Book III, is the culmination of my journey—a journey that has taken me from the neighborhoods of Brooklyn, Illinois, through the harsh confines of the Illinois Department of Corrections, to the forefront of the civil rights and Ferguson movements. In this third installment of my memoir, I recount the experiences that have shaped me as an aboriginal/melanated, or so-called African American/Black man in the United States. My story is a tapestry woven with threads of personal struggle, systemic oppression, relationship trauma, and relentless activism. It is a story of a man and natural leader who refused to be broken by the forces of injustice and revenge and who instead transformed his pain into a powerful call for change.

Yahkhahnahn Ammi

In Live or Die Tryin' Book III, you will walk with me through five main narratives:

*Trials and Tribulations with the American Legal System.

*My false arrest based on accusations of sexual assault and domestic violence.

*Losing custody of my children due to these false allegations and my juvenile record from over twenty years ago.

*The fight for my freedom and justice.

*Career opportunities and my right to travel taken away.

Reflections on the oppressive nature of the American legal and political systems. Throughout this memoir, I detail my involvement in the civil rights and Ferguson movements, shedding light on the internal conflicts and external pressures that defined these pivotal moments.

You will read about the challenges I faced as an aboriginal or so-called Black activist and founder of the Black Lives Matter Inc., organization in Missouri and the efforts by law enforcement and political adversaries to dismantle my advocacy work.

I am driven by a profound desire to share my story not just as a personal testament but as a beacon for others who face similar struggles. My life has been a series of battles against a system designed to oppress, marginalize, and silence voices like mine. By telling my story, I aim to illuminate the realities of racial and political injustice, inspire resilience, and call for continued resistance against systemic oppression.

This memoir is not just about my past—it is about the ongoing fight for freedom and justice. It is about the importance of standing up against injustice, no matter the cost. My journey is a reflection of the broader struggles faced by so-called African Americans or Blacks in the United States and it is a call to action for all who believe in equity, equality and human rights.

Live or Die Tryin' Book III concludes with my release from prison in 2003 and my continued pursuit of liberty. As I navigate through a failed marriage and relationship trauma, I take accountability for allowing these experiences to affect my life due to my choices in partners. I offer my final reflections on the importance of fighting for freedom and justice. This memoir is a powerful and moving account of one man's fight for justice, equity, and equality, offering a unique perspective on the civil rights movement and the ongoing struggles faced by African Americans for their human rights in the United States. I invite you to join me on this journey. Together, we can continue the fight for a more just and equitable world.

CHAPTER 1

Family Reunion

"Family Reunion" - The O'Jays

After a decade behind bars, freedom felt like a stranger, and my family like distant memories.

By the age of 24, I had already spent a decade in prison, having been incarcerated since I was 14. Due to an alleged violation of prison rules, my release date was extended by two months—from August 2, 2003, to October 31, 2003. My story is one shaped by the school-to-prison pipeline, a wrongful conviction, and a journey of personal redemption, fueled by an unwavering commitment to justice. It was just days before my release from Pontiac Correctional Center, a maximum security prison in Pontiac, Illinois. This chapter isn't the story of my entire prison experience, but rather a glimpse into my last few days before release. I had been sentenced to 16 years for attempted first-degree murder, charged as an adult just two weeks after turning 15 because my so-called friends put all the blame on me to get a lesser prison sentence. Those snitches never got stitches. While I don't deny my participation. I am innocent of what they claimed I had done. I would never kill or attempt to kill anyone. The years in prison had exposed me to unimaginable experiences. Prison provided the tools I needed for personal growth. It taught me that no weapon is more powerful than a pen. Prison taught me conflict resolution, and survival.

It shaped my perspective on life. Despite the isolation and time spent in segregation, I found solace in aligning with fellow prisoners dedicated to social justice advocacy. Together, we organized, spoke out against human and civil rights violations, and reached out to various organizations and representatives, including the President. These experiences inside prison, where my own and others' rights were often violated, fueled my determination to continue advocacy work upon my release. Though initially seeming futile, the skills I gained proved invaluable for my future endeavors. Prison enhanced my character development and personal growth.

The last few days before my release were filled with anticipation, fear, and uncertainty. Prison in general and Pontiac Correctional Center was a harsh and unforgiving environment, making survival a daily challenge. Tension was palpable, especially as my release date approached. Every interaction with guards and fellow inmates was a delicate balance to avoid further trouble and ensure I made it out on time. As I counted down the days to my release, memories of the past decade flooded my mind. Each memory served as a reminder of the journey that had led me to this point. These reflections were crucial in understanding the depth of my experiences and the person I had become.

It was six o'clock in the morning. There were no lights on, and everyone was quiet. The prison guards were in the middle of their shift change, the guards would begin their rounds and count fellow prisoners in another thirty minutes. The night before my release from my bid, I was haunted by the memories and the desperate cries of Lil X-Man, a childhood friend.

His pleas several years ago for help echoed through my mind and the prison halls of Statesville Correctional Center, in Joliet Illinois, a stark contrast to the hopeful reunion I longed for with my family. As I lay awake, uncertainty and anticipation intertwined.

Would my family embrace me after a decade of separation, or had the years driven an insurmountable wedge between us? Reuniting with my family after ten years of separation and my time in prison was a bittersweet journey of hope, fear, and the struggle to rebuild fractured bonds.

One night, I witnessed the system's brutality firsthand against Lil X-Man, a childhood friend of mine. He had been locked up too long, and it began to break him. After a fight with his cellmate, he faced the threat of becoming someone's 'property.' Refusing to submit, he called for help, demanding a transfer or isolation. When the guards arrived, his defiance provoked their wrath. They slammed him against concrete walls and floors, his cries echoing through the halls.

The guards viciously beat Lil X-Man, who was handcuffed and defenseless. Shouts erupted from the prisoners, and I joined in, demanding the officers stop. In that moment, we stood together, defying a system built to crush us. X-Man's cries embodied the brutal reality we all faced—a system designed to strip us of dignity and silence those who dared to resist.

Our protests were met with silence as they dragged Lil X-Man to the hole to hide their abuse. As a neutron, unaffiliated with gangs, X-Man's fate remained unknown. His cries still haunt me, a stark reminder of the system's cruelty.

I struggled with insomnia, unable to sleep for four days. My mind was filled with a whirlwind of emotions—anxiety, nervousness, excitement, fear, and concern for the friends and family I would leave behind. The weight of the past nine years loomed over me. It was time for a new beginning, a fresh start in a new place and environment. My journey would not be complete until I repaired the broken familial relationships and secured a stable future. I had been denied certain tools while in prison, but I could not let that stop me. I had plans to leave this place behind because God gave me a second chance at life. If I could just survive one more day, I would be going home, although to a strained family relationship dynamic. The time I spent in prison away from my family had torn us further apart. Would I be looked upon as the big brother that I am, or would I be treated as a guest or an outsider?

The Day of Release. Friday, October 31, 2003, was my release day. I had no rights. I could not cast a vote because of my felony conviction. I would have to wait three years before I could go to the polls or vote for a presidential candidate. None of this made sense to me. I paid my debts to society. Well, at least I had my freedom. I was filled with a mix of anxiety and excitement because today, I would be released from prison after serving a total of nine long years away from my family. It was a day I had dreamt of, but its arrival felt surreal. I kept my release date a secret from most fellow prisoners to avoid any potential trouble. Throughout my time in prison, I endured hardships, including losing two months of freedom due to infractions. The sound of the iron bars clanking as the officers checked for security breaches every morning would soon be a distant memory.

As the clock neared 7 am., the guards conducted their count, walking down the halls, calling out our names, and ensuring we were awake and accounted for. After the count, a guard came to my cell and uttered the words I had longed to hear, "It's time to bunk and junk. You're going home today." I swiftly packed my belongings, stripping my mattress and gathering my few possessions. Within minutes, I was ready to go. An hour later, the guard returned, and I followed him down the familiar corridor for the last time. Exiting the corridor, we went through a series of gates and doors, each locked behind us by vigilant guards. Finally, we arrived at a small office where I was handed clothes that my family had bought for me. I was forced to sign a piece of paper waiving my rights to the restitution owed to me by the prison, leaving me with a mere $50 check. I was preparing for freedom. Six months prior to my release, I had to secure a job and provide the prison with a release address.

My grandmother "Mama" (Jackie), whom I affectionately referred to as 'Mama,' became my parole home in Illinois. Especially since my biological Mother (Faith), her second husband Kenny and my siblings had moved to St. Louis, Missouri, over the years. I would be placed on parole for three years, obligated to pay restitution to the prison and to the alleged victims family for the crime I was accused of at age fourteen, and to add insult to injury I had to attend drug counseling at D.A.R.T., despite not having a drug related case. This contradiction left me disillusioned with the system, eagerly anticipating the end of my parole obligations. As I walked

31

out of the prison doors, a free man, I felt a mix of relief and gratitude. My immediate family came to pick me up. We drove to my grandmother's house in Brooklyn, Illinois, where I would be staying temporarily. I had envisioned a grand welcome home party, eager to reunite with friends and family. However, upon arriving at Mama (Jackie's) house, I realized the party I had imagined was not to be. It was a bittersweet homecoming.

Reuniting with my family after years apart brought a mix of emotions. Seeing both my grandmothers Bernadine, (My father's mother) and mama (Jackie, my mother's mom) filled me with joy, but the reality of everyone moving on with their lives left me feeling like an outsider. The strained relationship with my mother (Faith) before my incarceration added to the complexity of the reunion, leaving me yearning for the close knit family I once knew. Despite the lack of a grand celebration, I was grateful for the simple joys of freedom: the blue sky, the autumn breeze, and the sight of leaves falling from the trees. I relished the thought of a hot shower, a luxury I had long been denied. As I settled into my new life, I reflected on the journey that had led me to this moment and looked forward to the future with hope and determination.

Cooking at Mama (Jackie's) house was a liberating experience. It was the first time that I had the freedom to cook for myself in a kitchen.

As a vegan, I now had to learn to cook vegan meals, and it was a challenge I embraced eagerly. Cooking felt like a return to my childhood, where simple meals like eggs were the extent of my culinary skills. Now, as an adult, I was determined to master the art of vegan cooking. Mama (Jackie) and I would watch television shows, and that became our bonding time. We enjoyed watching

Yahkhahnahn Ammi

"Wheel of Fortune" together, challenging each other to solve puzzles before the contestants could.

Mama (Jackie) also watched the Trinity Broadcasting Network, a Christian programming channel, which was her favorite pastime. Watching TV became part of our daily routine.

I had never experienced big city life, and I felt drawn to it. My job at Building Butlers required me to work in St. Louis, where I would receive my first physical check. My stepfather Kenny and I worked at the Jewish Community Center in Creve Coeur, a suburb of St. Louis, Missouri. My duties included cleaning toilets, sinks, faucets, and mirrors, as well as sweeping, mopping, stripping, waxing, buffing the floors, and taking out the trash. Our routine extended to vacuuming corridors and offices, dusting furniture, and maintaining cleanliness throughout the entire Jewish community center. Despite the mundane nature of the work, I was grateful for the opportunity. Working in the Jewish community center gave me a firsthand experience of Jewish life outside of prison. However, my enthusiasm was met with mixed reactions. Some were impressed by my Hebrew fluency, while others felt threatened by it. As a melanated Jew, I often faced resistance and discrimination. Despite these challenges, I remained determined to find my place within the Jewish community. I explored different synagogues in St. Louis, seeking acceptance and belonging. I thought things would be different on the outside. I never imagined I would experience work challenges and cultural clashes among fellow believers.

My excitement and eagerness to learn led to my downfall. I failed to separate my personal interests from my professional responsibilities, and it ultimately cost me my job. Despite my sincere intentions, I encountered resistance and discrimination from some non-melanated Jews, who made it clear that I was not fully accepted as part of their community. Despite the setbacks and discrimination, I remained determined to find my place within the Jewish community regardless of the color of my skin. I lost the job Kenny had helped me secure, leaving me feeling like a failure. However, I remained hopeful for the future. I was determined to find meaningful employment and rebuild my life after prison. Facing Rejection and Moving Forward would be a necessity if I wanted to live. I had to play by a familiar set of rules if I was to survive on the outside. It was a journey of re-discovering my hometown and self.

As I drove around St. Louis, I couldn't help but marvel at the city's beauty. There was something captivating about the way it was designed. The city seemed to exude a unique charm, and I found myself drawn to its vibrancy and culture. Despite my excitement about exploring St. Louis, I knew I had to find a new job quickly. I couldn't afford to be idle for too long. It was crucial to secure stable employment to support myself and demonstrate to my parole officer that I was committed to rebuilding my life. The journey had just begun, and I was determined to make the most of this second chance. I had a lot to prove to myself, my family, and the world. The path ahead would not be easy, but I was ready to face the challenges and embrace the opportunities that lay before me.

Returning home after nearly a decade in prison was a bitter-sweet experience. The reunion with my family was both joyful and challenging, filled with mixed emotions and the realization that life had moved on while I was away. Adjusting to freedom, navigating the complexities of strained relationships, and facing rejection from parts of the Jewish community were significant hurdles. Despite the setbacks, I remained hopeful and determined to rebuild my life.

Cooking at mama's house and exploring the vibrant city of St. Louis provided small joys and moments of solace. The journey ahead was uncertain, but I was ready to face it with resilience, hope, and the unwavering belief that a better future awaited.

* * *

Personal Life Lesson Reflections

In this chapter, after nearly a decade behind bars, I walked into the free world on October 31, 2003, with the weight of a fractured past and a heart full of hope. Being reunited with family after such a long separation was bittersweet. While there was joy in seeing my loved ones, there was also the painful realization that life had moved on without me. I was no longer the boy they remembered; I had changed, and so had they. Prison may have stripped me of time, but it also instilled resilience and a determination to rebuild my life and relationships.

As I re-entered society, I realized that freedom was about more than just physical release from prison; it was about emotional and spiritual renewal. I had to navigate complex family dynamics, societal expectations, and my internal struggles—all while trying to reintegrate into a world that felt foreign. My time in prison shaped me into a man who knew how to persevere, but it was outside those walls where the real test of my strength began.

Learning to face rejection, rebuild trust, and rediscover my identity were crucial steps in my journey toward redemption.

Takeaways

Freedom is More than Just Physical Release

Leaving prison isn't just about regaining your physical freedom; it's about emotional and spiritual freedom as well.

True freedom comes from reclaiming your identity, forgiving yourself, and rebuilding your life one step at a time.

Family Reunions Can Be Both Joyful and Challenging

Coming home to family after a long absence can stir up mixed emotions.

While there is joy in reconnecting, the time spent apart can create gaps that take time and effort to bridge. Rebuilding relationships requires patience, understanding, and sometimes, the willingness to confront old wounds.

Hope is the Guiding Force in Life's Transitions

Despite the uncertainty and fear of the unknown, holding onto hope is what sustained me. Hope allowed me to envision a better future, even when the road ahead seemed full of obstacles. It's important to always cling to hope—it is the force that propels us forward, no matter how dark things may seem.

Yahkhahnahn Ammi

Final Reflection

Returning home after prison was a complex and emotional experience. Reuniting with my family and facing the reality of life outside those walls required courage, resilience, and hope.

The journey was far from easy, but it taught me that every challenge is an opportunity to gain experience, heal, and rebuild.

CHAPTER 2

Take Me Out to the Ballgame

"Take Me Out to the Ballgame"- St. Louis Cardinals Fans

Stepping onto the field at Busch Stadium wasn't just about selling refreshments; it was about reclaiming a dream that had once slipped through my fingers.

The roar of the crowd, the scent of freshly cut grass, and the crack of the bat—all sensations I had only dreamt of experiencing. As I stepped into Busch Stadium, the iconic home of the St. Louis Cardinals, I wasn't just there to work; I was fulfilling a childhood dream that had been deferred for far too long. Standing in Busch Stadium, selling refreshments to Cardinals fans, I realized I was living the dream my father had once promised me.

As a child, I harbored dreams of playing baseball like my father, who almost made it to the Negro league but had to put his dreams and baseball career on hold. He had promised to take me to my first baseball game. All my life, I dreamt of meeting one of my idols, the legendary St. Louis Cardinals player Ozzie Smith.

Yahkhahnahn Ammi

His mesmerizing back flips on the field captivated me and made me try to emulate him. I longed to be a pitcher for the Cardinals, but a lack of guidance hindered my aspirations. My athletic skills were lacking without a coach or mentor, and I struggled to excel in sports.

My first real opportunity to play baseball came at age twelve, after years of pleading with Coach Love from Brooklyn (Illinois) for a chance to join the team. Finally, he relented, agreeing to let me play one game if I could gather the team for practice. Eager to prove myself, I rallied the players early on that warm Saturday morning and eagerly took the field. In the outfield for the first inning, I fielded a ground ball and confidently threw it to the pitcher, feeling a sense of accomplishment. As the game progressed into the second inning, I watched seasoned players confidently step up to the plate, awaiting the perfect pitch to send soaring out of the park.

When my turn to bat arrived, I was a mix of nerves and excitement. Encouraged by my teammates' chants of, "Hey, batter, batter, batter, swing!" I swung with all my might, hoping for a home run. It was going, going... not gone; it stopped short. My hit was a ground ball that slipped past the pitcher and into the outfield, not the grand slam I had envisioned. Saddened, I took off running for first base as fast as I could, and boy, was I pretty fast. The team cheered me on. The next batter came up, and the pitcher watched me lead off first base as I danced back and forth, waiting for an opportunity to steal my way to second base. I had timed it perfectly; I took off like a jet running to second base. I made it, and my team was excited. The bases were loaded. We had two outs. The next batter could bring us in with a home run. I prayed. He hit the ball, and I ran to third base; I ran so fast that I overran third base. That's when the other player tagged me with the ball.

I did not know the fundamentals of playing baseball, and it had caused us the third out and possibly the game. I felt miserable, and I never played baseball again. I would only pitch to an imaginary catcher in my backyard for years while wearing my Darryl Strawberry glove.

Fast forward to my adult years where, after serving time in prison, I faced numerous challenges. I eventually enrolled in the St. Louis Job Corps and graduated. Shortly afterward, I was inducted into the St. Louis Carpenters Union. Balancing carpenter school, which was manageable as I only had to attend apprenticeship school every six months, was crucial. The school paid for my attendance, which helped cover bills and family essentials. However, maintaining stable employment proved difficult. After getting fired from a warehouse job, I received a disheartening letter stating, "Due to the nature of the offense committed, you are no longer employable." This pattern was repeated with another warehouse job, and the termination letter echoed the same sentiment. This rejection was a common theme among Illinois employers, leaving me frustrated and disheartened. Seeking a change from the cycle of temporary jobs, I wanted stable work. The grind of long, arduous hours never seemed to provide enough to cover basic necessities such as rent, bills, clothing, and food.

Despite these challenges, a glimmer of hope emerged when I found the perfect opportunity for seasonal work. I underwent interviews, completed training, and became certified as a food and beverage handler at the St. Louis Cardinals' Busch Stadium, eager to seize this chance for stability. Working as a seasonal independent contractor at Busch Stadium, selling food and beverages during home games, was an exciting experience for me. I cherished the opportunity as a devoted fan of the team, drawn not only to their play but also to the values they represented. Having never attended a professional baseball game before and getting to wear the Cardinal red made this opportunity a perfect match. Witnessing my beloved team competing against rivals was a dream come true.

During the seventh inning, I would hear "Take Me Out to the Ballgame," and I sang along to the lyrics as I remembered them as a child. In St. Louis, all of the fans joined in. If there was ever a time our team needed to win this game against the Pittsburgh Pirates, it would be now. I yelled, "Get your ice-cold beers," and then I sang out loud. This experience taught me valuable lessons in perseverance and determination. Despite my initial shortcomings, I continued to pursue my passion for baseball, driven by hard work and dedication. While my dreams of becoming a professional player may not have materialized, the experience instilled in me a deep appreciation for the sport and the importance of never giving up on my aspirations.

> *Take me out to the ball game,*
> *Take me out with the crowd;*
> *Buy me some peanuts and Cracker Jack,*
> *I don't care if I ever get back.*
> *Let me root, root, root for the home team,*
> *If they don't win, it's a shame.*
> *For it's one, two, three strikes, you're out,*
> *At the old ball game.*

My role allowed me to intimately explore Busch Stadium, navigating its steps, corridors, and concession stands, engaging in what I truly enjoyed—conversing with people and selling refreshments. This job marked a first for me, and it proved to be incredibly enjoyable. I developed a knack for salesmanship, so much so that I often joked I could sell people their own shoes given the chance. I called out to fans, enticing them with cries of "Get your ice-cold beer here!" or "Peanuts, popcorn, hot dogs, nachos!"

My enthusiasm was unwavering, even as my voice waned by the end of each shift. Yet, despite the vocal strain, the experience was deeply fulfilling. Accomplishing three significant things made me particularly happy.

Firstly, I fulfilled my dream of watching my favorite team in action, despite their frequent losses. Second, I relished the opportunity to interact with fans, whose energy and passion for the St. Louis Cardinals were truly remarkable. Lastly, I took pride in selling them products, knowing I could bring smiles to their faces with each purchase. After each shift, I dutifully accounted for the sales made, subtracted the tips, and was pleased with the substantial earnings. These tips, along with the proceeds from my sales, were instrumental in meeting my household responsibilities. Money was tight, so I juggled multiple jobs, including warehouse work, temporary positions, and personal training sessions. When not otherwise occupied, I served as a fitness facilitator at recreational facilities in St. Louis until that position concluded. Through this experience, I honed my customer service and sales skills, learning valuable lessons in perseverance and dedication. The camaraderie among fans and the joy of contributing to their game day experiences made every moment worthwhile, leaving me with cherished memories of my time at Busch Stadium.

Yahkhahnahn Ammi

Although my father never took me to the ball-game, I imagined what his presence would have been like.

* * *

Personal Life Lesson Reflections

In this chapter, standing in Busch Stadium, selling refreshments to cheering Cardinals fans, I found myself fulfilling a childhood dream that had once felt out of reach. My father, who never got the chance to take me to my first baseball game, had planted the seeds of that dream. Life's struggles—poverty, incarceration, and the absence of a mentor—had dimmed its light.

However, here I was, surrounded by the sights and sounds of the ball park, living a version of that dream. In many ways, this experience was a symbol of the resilience I had cultivated through the years.

While I never became the professional baseball player I aspired to be, standing at Busch Stadium taught me that dreams have many forms. Sometimes, achieving them requires adapting to the reality that life presents. It taught me that success isn't only found in the grand gestures but also in the small victories, like fulfilling childhood promises to yourself and embracing the joy of the present moment.

Takeaways

Dreams Can Take Different Forms

You may not always achieve your dreams exactly how you envisioned them, but that doesn't mean they aren't worth pursuing.

My dream of playing professional baseball didn't materialize, but standing in Busch Stadium still allowed me to be part of the game I loved. Be open to different versions of your dreams—they might bring fulfillment in unexpected ways.

Perseverance in the Face of Adversity

Life's challenges—whether poverty, incarceration, or constant rejection—can delay your dreams but don't have to derail them entirely. My path wasn't smooth, but through perseverance, I was able to create a life filled with meaning and small triumphs.

Even when circumstances seem impossible, perseverance can lead you to places you never imagined.

Redefining Success

Success isn't always about reaching the highest pinnacle but about appreciating the journey. For me, success was about learning how to be present in moments of joy, even when life didn't go as planned. Working at Busch Stadium wasn't glamorous, but it was fulfilling, and that taught me to redefine what success looks like for me.

Resilience Comes from Small Wins

Resilience isn't built on grand victories; it's constructed through small wins and everyday perseverance. Selling refreshments at Busch Stadium and hearing the cheers of the crowd brought me joy during a difficult period in my life. Those moments of joy helped fuel my resilience as I faced other challenges head-on.

Yahkhahnahn Ammi

Honor the Legacy of Those Before You

My father never made it to the Negro leagues, and he couldn't take me to my first baseball game as he had hoped. Still, standing in that stadium, I felt like I was honoring his legacy. Even if you can't achieve your dreams in their original form, finding a way to honor the spirit of them is powerful. I was able to do that in Busch Stadium, and it filled me with a sense of pride.

Seize the Moment

Life often gives us small windows of opportunity, like my chance to work at Busch Stadium. Seizing those moments can lead to unexpected happiness and fulfillment. Don't wait for the perfect opportunity—sometimes, what's in front of you is enough to give you a piece of your dream.

Final Reflection

Sometimes, life doesn't unfold the way you expect. The professional baseball career I once dreamed of never materialized, but working at Busch Stadium still gave me the chance to engage with the sport I loved. In those moments, I learned that resilience is built on adaptability.

CHAPTER 3

Why Did I Get Married?

"Let's Get Married" - Jagged Edge

Emerging from the shadows of poverty and prison, I sought not just love, but a legacy that would heal the wounds of my past.

Growing up in poverty, my childhood was marked by a struggle for basic needs. In an environment where showing emotion was a sign of weakness, I learned to suppress my feelings early on. My structured upbringing, influenced by family members who served in the military, clashed with my natural curiosity and distaste for rigid rules. At fourteen, my life took a drastic turn when I was incarcerated. The harsh realities of prison life reinforced the need to hide my emotions. Crying or showing any form of vulnerability could be perceived as a weakness, putting my very survival at risk. Despite this, I never lost sight of my dream to one day have a family of my own. Upon my release at 24, I kept the defensive mindset I had adopted in prison. Opening up to others, especially women, was a challenge. I sucked at relationships, not knowing how to express my feelings or thoughts. But my desire for love and a legacy remained strong, driving me to seek out meaningful connections despite my fears.

I embarked on a quest to find my soulmate, navigating the emotional complexities of reintegrating into society. My up bringing had left me unprepared for the realities of adult relationships, sex, and marriage. Yet, my determination to find love and build a family led me to embrace life as a family minded man, committed to a monogamous relationship with my future wife.

During my time in prison, I experienced profound personal growth. The challenges I faced taught me the importance of commitment, trust, and unconditional love. These lessons became the foundation upon which I looked to build my future relationships. Despite the stigma of my past, I was determined to find love and set up a legacy. My journey was fraught with unanswered questions: How could I love someone if I never learned to love myself ? Could I remain faithful to one woman for the rest of my life? These questions weighed heavily on my mind, but my faith and resilience kept me moving forward.

Lacking close relationships with married family members, I sought guidance and support wherever I could. My grandfather Abraham had been murdered at a young age.

When mama remarried, I had a stepgrandfather and protector. Cleo was my closest role model. Despite these challenges, I turned to God and prayer, trusting that divine guidance would lead me to the right path.

I wanted to get married because I was unbalanced, a void needed to be fulfilled. I wanted what most men seek in life: love, money, and respect. But more than that, I wanted to break the cycle of fathering children outside of wedlock, following in my grandparents' footsteps by marrying first. My journey was about more than just personal fulfillment; it was about honoring my family and creating a legacy built on love and commitment.

* * *

Personal Life Lesson Reflections

In this chapter, marriage is often seen as a union of love, but for me, it was also a path to healing, redemption, and building a legacy. After spending my formative years behind prison walls, where expressing emotions could be fatal, I emerged with a hardened heart yet a deep yearning for love and connection. I realized that marriage was not just about finding a partner but about finding a way to counteract the hate and hardships that life had thrown my way. My journey from prison to marriage was about more than just finding love—it was about creating a life filled with purpose, commitment, and the hope of breaking cycles of pain and poverty.

Takeaways

Marriage as a Path to Healing

For someone who has faced intense hardships, marriage can serve as a powerful healing force. It's not just about finding someone to love but about finding someone who can help you heal the wounds of your past. My journey from incarceration to matrimony was a testament to the power of love to transform and heal even the most scarred hearts.

The Importance of Emotional Vulnerability

In prison, showing vulnerability was dangerous, but in marriage, it's essential. I learned that to build a lasting and meaningful relationship, I had to unlearn the survival tactics of hiding my emotions and embracing the courage to be vulnerable. Marriage taught me that true strength comes from opening up and letting someone see the real you.

Breaking Generational Cycles

My decision to get married was rooted in a desire to break generational cycles. I wanted to create a family built on love, commitment, and respect—values that I didn't always see growing up. By marrying before having children, I looked to set up a legacy of stability and honor, something that would endure for generations.

Commitment is Built on Self-Love

Before you can truly love someone else, you must learn to love yourself. My time in prison forced me to confront my own worth and value, and it was through this journey of self-discovery that I became ready to commit to someone else. Marriage is a reflection of the love you have for yourself, mirrored in your love for your partner.

Resilience and Faith as Foundations

My faith played a crucial role in guiding me toward marriage. Despite the stigma of my past and the challenges of reintegration, I relied on prayer and divine guidance to lead me to my future wife. Marriage, for me, was an act of faith—a belief that despite my past, I was worthy of love, commitment, and a future filled with hope.

Marriage as a Legacy

I didn't just want to get married for love; I wanted to build a legacy. I saw marriage as a way to establish a foundation for future generations, a way to honor my family's history while creating a new path forward. My marriage was not just about two people coming together but about creating a life that would have lasting impact on our children and beyond.

Final Reflection

Marriage, for me, was a transformative experience. It was about more than just finding love—it was about healing from the past, embracing vulnerability, and building a legacy. Despite the challenges I faced, from poverty to prison, I found strength in the commitment I made to my wife. In doing so, I discovered that within every person lies enough love to counteract the world's hate, and marriage was the vessel through which I could share that love and create something beautiful and lasting.

CHAPTER 4

The Birth of a Nation

"Be Healthy"- Dead Prez

From the crucible of poverty and prison, I emerged determined to build a life of love, resilience, and legacy, with Selena by my side.

I threw myself into the program, choosing to study at the Home Builders Institute (HBI) and simultaneously working toward my General Education Development (GED) certificate. For the first time in years, I found myself back in a classroom setting, surrounded by the hum of learning. It wasn't easy, but I was determined to better myself, to seize this opportunity with both hands.

My passion for cooking, especially vegan dishes, led me to volunteer at Eternity Vegetarian Deli and Juice Bar. What started as a volunteer role soon became a part-time job, and I found joy in the rhythm of the kitchen, the sizzle of vegetables on the grill, and the smiles of satisfied customers. Eternity was more than just a deli—it was a community hub, complete with a salon called Natural Creations where I could get a fresh haircut before heading to my evening shifts. The location was perfect, the atmosphere vibrant. It was a place where I could breathe.

Back at the Job Corp center, I didn't just hit the books—I ran for Student Government President. Though I didn't win, I was elected Sergeant at Arms, a role that taught me the value of leadership and the importance of representing my peers. Every day was a new lesson, a new challenge, and I embraced them all. As the year progressed, I focused on my studies, preparing for the GED test with everything I had. When the day came to take the test at Harris-Stowe State University, I was nervous but hopeful. Weeks passed as I anxiously awaited the results. My GED teacher had one piece of advice: score high. And I did, in nearly every subject. But a few missed math questions meant I didn't pass. When the scores were posted, my heart sank. The high marks in other subjects were little comfort—I had run out of time to retake the test before graduation. It was a crushing blow. But life didn't stop, and neither did I.

I continued working at Eternity, picking up odd jobs and volunteering at the St. Louis City Department of Recreation, where I began to excel. I was nearing the end of my parole, with just one more year to go. The final six months would be the easiest, only requiring me to mail in reports of good behavior. Freedom was on the horizon, but it felt like an eternity away.

It was a sunny Tuesday afternoon while at Job Corps when I first laid eyes on Selena, a woman who would soon capture my heart. Reminiscent of the iconic actress Pam Grier, Selena exuded a warmth and kindness that drew me in instantly. Her smile was radiant, and her laughter was like a soothing melody. As our eyes met across the room, I felt a flutter in my chest—a love at first sight that seemed fated. We bonded over our shared experiences of overcoming life's challenges, including strained relationships with our parents and the added pain of her father's passing. Her resilience shone through, and together, we forged a deep connection built on understanding and shared aspirations. What began as a friendship blossomed into a love that fueled our journey of personal growth.

Before meeting Selena, I briefly dated other women after my release, although it was nothing serious each relationship taught me valuable lessons. Selena, however, was different. She touched my soul, and our connection was forged in the fires of passion, respect, and a shared desire to build a life together. As my journey continued, I was reminded every day of the power of love and the joy of finding someone who completes me. Our marriage was a testament to overcoming adversity and the beauty of building a life together. Over eight transformative months, we laughed, cried, and supported each other through life's trials.

Our conversations revealed a depth of understanding that only true soulmates could share. I was a committed vegan, and Selena's decision to embrace a meat free lifestyle further cemented our bond. One evening, as we watched the sunset together, I turned to Selena and said, "I can't imagine my life without you." Her eyes sparkled with tears as she replied, "I feel the same way." With the glow of the setting sun as our backdrop, I proposed, and through tears of joy, she said yes.

Meeting Selena was another pivotal moment. Her vibrant character, resilience, and military service earned my deep respect and admiration. On December 22nd, 2005 surrounded by loved ones, Selena and I exchanged vows in a small, intimate ceremony—a celebration of triumph and love. Our journey taught us the true meaning of perseverance and commitment.

As we pledged to support and uplift each other for a lifetime, we knew that our love was the greatest triumph of all. Our marriage became a testament to the transformative power of second chances. My release from prison not only marked my freedom but also defined my life with themes of perseverance, redemption, and unwavering belief in the power of love.

I had found my soulmate, and together, we embarked on a shared journey. This is why I got married – to find love, create a legacy, and embrace the happiness of a committed partnership. Our commitment to one another was soon tested when Selena discovered she was expecting our first child. The joy was indescribable, but it was soon overshadowed by tragedy. We suffered a miscarriage, a loss that shook us to our core. In the midst of our grief, we found strength in each other. *"We'll keep trying,"* Selena whispered, her hand tightly gripping mine. *"Our love is stronger than this."*

When Selena became pregnant again a year and six months later, our hope was renewed. I was the happiest man alive, and my health was perfect after six years of being vegan. We prepared meticulously, planning a natural birth and a naming ceremony, adhering to our Biblical principles. The day our son Prince Avatar was born that January was a day of immense joy and relief. I documented every moment with countless pictures and videos, capturing the miraculous event. Holding 'Prince' Avatar for the first time, I marveled at his tiny fingers and the way he clung to my finger. "He's perfect," Selena said, tears in her eyes. After the birth, I took on the role of the cook, bringing Selena whatever she craved. I cherished the quiet moments alone with her and our newborn son, even as family and friends visited our home with love and support. Despite our joy, the struggle was real. I struggled financially as a husband. The responsibility of being a new father weighed heavily on me.

Without transportation, I desperately needed to buy a car. I did not have a credit score. It was all bad. I was barely making ends meet. I was still on parole, I had to pay restitution to the alleged victims family, to the prison and parole monthly for three years. If I did not it would be considered a violation of my parole, that meant that I could be sent back to prison to serve the remaining sentence. Living in a two-bedroom apartment in Brooklyn, Illinois, I felt the weight of my responsibilities. Yet, I was proud of the stability I was beginning to build. I enrolled in the United Brotherhood of Carpenters Union and was attending the Carpenters Joint Apprenticeship Program as a union carpenter apprentice. Marriage had been a dream of mine since childhood. Selena, with her infectious laughter and genuine caring spirit, fulfilled all my desires. I felt complete, knowing I had found the person I could love with all my heart. I believed God had guided us toward marriage before starting our family, and I felt a responsibility to be a role model, not only for our children but also for my siblings. Selena and I grew together as the years passed, and our love deepened as our family flourished. We faced challenges, weathered storms, and celebrated triumphs, all while holding onto the unbreakable bond we shared. Our love story became a testament to the power of love, commitment, and finding a partner who compliments and uplifts our spirits.

* * *

Personal Life Lesson Reflections

In this chapter, in life, adversity can either break you down or build you up. For me, it was a journey through poverty, prison, and eventual freedom that forged my resilience and determination. The experiences of prison didn't just strip me of my physical freedom but pushed me toward personal growth, self-love, and a desire to build a meaningful life. When I met Selena, I found not only love but a partner with whom I could share my vision of a healthy, purposeful life. Our relationship, tested by loss and hardship, became a testament to love's ability to heal and rebuild, even in the face of adversity.

Takeaways

Resilience is Built Through Adversity

Life's hardest moments often provide the greatest opportunities for growth. My time in prison taught me the importance of self-respect and determination. It allowed me to discover my inner strength, which became the foundation for everything I've built since—my education, my career, and my family.

Love as a Source of Healing

My marriage to Selena was a turning point, not just because I found love but because we found healing in each other. Despite our individual struggles—mine with reintegration and hers with grief and challenges—we created a life together that was rooted in mutual respect and commitment. Love became our anchor, helping us navigate the storms of life.

Yahkhahnahn Ammi

The Power of Second Chances

Life doesn't always go according to plan, but when we get second chances, they can be transformative. After leaving prison, I found myself at a vocational school, where I met Selena and discovered a new path forward. Second chances are about redemption, not just for our past mistakes but for the opportunity to live the life we've always envisioned.

Family is a Sacred Commitment

Marriage, for me, was about creating a legacy—a bond that extended beyond just Selena and me. It was about building a family that reflected love, health, and values. Even when we faced the heart-wrenching loss of a child, we grew stronger and more committed to each other, knowing that the love we shared would help us through the darkest times.

Perseverance Through Financial Struggles

Being a husband and father came with its share of challenges, particularly financial ones. I struggled with the weight of providing for my family while trying to keep stability and security. Yet, even during the toughest times, I found pride in my ability to support my loved ones, whether through cooking for my wife after childbirth or ensuring our home was filled with love and care.

A Healthy Life is a Holistic Life

My commitment to a vegan lifestyle wasn't just about physical health; it was a reflection of the values Selena and I shared. We built a life centered around health, spirituality, and shared principles, creating a family that was nourished in every sense of the word—body, mind, and soul.

This chapter is a reflection on the importance of resilience, love, and the transformative power of family. Through my journey with Selena, I learned that no matter the hardships or losses we face, love can heal, strengthen, and carry us through.

CHAPTER 5

I Had a Dream

"Retrospect For Life"- Common

Have you ever dreamt of a life so vivid it felt like destiny was calling, only to wake up and find that reality had something far more complex in store?

Have you ever imagined finding out you're a father—or not—on national television? I grew up in poverty, dreaming of a better future, but life had its own plans. I remember those afternoons spent glued to the TV, watching the Maury Show. It was a real roller coaster ride. Mothers and fathers would often come on the show to argue, fuss, and fight about whether or not the father was the child's biological father. The tension was palpable, the stakes high. With his calm demeanor, Maury would open that envelope, and the truth would spill out. Sometimes, it was revealed that the man in question was indeed the biological father, leading to tears of joy or sighs of relief. Other times, the DNA test would show that the alleged father was not biologically related to the child, and chaos would ensue. The drama, the emotions, the confessions—it was all so raw and real.

Watching these episodes, you couldn't help but laugh at some of the outrageous reactions yet feel deeply for the people involved. There was a strange mix of humor and seriousness that kept you hooked.

Now, imagine my relief when I found myself in a similar situation, but without the national TV audience. My ex-girlfriend, Whitni, had called me years after we broke up, asking for a paternity test. The suspense was real, and my heart was pounding. When the results came in, it was revealed that I was not the biological father of the child. The year following my breakup with Whitni was a challenging one. Dating felt daunting because I knew I wanted more than casual encounters. I craved substance, a connection with someone who would value me as much as I valued them. It wasn't easy, but it was worth it. A year later, I met the woman who would become my wife. We took our time dating and courting each other, and two years into our relationship, we welcomed our first child. This experience of building a family brought immense spiritual and personal growth. My marriage has made me a better person, a stronger person, more patient and loving. Reflecting on my past relationships, I realized how much I had evolved. However, the path to this growth wasn't without its challenges. When Whitni called me years later, my life had changed dramatically. I had moved on, built a new life, and started a family. Yet, her call shook me to my core. Whitni mentioned she had given birth to Brianna several years ago and thought I was the father of her child. Whitni and I had not been together in years. I had a child who was potentially mine. In that moment, fear, hope, and love all collided within me.

Yahkhahnahn Ammi

I had a dream that I thought brought clarity, closure, and a new beginning in my life. I had a dream that my wife Selena and I were blessed with a baby girl. In the dream, she had beautiful brown skin and a head full of hair.

This dream became a topic of conversation with my wife after the birth of our son, whose description did not fit into the dream, as she was expected to give birth to our daughter in a few months. However, when our daughter arrived, I noticed she also didn't have as much hair as the dream depicted. This raised questions, making me wonder if we were expecting a fourth child (our first child miscarried) or perhaps twins. This dream felt like a message, a glimpse into our future. It filled me with hope and anticipation. Dreams have always been significant to me.

They often carried meanings and lessons from my subconscious, guiding me through life's uncertainties. Months later, Whitni contacted me by phone one day and said, "*Someone wants to talk to you.*" The little angelic voice was a baby girl who said, "*Hi, Daddy.*" I was shocked, conflicted, and speechless. I did not know what to say. Whitni revealed that the child was three years old at the time. She said, "*You are the father.*" After we hung up, I shared this information with Selena, explaining my past involvement with Whitni and the possibility of being the child's father. The dream did not prepare me for one of those momma's baby, daddy's maybe situations. I wondered, "Was this the baby I had a dream about?" Hearing Brianna's angelic voice call me "daddy" over the phone was heart-wrenching. My mind raced with questions and concerns. Why had Whitni waited so long to reach out? How would my wife react? Would she think I had been unfaithful? The fear of my marriage unraveling was overwhelming, but so was my desire to do right by Brianna if she was indeed my child.

My wife Selena, supportive as ever, said, "*If it's your baby, we'll get through this together as a family.*" Arrangements were made for Whitni to bring the baby girl over, and I finally had the chance to meet Brianna. She was the beautiful, chocolate-brown skin child I had dreamt of, with hair all over her head. Meeting Brianna for the first time was surreal. Holding her in my arms, I felt an overwhelming sense of responsibility and love. It was as if the universe had given me a second chance to correct the past and to be the father I always wanted to have.

To ensure clarity, my wife suggested a paternity test despite the baby resembling me. Whitni allowed Brianna to spend weekends with us, and I began considering her as my own daughter. This situation took a toll on my wife, though she never expressed negativity. We believed we would get through it, not realizing the impact it had on everyone involved. When the paternity test results came back several months later, indicating a 99.9% chance that I was not the biological father, I was relieved yet hurt. I had introduced Brianna to my immediate family, including my grandparents. As time passed, it became apparent that Whitni, a student at the time, had been involved with someone else, a staff member at St. Louis Job Corps shortly after we broke things off. Unfortunately, that person was deceased, and there was no way to obtain DNA for a paternity test. Selena supported me through difficult times, such as the paternity test for Brianna, showcasing her love, determination, and understanding. Reflecting on our journey, I am filled with gratitude for the lessons learned and the love that has carried us through. Our story is one of resilience, hope, and the transformative power of love. It is a reminder that no matter where you start, creating a beautiful life with the one you love is never too late. Despite the test results and the dream, I maintained a healthy relationship with Brianna, treating her as my own.

It was a bittersweet revelation. I was not her biological father, yet I felt a deep connection to Brianna. I realized that fatherhood transcends biology; it's about love, commitment, and being there through thick and thin. Whitni and I promised to maintain open communication with Brianna. I fought hard to keep Brianna in my life, encouraged her family to stay in touch, and allowed her to spend weekends with my family. However, that did not happen, and we lost contact.

Seven Years later, after reconnecting with Whitni's family, I saw Brianna, She was 10 years old. Her mom let her spend the weekend with my children and I. We lost contact. The next time I saw her she was almost a teenager. She was twelve years old. Our interactions were always positive. Brianna enjoyed spending time with me and my other two children. We lost contact again. That was the last time I had seen her. I learned of Whitni's passing recently. Whitni left behind several children, and I tried to reach out to Brianna for years but because I could not reach her mother I lost contact with Brianna, and her family. It took me six years to get in touch with her family members again. I recently discovered that my almost 18-year-old has her first job and works at a fast-food restaurant. I am very proud of Brianna, and my heart goes out to her. I want Brianna to know that I love her and will always be here for her whenever she needs me. Reflecting on my journey with Brianna, I am filled with pride and gratitude. Despite the uncertainties and heartaches, just like her mom, she has grown into a resilient and beautiful young woman. Her strength inspires me, and I am committed to being a constant support in her life.

Navigating this journey without the guidance of a loving father and dealing with the loss of her mother has been an unimaginable path for her. Despite these challenges, I want Brianna to know that I am incredibly proud of her accomplishments. I encourage Brianna to reach beyond the stars for success and want her to understand that she is loved and will always be cherished. I cannot fathom the hurt and confusion Brianna must have gone through, growing up without either parent in her life. My Brianna faces the challenges of growing up without a mother or a father. In my heart, I hold onto the dream that one day, we will all be reunited as a family. Looking back, this experience has taught me the true essence of family. It's not defined by blood but by the bonds we create and nurture.

My dream was not just a glimpse of the future but a reminder of the power of love and resilience. I am hopeful for the day when Brianna and I can reunite, and until then, I will keep the dream alive in my heart. This journey has been one of vulnerability and honesty, facing my fears and nurturing my hopes. It is a testament to the growth and resilience that love and family brings into our lives. As you read on, I hope you find a part of your own story in mine that resonates with you on a deeper level.

* * *

Personal Life Lesson Reflections

In this chapter life can unfold in the most unexpected ways, leading us down paths we never imagined. For me, that path led to a paternity test, unexpected dreams, and the realization that fatherhood goes beyond biology. My journey through doubt, heartbreak, and eventual acceptance taught me invaluable lessons about resilience, love, and what it truly means to be a father. Despite the emotional roller coaster and the uncertainty of Brianna's paternity, I discovered that the essence of family isn't limited to blood but is defined by the love, commitment, and bonds we nurture.

Takeaways

Fatherhood Goes Beyond Blood

The experience of connecting with Brianna, even without being her biological father, taught me that fatherhood is much more than DNA. It's about being present, loving, and providing guidance to those who look up to us, whether they are our children by blood or by heart.

Dreams Can Be Messages

The dream I had about a baby girl felt like a glimpse into my future, filling me with hope and reflection. Dreams have a way of offering clarity and sometimes serve as a subconscious guide to help us navigate life's uncertainties. They remind us to stay open to the messages life sends us, whether through dreams or intuition.

Love and Resilience are Intertwined

My journey through love, heartbreak, and uncertainty showed me the power of resilience. Love, in its truest form, requires the strength to withstand trials and challenges. It was love that kept me committed to Brianna and my family, despite the paternity test and the distance that life created between us.

Honesty and Communication are Crucial

When Whitni reappeared with Brianna, I was honest with my wife Selena, and her support was unwavering. This honesty and openness helped us weather the emotional storm together. Communication builds the foundation for trust, especially when life throws unexpected challenges our way.

The Power of Forgiveness

The journey with Brianna, and the uncertainty surrounding her paternity, required me to forgive past mistakes and misunderstandings. Forgiveness—both of myself and of others—became essential for moving forward, embracing love, and creating space for healing.

Family is What We Make It

My connection with Brianna, despite not being her biological father, reminded me that family is about the bonds we create through love, support, and commitment. It's not always about who shares our blood but about who shows up and loves us unconditionally.

This chapter is a testament to the power of love, dreams, and resilience. It reflects the unpredictable nature of life and the importance of embracing love wherever it presents itself. Through my experience, I've learned that family is more than just a label—it's a commitment to love, nurture, and support one another, no matter what.

CHAPTER 6

PTSD & Resilience

"You Are Not Alone"- Michael Jackson

Unbeknownst to me, the woman I loved was silently battling demons of her own—demons that would test the very foundation of our marriage and reshape the course of our lives forever.

In a world where strength is often demanded, I discovered that true resilience lies not in the absence of struggle, but in the unyielding determination to face the deepest fears of a broken heart, a shattered marriage, and the love for my children. In the midst of chaos and heartbreak, I discovered the unyielding power of resilience and the silent strength that emerges from facing the haunting shadows and deepest fears of PTSD.

I had been completely unaware that my wife was taking psychotropic medication, had suicidal ideations, and had a history of mental illness. Selena and I seemed to have it all: a loving marriage, a roof over our heads, our beautiful son, Prince Avatar, and a child she would soon give birth to. Reflecting on my own journey post-incarceration, I realized that the challenges I faced were not just personal but also deeply affected my relationships, particularly with my wife, Selena. Our story highlights the importance of communication, mental health awareness, and the power of resilience in overcoming adversity.

Underage prosecution is both traumatizing and abusive. Putting children into the adult criminal justice system puts them at greater risk for suicide and sexual and physical violence. These types of cruel and unusual punishment can cause irreversible trauma. When eight-year-old children can be charged and sentenced as adults and sentenced to 241 years or more to serve in prison, we must ask how our society is failing them. It is horrific that 13 and 14-year-old children like Lionel Tate can be sentenced to die in prison.

After leaving prison, I was both fascinated and freaked out by the new world and especially technology. I eventually bought a cellphone, marking a significant upgrade from the pagers I used to wear on my waist. With the cellphone, I could make direct calls, a convenience I had not yet experienced. Additionally, the music world had turned to CDs instead of old-school cassette tape players and boom boxes. Despite the many challenges of reintegrating into a changed world, I never resorted to violence and always walked away from confrontations. I felt easily agitated but coped by creating structure and distancing myself from others. I knew I needed help. I did not know how to cope with the trauma I had experienced during my lifetime, and when I could not find it, I did what most men I knew did: kept my feelings bottled up. Prison and life had taught me that I had to be tough and not show any signs of weakness.

Even though I felt fulfilled as a husband and father, my past brought severe challenges to my mental health. I experienced

Yahkhahnahn Ammi

PTSD, a distorted sense of self, and difficulties in relationships. I avoided places around Brooklyn where loved ones had been murdered and had flashbacks of my time in prison, leading to sleep disturbances. Separating my past trauma from my new life outside of prison was a constant struggle. This often resulted in memory lapses and low self-esteem.

I felt constantly on edge and tense. I managed my aggression through gym workouts, mentoring youth through Stop the Violence campaigns, and cooking.

During that time, Selena and I both realized that we had kept secrets from each other for years. These were the types of secrets that could either bring us closer together or tear us apart. The truth was as shocking as the lies we told each other. Fate had another surprise in store for us. Less than a year later, Selena was pregnant (with our second child since marriage) for the third time. I worked, went to school, cooked, and took on most of the chores around the house, although my wife often beat me to them. We kept a clean house, and cooking became a therapeutic outlet for my emotions. The nerve-wracking unraveling of our family panicked our children. One day, I caught Selena flirting privately on the phone in our son's bedroom (as he slept) with someone she claimed was just a friend.

"Why did I put up with it? How was I supposed to stop it without coming across as controlling, pathetic, and weak? What if it was a girlfriend or an ex-lover of hers? She had mentioned after we got married that she was bisexual, but she did not mention having any male friends, so I ignored it. I noticed that the calls started happening more frequently, and that's when I asked, "Who was that on the phone?" I demanded, the tension palpable in the air as

69

each word hung between us, heavy with unspoken resentment and suspicion.

"Just a friend," she replied, her voice tight with defiance. "We're just friends. Why does it bother you so much?" she shot back. The exchange was fraught with frustration and misunderstanding, and neither of us was willing to confront the deeper issues plaguing our relationship.

"What friend?" I asked. She confessed, "He's an ex-boyfriend from the military." She admitted to talking to several of her ex-military lovers.

"Why do you always talk to your exes?" I pressed, frustration seeping into my words as I struggled to contain my emotions.

The scene had been set in the apartment, the air heavy with the scent of betrayal and longing. As the soft glow of scented candlelight cast long shadows across the walls, the room was infused with the scent of essential body oils that lingered in the air, a constant reminder of my wife's presence even in her absence. Anger, hurt, and a burning desire for revenge surged within me, fueled by the sense of betrayal that gnawed at my heart. Was I inadequate?

Was my crumbling marriage at stake because I wasn't enough for her? These thoughts plagued me, relentless in their assault on my psyche.

I told her I wanted to talk to him. After a brief conversation, he agreed not to call anymore. I was not having any of it. I also had a conversation with the other ex-boyfriend. She asked, "*Why did you say that to them?*" You could not be serious right now. I thought. I told both of them not to call my house every day.

I said, "I don't mind my wife talking to old friends, but you will respect my house and accept that whatever you had together in the past is over with." They both agreed. I was relieved. As I looked at my wife, there was an uncomfortable silence. I needed some fresh air. I couldn't seem to take my eyes off Selena. I was angry inside, but she only saw my frustration.

She continued talking on the phone. I had never had such suspicions before, or perhaps I had overlooked them.

What was I not fulfilling? Why were others the recipients of her attention instead of me? I thought we were a striking couple. We looked good together. I was always committed to my family, and she was aware that my children meant the world to me.

I grew quieter at home, distracted by my wife's secret phone calls with her friends. I was moody; however, I did not articulate how I felt. Selena's energy seemed to have waned, and she slept more often. Several months later, I noticed signs of depression in her. One day, while checking on her and Avatar napping in the bedroom, I found prescription pills scattered on the floor, along with an empty bottle. She had hidden inside the closet while our son slept on the bed, and it appeared she had overdosed. Despite the urgency of the situation, I didn't call the Granite City ambulance, as they did not service our area. I pulled her out of the closet, laid her body flat on the floor, checked her breathing just as I had been certified to do through the American Red Cross and finding she was alive, I put both her and the baby in the car. I called the hospital and drove to Gateway Regional Medical Center in

Granite City, making the trip in just ten minutes. She was admitted and kept under observation until she could be discharged. Thankful that she was alive, I was relieved that I had found her in time to get her medical help.

Before finding Selena lying inside the closet floor, I had no idea about her prescription medication abuse, suicidal thoughts, or mental health history. While in the hospital, I checked on her regularly until her release three days later. Though happy she was coming home, I was concerned. It seemed she wasn't getting the help she needed, especially as she was pregnant with our daughter. When I arrived to pick her up, she was in tears. Despite my attempts to comfort her, she remained silent.

Driving home, I felt relieved yet uneasy. Something felt wrong, but I couldn't pinpoint it. Although she insisted she was fine as we drove, she suddenly tried to jump out of the moving car. I stopped the car, shocked and confused. It was clear she needed more help. Feeling helpless, I suggested returning to the hospital, but she refused. We needed counseling.

I was determined not to give up on my wife or our marriage. Trying my best to be a supportive husband, we sat and talked for about twenty minutes before driving to a nearby park, holding hands as we walked. "Selena, you are not alone. You don't have to feel lonely, deeply sad, or angry because I am here. A family that prays together stays together," I assured her, offering comfort. I scheduled appointments with our minister and rabbi, and we attended marriage counseling. During these sessions, Selena admitted she was unhappy. I wanted to blame myself, but she made it clear to both me and our counselor that this wasn't the case.

Yahkhahnahn Ammi

Hearing this, I felt somewhat relieved, though deep down, I knew I had contributed to her stress, as we were living in poverty, and I couldn't financially provide for her in the way I thought I should.

Meanwhile, Selena's belly grew as she was due any day. Excited that we would give birth to our third child eleven months later. As our family grew, I could not have been prouder or more fulfilled.

We planned to keep the same birth plan, except this time, there would not be a circumcision, as we were expecting a girl. When Selena experienced labor pains, we drove to see her doctor, who told us it was not yet time to deliver and that we needed to wait. One month later, we were at home when her water broke. Selena called her doula friend and told her to meet us, and then I called the hospital. I updated and notified the hospital that we would be arriving soon. I drove to DePaul Hospital with my four-way emergency flashers on. Our daughter's birth was the longest. Princess Tiana was finally delivered on that beautiful day in December, bringing tears to my eyes. I took many photos to document this special occasion, just as I had done when Avatar was born. As our family grew, I could not have been prouder or more fulfilled. I loved my family.

One day, my wife and I discussed the possibility of her having Post-Traumatic Stress Disorder (PTSD) three months after the birth of our third child. I was concerned that I might not be able to support her adequately, as I had not sought help with my own issues. However, I was determined to be there for her as much as possible. While I accompanied her to a few postnatal doctors' appointments, I was unaware that she was also secretly seeing a psychiatrist at Behavioral Health Chestnut Family Health Center. I did not fully comprehend the impact her condition was having on her and our marriage. At that time, I was not very talkative and had not yet found an effective method of communication. Nonetheless, I tried my best to provide support and be understanding. Selena had another doctor's visit.

We took our children to Ms. Roundtree's home daycare, and then I dropped Selena off at Gateway Regional Medical Center and picked her up after the appointment.

I did not know why, after giving birth, she had scheduled frequent doctor's visits. Selena always assured me that she was fine and that the appointments were follow-up visits. Things had improved between us until after that doctor's visit, or was I naïve?

Something seemed to be bothering her as she sat quietly inside the car. Tears fell down the sides of her face. I asked what was going on and how her doctor's visit turned out. I also asked if she was ready to go home or grab something to eat. Instead, she decided that she wanted to visit her side of the family, who lived in St. Louis for a few weeks. I assumed she needed that time to be with her family. After some discussion, I agreed that I would drop her off. She wanted to drive, but I told her that I would drive. I needed to buy gas and check the tires before we picked up our children from daycare. Then we would head home so she could pack some clothes. Holding her hand, I reassured her, "Everything is gonna be alright." The gas indicator light came on and I pulled into the BP gas station near the McKinley Bridge. Selena started crying again, deepening my concern. I got out of the car, added the fuel, checked the tires, then got back into the car. I inserted the keys in the ignition when suddenly she pulled them out of it. "What are you doing?" I questioned her, stunned.

Yahkhahnahn Ammi

"I want to drive the car," she insisted. Recognizing she was not in a fit state, I retrieved the keys from her. Despite my efforts, she persisted, prompting a tense exchange with her assaults of punching and hitting me. Amidst the chaos, the situation escalated when two white male police officers arrived, guns drawn, demanding identification and vehicle registration. To my shock, I discovered there was an outstanding warrant out for me for a ten-year-old traffic violation. Placed in the back seat of their police car, I managed to grab my cell phone from my pocket to call my friend Lisa. I was put in a holding cell on a twenty-four-hour hold.

I felt helpless, reaching out to contacts for assistance. Despite my attempts to contact Selena, there was no response. Ultimately, with the help of my rabbi and my friend's mother, I was able to secure my release.

Selena had gone with our children, and I had no idea where she was. I wondered, "How did we get here? If I had been more attentive, could I have prevented the phone conversations with her alleged girlfriends?" My logic was simple: she had friends before me, and I didn't want to control who she talked to. I did have conversations with two of her ex-boyfriends whom she had served with in the military, but I wasn't jealous. I simply asked them to respect our marital home by not calling and speaking to my wife daily. Despite this, she had the nerve to ask me why I had confronted them. One of the men stopped calling out of respect.

Now, I thought that all of that was behind us, but it was not. I had to remain focused. It had been three days since I last saw or spoke to Prince Avatar and Princess Tiana. Tormented, I asked God, "Why is this happening to our family, and why have we been under attack?" I did not get any response. How did I let it happen? I thought I was doing everything a husband was supposed to do.

I provided for my family, kept a roof over our heads and food in the home, and protected my household. I worked two jobs and gave up attending carpentry school because I could not fully concentrate or pass the math exams with all the dysfunction at home. I discovered that love alone could not sustain or bring happiness to a marriage.

I couldn't say for sure if Selena was on drugs, but I couldn't ignore the signs either. Something was clearly wrong, but she kept me at a distance, shutting me out whenever I tried to reach her.

I began to realize that it was probably time for both of us to seek help—not just for the PTSD we both carried but also for the mental health concerns that Selena seemed to be grappling with, though they remained unnamed and elusive. Talking to Selena about her past was always difficult. The walls she had built around herself were high and impenetrable, shaped by years of trauma. She had served in the military, fought in wars for America, and those experiences had left deep scars. We never sought counseling together for the traumas we carried. Looking back, I know that was a mistake.

It was easier for both of us to bury our pain, but in doing so, we became strangers to each other, locked in our own private battles. But it wasn't just Selena carrying the weight of buried trauma—I carried my own too. From being molested as a child to enduring both mental and physical abuse from my stepfather Goliath from the age of six to thirteen, those early years were marked by pain I never fully addressed. The trauma didn't stop there.

Yahkhahnahn Ammi

At fourteen, I was locked up, isolated from my family, and spent the next nine years of my life behind bars.

By the time I was released at twenty-four, reuniting with my family felt like stepping back into a world I no longer recognized. Both Selena and I were burdened by the weight of our unresolved pasts, yet we buried it all deep inside our hearts. Instead of confronting our pain, we let it fester, allowing it to shape our relationship in ways we couldn't fully understand.

It wasn't until much later that I learned Selena had secretly been receiving some kind of mental health counseling before she took off with our children. This revelation made sense of some things, but it also opened up a flood of questions. Why hadn't she told me? Why did we never take that step together? The more I reflected on it, the more I realized that healing could only come from confronting our pasts together—something we had never been able to do.

Both of us were carrying the weight of wounds that hadn't healed, and without facing those wounds head on, we were bound to keep hurting each other, even unintentionally. Throughout our marriage, I endured psychological, financial, and physical abuse from Selena. Upon her return, she deliberately ran up all the utility bills excessively and intentionally, leaving me unable to pay them, which put us at risk of eviction. I was forced to relinquish my role as head of household for the utility bills and with the St. Clair Housing Authority, due to her irresponsible behavior and I sought to have her held accountable for the utilities.

I had always thought that being head of household meant that I had to pay all of the bills or that I was only responsible for the finances of the household.

Today, I know that is not true. However, many men have been miseducated about what manhood is and means. It is more than financially/physically taking care of the house. That is part of it but certainly not all.

Selena called me crying two days after taking our children. She said, "I am bringing the babies back home to you tomorrow because I am not ready to be a mother. I'm not ready to take on the responsibilities. The children can stay in your care until I can get myself together." I told her that I wanted us to co-parent, but I was relieved that she decided that it was in the best interest of our children to remain in my care.

Selena brought our children back home the following day, demanding that I refuel the car and buy them food and diapers. I obliged for the sake of my family and because I missed my angels. I was excited to see them. Selena wanted to stay at our apartment, so I decided to temporarily stay at Mama Jackie's house, which was just up the street. I took our children with me everywhere I went. Initially, I used a double stroller to push them around. People would often comment, saying, "You've got your hands full!" and we would share a laugh. Eventually, I invested in a baby carrier and a backpack style carrier. This allowed me to carry them hands-free, with my daughter on my chest and my son on my back.

I was now called Super Dad. When people remarked, "I see you've got your hands full," I would respond, "No, my body is full. My hands are free." This became a humorous exchange between me and others, turning a difficult situation into a lighthearted moment. Raising our children as a disciplined single father, while technically still married, was challenging. The situation was chaotic, but I did my best to navigate it for the sake of the children. I wanted to give my children everything that I never had: an active father who showed genuine love, guidance, and protection. Selena was gone for months without calling to check on the children.

When she did occasionally call, they were brief interactions, and then, like the wind, her conversations drifted off. The months finally turned into a year since we had seen her. I hoped Selena was doing well and getting the support that she needed. Meanwhile, our children were without a mother, and I had lost another job. I was struggling. I had, in all actuality, become a single father. Never in a million years would I have imagined that this would be my life. I was married with children and alone, trying to figure it all out without my helpmate. Being single was not my heart's desire.

In the meantime, I found another outlet—political canvassing. I began volunteering in St. Louis and East St. Louis, knocking on doors, and spreading the word for politicians. One name stood out among the rest: Senator Barack Obama. There was a buzz in the air, a sense that something monumental was happening. I dared to hope that he would become the first Black president during my time, the first that would get my vote.

For me, the decision was clear. It was time for change. Election day arrived, and for the first time in my life, I entered the voting booth.

It was an overwhelming experience, not knowing exactly what to do, but determined to make my voice heard. As I cast my vote, I allowed myself a moment of pride, telling myself that my vote could be the one that made history.

When Barack Obama was elected and later sworn in as President of the United States, I felt a surge of hope. My vote had mattered— or at least that's what I told myself at the time.

But as the years went by, I couldn't help but wonder: how much had really changed? The election of a Black president was historic, yes, but the struggles I faced as an ex-felon in a society slow to forgive hadn't disappeared. The hype of the moment was bittersweet, a reminder that real change is often slower and more complex than we want it to be.

Looking back, I see that time in my life as a period of growth and resilience. I faced disappointment, yes, but I also found strength in myself I didn't know I had. I learned that progress isn't always measured by immediate success, but by the determination to keep moving forward, even when the road is rough.

* * *

Personal Life Lesson Reflections

In this chapter I saw that in the depths of my most difficult moments, I confronted the harsh realities of PTSD and the impact it had on my life, my marriage, and my family.

My wife's struggles with mental illness and my own battle with trauma revealed the complexities of resilience. Together, we faced the consequences of suppressed pain, and I learned that the strength to endure comes from within, even when the weight of the world feels unbearable. Through the struggles, I found clarity in my role as a father, and I realized that love, faith, and perseverance were the cornerstones of my survival.

Takeaways

Resilience is Built Through Hardship

The challenges I faced—coping with PTSD, my wife's mental health struggles, and the chaos within our marriage—taught me that resilience isn't born from comfort. It's forged through the hardships that test our will to survive and our ability to move forward despite fear and pain.

Mental Health Awareness is Crucial

My wife's secret struggles with depression and medication abuse were shocking revelations. This experience opened my eyes to the importance of being aware of mental health, both my own and that of my loved ones. Ignoring or downplaying these issues only allows them to fester and worsen.

Communication is Key in Relationships

Secrets and lack of communication eroded my marriage. I learned that true connection with a partner requires honesty, openness, and an ongoing commitment to working through the problems together. When communication breaks down, the foundation of a relationship weakens.

Support is Essential—You Are Not Alone

Despite the weight of trauma and emotional pain, I discovered that support systems—whether through counseling, faith, or loved ones—are vital. No one should have to face their battles alone. Reaching out for help is not a sign of weakness but a step toward healing.

Fatherhood as a Source of Strength

My role as a father became my anchor during this turbulent time. Even as my marriage faltered, the love and responsibility I felt toward my children gave me the strength to persevere. Fatherhood grounded me, gave me purpose, and helped me find resilience amidst the storm.

This chapter reflects the complexities of navigating mental illness, trauma, and family life. It shows that healing and resilience often require facing painful truths, seeking help, and finding strength in our roles as parents and partners.

The power of resilience is not in avoiding challenges but in facing them head on, learning, and growing stronger in the process.

CHAPTER 7

Ms. Contagious

"Give It To Me Baby" – Rick James

In the chaotic dance of desire and deception, Ms. Contagious was the melody I couldn't resist, even as it led me further from the truth I refused to face.

In the depths of our struggles, amidst shattered trust and hidden pains, I found myself drawn to her allure, a beacon of light in my darkness: Ms. Contagious. Truth be told, our imperfect life began to crumble not when I discovered Selena's secret struggles with mental illness but when she uncovered my job struggles due to my criminal past, and I found out about her flirtations with ex-lovers, despite my efforts to comfort her and manage my own battles.

My actions to seek comfort and validation outside of my marriage were driven by a deep seated desire to feel wanted and desired. Childhood insecurities, trust shattered by previous relationships, and my wife's abandonment made it difficult for me to connect with her on a deeper level. Selena often masked the pain of past betrayals herself. I have to admit, witnessing my wife talking and flirting on the phone with her ex-boyfriends made me feel a certain way. I wanted to even the score, so I began talking to other women on the phone, hoping to fill a void and experience what she had felt. It was immature, I know, but at that moment, I wasn't thinking clearly. We were still newlyweds, and our marriage was deteriorating faster than either of us realized. I rationalized that talking to other women was okay since my wife didn't seem to have a problem talking to other men. I wasn't trying to control her; a man could never control a woman, only himself and his actions. I had to be responsible for me.

While separated from my estranged wife, I saw another woman again. It was a cold winter day, and I desperately needed food for our household. Thankfully, there was no snow on the ground. I drove my children from our apartment in Illinois to 11 South Euclid Avenue to grab a bite to eat at Eternity Vegetarian Deli & Juice Bar, the restaurant in St. Louis where I worked as a part-time cook and waiter. Shortly after eating our food, I noticed her. She walked in, looked in my direction, waved, and smiled at me. I nodded in acknowledgment, playing it cool. She stood at the counter and ordered her food, then came over and asked if she could sit at our table. I agreed.

I met Ms. Contagious several years before meeting my wife. She had invited me to watch her perform at Legacy, a place where artists perform spoken word. How can I describe her? The words fail me, or better yet, they just don't fit in my mouth. She was an attractive, well-known spoken word artist, one of the most talented I had ever seen. An international poet. Her melanated skin, her classy walk, her great personality. She wore her hair in locs that fascinated me and drew me into her energy. She was contagious. Intoxicating. When she spoke, she lured me in.

She was explicit. The first time I had ever seen her was when I was working at the Vegetarian Deli and Juice Bar several years ago. Ms. Contagious frequented. I saw her about a year later after my marriage had gone awry. We sat and talked. She revealed that she had feelings for me and wasn't certain if I felt the same way. It was as though she had read my mind, and suddenly, the song by Alicia Keys, "You Don't Know My Name," harmonized in my mind. Her next words played like a melody as she spoke, "*You never stepped to me, but had you approached me back then, I would have cheated on my husband. He had been an asshole towards me. He cheated on me so many times, got me out here looking bad.*" Wow. I was at a loss for words. He needed his ass kicked, I immediately thought. I assured her that I certainly did have an interest. I did not reveal that my marriage had soured. I followed up with, "Once I found out you were married when I first saw you, I just couldn't.

I had boundaries that I would not cross. That was not something I could ever bring myself to do—have an affair with a married woman." We exchanged phone numbers, and after talking on the phone frequently, we decided to meet. She invited me over to her place to talk.

One evening, she drove to my house, parked in the parking lot, and waited for me to come outside. My wife had recently come home after being gone for fourteen and a half months. We were not on talking terms. She slept in one room with our children while I slept in our bedroom. The marriage had been over for quite some time. In my eyes, there was no repairing it. I wanted my pound of flesh.

I wanted revenge. As far as I was concerned, I was a single man out here in these streets in search of love, companionship, and loyalty. I just wasn't sure if it existed. Ms. Contagious was not aware of what was going on behind closed doors, and I did not tell her. Because "What goes on in this house stays in this house." All Ms. Contagious knew was that I was a married man.

I got dressed, took a last look in the mirror, sprayed on some cologne, and grabbed my black aviator bomber sheepskin leather jacket, which, incidentally, I had given to my wife as a gift prior to our separation. I could not believe that I was actually "outside." It started raining. I got in her car, we hugged and drove back to her second-floor multi-unit apartment.

Our energy was electrifying, magnetic even. We kissed, we embraced. Our clothes came off quick as lightning. We were all over each other. It was passionate. It was fiery. It's what I felt I needed. The way her body responded to me was as if she had longed for my touch for an eternity. I whispered, "I wanna Rock Wit U," as I heard the heavenly sounds of "Awww baby" (in Ashanti's voice) from her lips as our clothes hit the floor. We found our way to her bedroom. We tossed and turned comfortably on her queen size bed, repeating, "Oh baby," kissing, hugging, nibbling, tasting each other's bodies as if we were eating chocolate covered strawberries.

I had never been with another woman since I had been married. I took a picture of her naked body as she posed, wearing nothing but my coat that I had gifted my wife. I didn't think much of it; we were caught up in the moment. I sought what I lacked at home—conversation, intimacy, and companionship.

Yahkhahnahn Ammi

I enjoyed every moment with Ms. Contagious. It had been a long time since I'd felt loved, appreciated, and admired; she catered to my every need, want, and desire. I had never experienced love from anyone like I had with her. The way she performed fellatio on me, deep-throating every inch of me, was nothing I had experienced before. I felt my toes curl. It was so good. I almost exploded with ecstasy. It was the most passionate lovemaking that I had ever experienced, "If only for one night." (Luther Vandross).

It was as though we were soulmates, reuniting. We spent hours making passionate love. Afterwards, we cuddled, talked, and laughed. When finally, she got up to shower, I joined her. After making love in the shower, we emerged and got dressed. The rain had stopped by the time we left the apartment. We walked down the stairs, got into the car, and fastened our seat belts. We talked as she drove me back to my apartment. I hugged her as we kissed. I told her to have a good night and to call me when she made it home safely. I walked into my apartment, went into my bedroom, took off all my clothes, and laid there in my boxers, thinking about Dru Hill's song, "The Love We Had," which stayed on my mind all night.

I saw Ms. Contagious once more, feeling compelled to reconnect with her. We arranged to meet at her place again, and this time, I drove there. She welcomed me warmly as soon as I arrived. We talked, kissed, and reminisced, reliving our previous encounter. It was thrilling, fulfilling, and truly remarkable. Afterward, just like before, we cuddled, shared more intimate moments, and showered together. As we dried each other off and moisturized our bodies, I felt a deep connection with her. We dressed and moved to the living room, where we sat on the couch, engrossed in conversation, looking into each other's eyes as if exchanging a silent, passionate dialogue. She shared more about her personal life, and I told her of my aspirations of publishing my first book and shared some of my work with her.

At some point after our second sexual encounter having just finished being intimate during our time together, Ms. Contagious secretly texted and invited some of her girlfriends over. As we sat together, one of them upon arriving said, "It smells like sex in here." They chuckled. Another one of her friends had the nerve to ask, "Aren't you married?" It was awkward. I felt a wave of disrespect wash over me. I was not embarrassed but deeply offended. I couldn't understand how or why Ms. Contagious had shared details of our intimacy with her friends, who were complete strangers to me. Who the fuck were they to assume anything about me?

This encounter with Ms. Contagious and her friends led to an unexpected turn in our relationship. I felt disappointed and betrayed. Why had she shared our personal business without my consent?

It can be devastating when trust is broken, especially after such intimacies had been shared. I was going through a difficult time, and it was during this period that I realized I had to focus on healing and moving forward. This incident changed the atmosphere. Ms. Contagious and her friends assumed I was having an affair, which was not exactly the case. I wanted to clarify that I was legally separated from my wife. While true that I did not owe her friends any explanation, I did owe Ms. Contagious one, but that wasn't the time or the place. I knew that the marriage between my wife and I had ended long ago. We were merely cohabiting in separate bedrooms in the same apartment, living separate lives.

Despite this, I felt betrayed by Ms. Contagious. After the deep connection and love we had shared, I couldn't believe she had broken my trust. This marked the last time I spoke to, saw, or made love to her. As I drove home, I felt as if my life had been shattered.

* * *

Personal Life Lesson Reflections

In this chapter, the complexities of love, desire, and betrayal took center stage. Amid the wreckage of a fractured marriage, I sought comfort and validation outside of my relationship, drawn to Ms. Contagious. The connection between us was undeniable, and it provided a temporary escape from the turmoil I faced at home. But the thrill of new intimacy came with its own set of complications, forcing me to confront my choices and the consequences of infidelity, broken trust, and unmet needs. What began as a passionate encounter eventually became a reflection of the deeper issues within me and my relationships.

Takeaways

Infidelity Doesn't Solve Problems

Seeking comfort outside of a troubled relationship may provide temporary relief, but it doesn't address the root issues. My time with Ms. Contagious distracted me from my marriage's problems, but it didn't fix them. Ultimately, these actions only added layers of guilt and complexity to an already difficult situation.

Emotional Vulnerability Can Lead to Poor Decisions

Being emotionally vulnerable often clouds judgment. During a period of deep loneliness and confusion, I made decisions that I later regretted. It's essential to recognize when you're vulnerable and to seek healing before engaging in new relationships or actions that could hurt others.

Be Honest with Yourself and Others

When I wasn't honest with myself about the state of my marriage or my feelings, I inadvertently misled Ms. Contagious and further complicated the situation. Transparency—both with yourself and others—is key to preventing misunderstandings and emotional harm.

The Importance of Boundaries in Relationships

Setting clear boundaries, both emotional and physical, is essential in any relationship. The lines between my failed marriage and my interactions with Ms. Contagious were blurred. Had I established clearer boundaries, I could have avoided further complications and betrayal of trust.

Healing Comes from Within

No outside relationship can fill the void created by internal wounds or a broken marriage. The love and attention I sought from Ms. Contagious were temporary fixes for deeper issues that needed healing from within. True healing requires introspection, time, and the willingness to confront difficult emotions.

Yahkhahnahn Ammi

This chapter highlights the dangers of seeking validation from external sources and underscores the importance of addressing personal issues directly. Through the thrill of newfound intimacy, I learned that true healing can only come from within and that escaping problems doesn't solve them—it only delays the inevitable.

CHAPTER 8

The Argument

"Ex-Factor"- Lauryn Hill

In the quiet hum of our home, a sudden jingle of keys shattered the stillness, marking the beginning of an unforgettable confrontation that would unravel the very fabric of our fractured family.

S ix months after my wife, Selena, had abandoned our marital home, I was left to figure out how to support myself and our children. I didn't have a steady job, so I turned to personal training, using my certification from the International Sports Science Association (ISSA). It was during this time, at one of the gyms I frequented, that I met Lisa. She had hired me as her personal trainer, but over time, our professional relationship grew into a close friendship.

Lisa was more than just a client; she became a lifeline during one of the most challenging periods of my life. She stepped in when Selena left, helping me raise my children in her absence. Lisa's presence brought stability, love, and support, particularly in moments when I didn't know how I could manage alone. As our bond deepened, she was not only a friend to me but a mother figure to my children, filling the void Selena had left behind.

However, that bond was tested when Selena, after a fourteen-month absence, returned home unexpectedly.

In the quiet hum of our home, a sudden jingle of keys marked the beginning of an unforgettable confrontation. Imagine the shock of seeing your estranged, now pregnant wife burst through the door after a fourteen-month absence, only to accuse your friend of infidelity and claim her place in a home she had long abandoned. In that moment, my life turned upside down, igniting a series of confrontations and revelations that would test the very fabric of our fractured family.

Can you imagine your spouse giving birth, breastfeeding two children, and then suddenly leaving you to raise them alone for what would turn out to be the first ten years of their lives, without any help or support? Selena missed significant milestones in our children's lives during her absence. She missed potty training Prince Avatar and his wobbly first steps at just eight months and his first words. She missed the delight of seeing Princess Tiana completely bypass the crawling stage and start walking. I vividly recall Princess Tiana's attempt to crawl, only to stand up and start running instead, which was a funny moment. Mama Jackie joked about someone being pregnant, and to my surprise, it turned out to be true—Selena had missed so many precious moments to bond with her children.

One day, while I was at home with our children, my friend Lisa and I were talking over a homemade vegan lunch I prepared. I had just put the babies down for a nap, and Lisa was sitting on the couch when I heard a key being inserted into the front door. I was not sure if it was someone trying to break in or not. I reached for the metal baseball bat I always kept in hand, but it was my wife, whom I had not seen for fourteen and a half months. I stood there momentarily stunned.

An obviously pregnant Selena wobbled into our apartment door as if everything was normal and immediately attacked Lisa.

I had to separate them. My wife had some nerve to suddenly pull this jealous act. She walked in pregnant, carrying another man's child in her womb, demanding to see her children, who were asleep as part of their daily routine. She was instantly jealous and vindictive toward Lisa. This woman had done more for our family than my wife had done in her absence. Selena did not even ask about our relationship. Lisa could have been my cousin, aunt, or anyone. She assumed that I'd had sex with Lisa, although she never asked, and I never denied or confirmed it.

Selena went into our children's bedroom and woke them up. They squirmed and cried when she tried to pick them up and hold them. They didn't know who their own mother was. It was sad; they kept running away from her and running to both Lisa and me. Lisa left crying and shaking her head.

Selena stayed that morning, comforting them, and by the evening, they wanted to sleep in the room with me. I sat with them for a while until they had gotten used to her. Selena spent the night in the bedroom with our children. As I lay awake in the quiet moments of introspection at night, consumed by guilt and regret, I found clarity amidst the chaos. Each mistake was a painful reminder of the consequences of my actions, pushing me to confront the truth about myself and my marriage. Through humility and acceptance, I began to see the possibility of a chance to rebuild my life with a newfound sense of purpose, even as the shadows of doubt lingered on the horizon.

The next morning, Selena asked if she could use my cell phone to make a call. I was hesitant, but I allowed her to. She called me into the living room, while our children were asleep in their shared bedroom. I had just checked on them and wasn't sure why Selena needed me. As she approached me, holding the cell phone in her hand, she asked, "Who is this lady in your phone?" I was already in the process of getting dressed to leave the house, and I was taken aback. I asked her why she was going through pictures on my phone. As I walked away from her, she followed me to the bathroom, where I stood in front of the mirror, getting dressed. She stood there, demanding to have the conversation, and all I could think was, "You've got to be kidding me right now. Are you serious?"

Selena continued to press me about the woman in my phone. I forgot to delete the photos of Ms. Contagious, and in a moment of weakness, I gas-lighted her. I lied, claiming that the woman wearing the coat in the picture was not wearing her coat but rather her own coat, which happened to resemble the one I had given her.

I couldn't bring myself to tell Selena that I had allowed another woman who I slept with to wear the coat I had given her. My wife didn't buy it. The reality hit me hard as I couldn't hide or deny any longer that the woman was wearing my wife's coat. When Selena found out the truth, she was furious. She looked at the phone, looked at the woman in the picture, looked at me, and then she slapped the holy shit out of me. It was not a regular slap; she slapped me hard. It was sudden, and I did not even see it coming. I could not even blame her. At that moment I questioned myself, I thought I deserved it. The reality is, no woman or man should ever put their hands on one another period.

The aftermath of her slap to the left side of my face caused it to go numb as I stood there in shock that she had put her hands on me. We were both against physical violence in our relationship. I had confided in Selena how domestic violence had destroyed my family as a child and my promise to fight against it and advocate for victims of domestic violence prior to our marriage. She knew I was an anti-domestic violence activist in Illinois and Missouri. Nevertheless, I was shocked that I had lied to my wife so easily and that my face stung like that. I heard ringing in both ears.

She had slapped me so hard it echoed throughout the apartment, leaving me frozen and lost in time from the effects. It took the love of God inside of me to keep from retaliating. In that moment, I wanted to slap her back. Gritting my teeth, I brushed past her and walked out of the house, only to be greeted by the police she had called while I was still in a haze from her assault. I guess she had anticipated a physical escalation. Thank God I had restraint. Her actions jolted us back to reality, and I was left reeling. Selena's message was loud and clear—I would never lie to her about anything else.

As I walked out the front door, I was greeted by the police. Selena had already admitted to slapping me. Despite their presence and her admission, I chose not to file charges. Instead, I simply left home, I let it slide, carrying only the weight and embarrassment of the moment and the decision to move on.

Yahkhahnahn Ammi

In the aftermath of our indiscretions, I grappled with faith in my wife, shaken by her seemingly innocent conversations with other men. The line between loyalty and betrayal blurred, forcing me to confront the consequences of my actions through introspection and self-reflection. Amidst the wreckage of our failed marriage, I questioned the very foundation of our relationship, searching desperately for a glimmer of redemption that remained elusive. Selena had been back for about two weeks, demanding to claim our children on her tax returns. Before leaving back to St. Louis, Selena and I had an argument over something minor and childish—the thermostat. I would set it to 77 degrees, and Selena would turn it up to 100 degrees, causing it to be increasingly hot in our apartment. Admittedly, Selena was anemic. It was winter time, and it felt like a sauna.

I was adamant about budgeting and keeping the house at a reasonable temperature for the family. I didn't want our children to get sick. She turned the thermostat up every chance she got, and I turned it down from 100 degrees to a safe temperature.

As we both touched the thermostat panel, it fell off the wall. It was a silly thing to argue about. This time, my wife and I both reached for the thermostat panel, and the cover of it fell to the floor.

Selena called someone on her cellphone in front of me and told that person, "I want my husband out of the house." It was crooked Officer Robinsome, who responded and arrived first at our apartment, and then other police arrived. He carried spare keys to apartment units because he was also employed in some capacity by the St. Clair Housing Authority. He entered the apartment forcefully and spoke to my wife, who showed him the thermostat panel that had fallen to the floor during our argument. I told

Robinsome to get out of our house. Our children stood there afraid, staring at the stranger in our living room. They watched Robinsome arrest and handcuffed me. Our son was only two, and our daughter was one year old. He placed me in the back of his police car, took me to the local police station, city hall in Brooklyn, and locked me in a holding cell with my hands behind my back.

I had flashbacks of the prison I had left six years before. I snapped. I kicked on the jail door. I demanded to know why I had been arrested. I was pissed. I felt the tears run down my face because I was so angry. I demanded to speak with the police chief.

Robinsome made several threats. He said, *"If you do not shut the fuck up, I'm gonna come in that cell and beat your ass."* Hearing the commotion, the police chief, who was my uncle, walked into the office. He had heard Robinsome's threat and was infuriated with him. The police chief told Robinsome, *"You will not threaten or put your hands on anyone locked up and in handcuffs, especially not my nephew. Take them goddamn handcuffs off, and release him, now!"* Robinsome had no idea that the Chief was my uncle. I was glad to see my uncle that day.

The Chief knew that Robinsome had been on some straight up bullshit and reprimanded him for arresting me over a civil matter. The charges were dropped. I could not understand why that officer had behaved towards me in that manner.

I did not follow up to see if he had been fired or suspended, I am sure his karmic patterns would eventually catch up with him. I found out that Robinsome later transferred to a different department. Perhaps he returned back to the Washington Park or the East St. Louis, Illinois police department where he came from.

Yahkhahnahn Ammi

I am unaware if it was because of that incident or an accumulation of them. This is an example of why we as melanated or so-called black men do not trust or cooperate with them. There should have been an investigation into his conduct, maybe there was, and maybe he would get fired, or transferred to a different precinct.

Once I was released, I called Lisa and asked if she could pick me up from the police station. I waited until she arrived and told her everything. After that incident, I didn't have any more issues with Robinsome, and the department dropped all charges he tried to bring against me.

Despite my efforts to avoid conflict, Selena persistently escalated trivial disagreements, leading to confrontations and calls to emergency services. Her vindictive actions left me homeless and deprived of access to my apartment and our children for over a month. She further exacerbated the situation by manipulating government services and agencies against me, falsely portraying me as a threat. Selena was not done playing her dirty little tricks. Anytime I went to the store for groceries or diapers, she would call 911 upon my return, claiming I was causing a disturbance and pretending that I did not live there. When the police arrived, they informed me that it didn't matter if her claims were true or false; if the police were called on a man, he had to leave. I was baffled. This pattern continued: she would call me every time our children needed something. Each time, I hoped for a different outcome. Then, she would take our children to visit her family in St. Louis. I felt like I was being pushed out of my home and away from my children. I would only hear from her when she claimed they needed food or diapers. Where was I supposed to go? That was my home, my family, and I was determined to protect what I loved! This is a teaching lesson to men and your rights that you have when it comes to your children and filing for full custody.

My wife Selena at that time was not mentally stable to care for our children and I had different events that proved that I should have been the custodial parent at minimum but because the state of Illinois, judicial biased laws that favored mothers as custodial parents it would have proven to be an uphill battle.

The police chief who was my uncle, the mayor, and everyone in town knew what type of person I was. I was a family man, a stand-up guy who didn't cause any problems. I kept my nose clean, minded my own business, and took up my responsibilities as a married man. I wasn't sleeping around with women in town. Once released from jail, I was told that I could not go back home unless I had orders from the court. So, I called Lisa to pick me up. We immediately drove to the courthouse. I explained to the judge what was happening. Although the judge did write an order, it stated that we were both listed on the Housing Authority subsidized housing as tenants and had equal access to the apartment. It was further ordered to contact the Housing Authority.

Lisa also drove me to the housing authority, where I informed them of what had transpired. I told them I needed to be removed from the household as my wife had taken possession of the house, and I didn't want to be responsible.

Because I was still a tenant on the lease, I had legal grounds to be there. I filed the paperwork to be removed from the apartment as head of household and to have Selena listed as the responsible party instead. After that was completed, we drove back to the police station and left them with a copy of the Judge's order granting me access to the apartment. A few days later, I returned home to check on Prince Avatar and Princess Tiana, bringing diapers, wipes, and clothes for them. Despite Selena's cold reception, I was thrilled to see my children. They were happy to see me, too, and I spent precious moments playing and laughing with them.

Selena seemed distant; she scoffed, walking away to the children's bedroom. Despite her attitude, I enjoyed the time with my little angels. Devastated and fed up with the ongoing drama, I reached my breaking point and filed for divorce in St. Clair County Court in Belleville, Illinois. After Selena was served with the divorce papers, she retaliated by filing an emergency order of protection against me, seeking to retain possession of the car and the apartment and to keep me away from our children.

In court, I refuted her claims, highlighting her abandonment and the disruptive behavior upon her return just two months prior, with support from witnesses, including our Rabbi. I pleaded for full custody of our children, emphasizing my role as their primary caregiver and the assistance I had received from various organizations. Despite the turmoil, I remained steadfast in seeking justice and protection for myself and our children, determined to navigate these challenges and reclaim what was rightfully mine. Fortunately, Judge Carson recognized the truth of the situation and vacated Selena's order of protection against me.

* * *

Personal Life Lesson Reflections

In this chapter, the fragile remnants of my marriage came to a head when Selena returned to our home after a fourteen-month absence. She was pregnant, carrying another man's child, and her presence sparked an intense confrontation that unraveled the fabric of our fractured family. The arguments, betrayals, and accusations that followed became defining moments, forcing me to reevaluate my marriage, my role as a father, and my own choices. Through it all, I grappled with intense emotions of anger, guilt, regret, and love, as I navigated the complexities of divorce, fatherhood, and personal responsibility.

Takeaways

Respect and Boundaries Are Crucial

Relationships demand mutual respect and clear boundaries. Selena's sudden return, her accusations, and her physical attack reminded me of the importance of setting and maintaining boundaries. Without respect, even the strongest relationships can crumble under the weight of unresolved issues and miscommunications.

Violence is Never the Answer

No matter how high emotions run, resorting to violence—whether physical or emotional—never leads to resolution. Selena's slap and my desire to retaliate showed how anger can escalate situations, but it is critical to practice restraint and deescalate whenever possible.

Yahkhahnahn Ammi

Introspection Leads to Growth

In the aftermath of our confrontations, I found myself reflecting deeply on my own actions and mistakes. Through introspection, I realized the importance of humility and the need to accept my flaws to become a better father and person. Personal growth begins when we face the consequences of our actions.

Effective Communication is Key

The breakdown of communication in my marriage led to misunderstandings, resentment, and mistrust. This chapter underscores the need for open, honest conversations in relationships, especially when faced with conflict. Clear communication can prevent unnecessary arguments and help resolve issues before they escalate.

Self-Advocacy and Legal Protection Matter

When navigating difficult relationships or legal battles, it's essential to protect yourself and assert your rights. Filing for divorce, defending myself in court, and advocating for my rights as a father were necessary. I took the necessary steps to ensure my safety and that of my children. Don't be afraid to seek legal recourse if the situation calls for it.

This chapter serves as a powerful reminder of the emotional and legal complexities that arise when relationships break down. While the journey is painful, learning to navigate conflict, assert boundaries, and pursue personal growth can lead to healing and a better future for you and your family.

CHAPTER 9

Betrayal & Legal Battles

"Contagious"- The Isley Brothers

I never imagined that betrayal would arrive wearing a police badge, but that night, with Officer Robinsome's car outside my window, my world was about to unravel in ways I could have never foreseen.

That night, I saw Robinsome's police car parked outside our bedroom window. My world crumbled, and the weight of betrayal crushed my heart. Discovering my wife's affair with a police officer shattered my life, sparking a battle that would test my strength and resolve. At that time Selena and I were not divorced and were still living in the same apartment with our children, that is when she called the police to have me escorted away. In fact, our children were inside the home when this affair took place.

The weight of betrayal sits heavy on my chest, a burden I never thought I would bear. When I discovered the affair between my wife and Robinsome, I was overcome with a mix of emotions -

shock, anger, and deep sadness. My trust was shattered, and my sense of security was ripped away. It wasn't just the betrayal of a spouse; it was a betrayal of the sanctity of marriage, of the vows we took, and of the respect I thought we had for each other. I felt violated, disrespected, and deeply ashamed as if I had been a fool to trust in something so fragile.

The affair with Robinsome was the ultimate betrayal. Not only did he breach his duty as a police officer by engaging in a relationship with my wife, but he also violated my trust and the integrity of our community. His actions were a slap in the face, a reminder that even those sworn to protect and serve could be capable of such deception and betrayal. As I grappled with the reality of the affair, I struggled to understand how my wife could betray me in such a profound way. I never revealed to her that I was aware of the affair because I wanted to believe that what was done in the dark would come to light on its own. But as I watched Robinsome's police car parked behind our apartment building, in the grass yard outside our bedroom single window (which was on the first floor) one late night, everything became painfully clear. My wife's actions spoke louder than words, and her silence on the matter only confirmed my worst fears.

The betrayal escalated when I realized the extent of the deception. Robinsome and my wife had orchestrated a plan to keep me away from my family while they continued their affair. They used the police force, a symbol of justice and protection, to enforce their deceit, further adding to my sense of betrayal and powerlessness.

I wanted to confront Robinsome, to demand answers and justice for what he had done. But I knew that my priority was to keep my children safe and out of harm's way. My anger and hatred towards my wife grew, and I felt a coldness in my heart that I had never experienced before.

The love I once felt for her was replaced by a burning desire for revenge, a need to make her feel the same pain and humiliation that I was feeling. The betrayal extended into the legal battles that followed. My wife's attempts to claim our children on her tax returns and her fraudulent actions only added to the chaos and confusion of our divorce proceedings.

But through it all, I fought for my children, justice, and the truth to be revealed. I had a meeting with the State of Illinois, "Welfare" Department of Human Services (DHS) office, who awarded me temporary assistance for needy families, and they pursued my wife for child support and the money she had illegally received from filing our children on her tax returns. Her actions forced her to flee to Missouri, leaving behind a trail of lies and deceit.

Returning home from the DHS office, I discovered that Selena had driven to the private daycare in Ms. Roundtree's home, causing havoc. Ms. Roundtree refused to let her take the children and called me about Selena's erratic behavior. She asked if Selena was on drugs. I could only say, "I am not sure. You know I have not seen my wife in over fourteen and a half months."

"I know; it put me in a tough position, and I felt bad, but I could not let her take the kids," she replied.

"You did the right thing by calling me," I told her.

Selena called me asking if I could refuel the car that she had taken from us. I said no. When I arrived at the apartment, I noticed she had also been there. She left behind a few pieces of important documentation that I would later use in court, critical for filing our divorce in Missouri. She took our children's clothes, all her clothes, and their diapers. She wanted to make me suffer by taking our children away from me, but Ms. Roundtree had put an end to her plans.

Unfortunately, Selena decided to leave Illinois in the middle of our divorce proceedings. She told me that she planned on living with her mother and family. Our attorneys moved to dismiss the case. This move led to the cancellation of all future court hearings and the dismissal of our case, as Illinois claimed they no longer had jurisdiction. Consequently, I needed to file for divorce in Missouri. I had to determine her current residence or find an address where she had been living for nearly two years prior. This marked a heartbreaking and pivotal moment in our marriage, signaling the beginning of the end.

Through the pain and turmoil of betrayal and legal battles, I learned valuable lessons that have shaped my perspective on life and relationships. I learned the importance of trust and communication in a relationship and the devastating consequences of betrayal.

I realized that sometimes, the people we trust the most are capable of hurting us the deepest.

My advice to anyone going through a similar situation is to stay strong, to fight for what is right, and to never lose hope. Betrayal may shake your faith in humanity, but healing and finding peace is possible. Surround yourself with supportive people who uplift and encourage you, and never be afraid to seek help when you need it.

The journey to healing may be long and difficult, but it is worth it in the end.

* * *

Personal Life Lesson Reflections

In this chapter, I faced the ultimate betrayal—an affair between my wife and a police officer, Officer Robinsome. This affair tore my world apart, not just because of the infidelity but because of the deeper betrayal of trust, family, and the sanctity of marriage. The affair revealed the fragility of relationships and sparked a legal battle that would test my resolve, endurance, and love for my children. As I fought through the emotional turmoil, legal challenges, and the fallout of the affair, I learned valuable lessons that reshaped my understanding of betrayal, trust, and resilience.

Takeaways

Trust Can Be Fragile

Betrayal by someone you trust can be one of the deepest wounds you'll ever experience. It teaches us that while trust is the foundation of any relationship, it can be fragile and easily broken. It's essential to value and protect that trust while also preparing to rebuild when it's shattered.

The Importance of Resilience

Betrayal can be emotionally devastating, but resilience is key to moving forward. Despite the heartbreak, legal battles, and feelings of powerlessness, I stayed focused on what mattered most—my children. Strength lies in persistence and finding the resolve to keep fighting for what is right.

Justice May Be Slow, But It's Worth Pursuing Legal battles, especially in the context of family and betrayal, are long and draining. Yet, pursuing justice and holding people accountable, as I did with my wife's fraudulent actions, can bring some measure of closure and balance to the chaos.

Lean on Support Systems

In times of turmoil, having a support system is critical. Whether it's friends, family, or people like Ms. Roundtree, whose actions protected my children, having others you can trust and depend on is crucial to finding the strength to continue.

Healing Takes Time

The road to healing from betrayal is long and difficult. It requires patience, time, and a willingness to confront pain head on. Surrounding yourself with positive influences and focusing on your well-being is essential to eventually finding peace and moving forward.

This chapter serves as a reminder that betrayal, while painful and disorienting, does not have to define the rest of your life. With resilience, support, and a commitment to healing, you can rebuild and find your way forward, stronger and wiser than before.

CHAPTER 10

Divorce, Custody, and Visitation

"Keep Ya Head Up" - 2Pac

As I stood in the courtroom, the echo of past betrayals reverberated through the sterile halls, and I realized this wasn't just a fight for divorce—it was a battle for my children's future, my soul, and everything I believed in.

The cold, sterile light of the courtroom bore down on me like an unyielding force, marking the beginning of a battle that would reshape my life and redefine the meaning of family. Each time the courtroom doors swung open, I braced myself for the tidal wave of revelations that would follow—secrets that shattered illusions, tested my resilience, and ignited a relentless fight for my children's future.

Divorce isn't just the end of a marriage; it's a war that ravages the mind, body, and soul. The process breeds jealousy, revenge, and hatred—all emotions that can destroy one's ability to parent effectively. In the summer of 2013, I found myself back in the family court of St. Louis, where another court date was set to determine custody of my children and finalize my divorce from Selena, my soon-to-be ex-wife.

As the courtroom drama unfolded, it became glaringly obvious that Selena had been evading her visitation responsibilities. It was clear that I was shouldering the weight of parenthood alone, and her erratic behavior and blatant disregard for our children's well-being only fueled my determination to fight for their safety and stability. Reflecting on my failed marriage, I wished I could rewrite certain moments. I would have cherished her more, communicated better, and nurtured our bond with more respect. In my immaturity, I had asked God for a wife, but I failed to consider the kind of partner I truly needed. Selena had her good qualities—she was loving, humble, and often respectful—but our differences ran too deep, leading us down the path to divorce. The divorce dragged on for over five grueling years, largely because neither of us could afford legal representation. The case sat neglected, gathering dust in the court system. Eventually, I gathered evidence—Selena's dishonorable military discharge and character references from community leaders—and filed them in court. Finally, after years of turmoil, we reached an agreement.

The judge signed off on the terms, but the real toll had been on our children. I had always dreamt of being the best husband and father, providing a loving home for my kids, but in many ways, I felt I had failed them. When the judge finally made a decision, it felt like a small victory amidst the chaos. He granted me sole legal custody of our children—Prince Avatar and Princess Tiana.

It was a hard-fought battle, especially as a Melanated or so-called Black man in Missouri, where the odds were stacked against me. Gaining custody as a single father, particularly in a system that often favors mothers, was no easy feat. But after years of fighting, I had won. I was given the authority to make decisions regarding their religious upbringing, education, and medical care. Although their mother was ordered to pay child support and granted weekend visits, I had legally become their primary caretaker.

By the summer of 2013, I had been their sole parent for nearly six years. The journey was full of challenges—Missouri's court system often presumes that mothers are the primary caregivers, and systemic biases against Melanated or so-called Black men only compounded the difficulty. But despite these obstacles, I stayed committed to providing my children with a stable, loving environment. My victory was a testament to perseverance, and I hoped it would inspire other fathers, especially Black fathers, to fight for their children's futures. However, the battle was far from over. Selena had abandoned our home five years earlier, only to resurface with new children from extramarital affairs—children she had tried to hide. Despite these revelations, the court ultimately granted me custody of our two children. Though Selena was permitted unsupervised visits, she often disappeared for months on end, only to reappear demanding to see our children. When Selena resurfaced, she insisted on having our children for the weekend, per the court order. Although I had reservations, I had no choice but to comply. After their first visit to her place on the Southside of St. Louis, my children returned home visibly shaken, unwilling to go back. Yet the court order remained, and I was forced to continue sending them on weekend visits. I documented each incident—her erratic behavior, their fearful reactions—but it wasn't enough.

Without legal representation, I had to go through the process all over again. On one occasion, Selena absconded with our children, vanishing from her apartment without a trace. Panicked, I contacted the police, seeking to file kidnapping charges, but was told that because she was their mother, no such charges could be filed. Despite my pleas, law enforcement offered little help, promising only to assign a juvenile detective to the case. Months passed without any progress, but I persisted, documenting every detail and searching for information on their whereabouts. In October 2013, I approached Patrick Henry Elementary School, a public school downtown, hoping to catch a glimpse of my children. To my surprise, I saw them walking alone through a dangerous neighborhood, presumably on their way to their mother's apartment. Overcome with relief, I called out to them, "Yeladeem!" (which means "children" in Hebrew). They turned, recognizing my voice, and joyfully ran to me. I scooped them up, hugged them, and kissed them—grateful to have them back in my arms. Concerned for their safety, I took them home with me. I notified the Sublet police detective and informed them that my children were once again in my care. Selena never reached out to inquire about them, and I decided not to tell her that I had regained custody. This marked a turning point in my fight for custody. I scheduled a pediatrician appointment to ensure they were unharmed, and though the results came back clear, I remained unsettled.

By 2016, Selena had not exercised her visitation rights in three years. She had absconded with our children, sold their cellphones, and cut off all communication. I eventually bought them new phones to maintain some connection with their mother. After years of neglect, Selena called. It was the fall of 2016, asking to be involved in their lives again. Her behavior during her limited visits left our children frightened and confused.

Violating court orders, she often vanished without notice, and each time I reported her actions to the police and courts, I was met with indifference. The law's blind spots—particularly when it comes to a mother's rights—left me feeling powerless.

Despite this, I stayed determined to protect my children. I sought medical evaluations to ensure their safety and did everything in my power to provide them with a stable, loving home. The road ahead would be long, but in the eyes of my children, I found the strength to continue. I vowed to continue fighting, standing as their guardian against whatever storms lay ahead. The courtroom battles tested every fiber of my being. I had to confront a system blind to the truth and a future filled with uncertainty. But through it all, I learned invaluable lessons. I realized that second chances are rare, and I vowed to build a better future for my children.

For anyone considering marriage, I implore you to ensure deep compatibility with your partner. Take the time to really get to know them and their family. And if you find yourself facing divorce, weigh your options carefully—seek counseling, and avoid advice from those who lack firsthand experience. Marriage and parenthood require commitment, and when they break down, the consequences can be devastating. But with perseverance, you can still provide a loving home for your children. My battle for custody wasn't just against my ex-wife—it was against a flawed system that seemed indifferent to the truth. Missouri's family courts often lean towards maternal custody, operating under the presumption that mothers are the best primary care-givers. But statistics show that only about 17.5% of custodial parents in the United States of America (U.S.) are fathers. The systemic biases, compounded by racial prejudices, make it an uphill battle for so-called Black men to gain custody of their children.

My victory was not just personal; it was a challenge to the system. It demonstrated that change is possible, even within a flawed system. It offered hope to other fathers—especially Black fathers—who find themselves in similar situations. Perseverance, advocacy, and an unyielding belief in the possibility of change can ultimately secure justice and equality in family law. As I reflect on the journey that led me here, I understand that the scars run deep, but they also remind me of the strength I found in the darkest times. My battle for custody has not only been about reclaiming my role as a father but about challenging a system that needs reform. It's a story of survival, resilience, and the unbreakable bond between a father and his children.

In Missouri, the presumption of paternity applies but can be contested under certain circumstances:

Presumption of Paternity: Missouri law presumes the husband is the legal father of a child born to his wife during the marriage (RSMo § 210.822).

Challenging Paternity: The presumption can be challenged by filing a paternity action in court, initiated by the husband, mother, child, biological father, or the Family Support Division. DNA testing may be ordered to establish the biological father's identity.

Time Limits: There is no specific statute of limitations for challenging paternity in Missouri, but it is advisable to act promptly as the court will consider the best interests of the child and the length of time the presumed father has acted as the child's parent.

Best Interests of the Child: Missouri courts consider the best interests of the child when deciding paternity issues, including the emotional and psychological relationship between the presumed father and the child.

Termination of Parental Rights: If paternity is successfully challenged and the husband is found not to be the biological father, his parental rights and obligations, including child support, may be terminated, subject to the court's determination of the child's best interests.

Acknowledgment of Paternity: If the biological father wishes to establish his paternity, he can sign an Acknowledgment of Paternity (AOP) form, filed with the Missouri Department of Health and Senior Services. This form can also be used to challenge the presumed father's paternity.

For married men in Missouri facing similar situations, consulting with a family law attorney is strongly recommended to navigate the legal process and understand the specific steps and considerations involved.

Selena concealed the whereabouts of the child conceived from her affair with officer Robinsome, which led to our divorce.

Yahkhahnahn Ammi

Despite this, the court ruled in my favor, granting me custody of our two children Prince Avatar and Princess Tiana, and the court allowed me to relinquish parental rights to the two children, a boy and a girl, Selena attempted to give up for adoption that I did not father. This decision was in their best interest, sparing them from the complexities of their parents' actions. I thought.

Standing before the judge in the St. Louis courtroom, the weight of the past six years pressed down on me like an anchor, threatening to pull me under.

My battle to retain custody of my two children, Prince Avatar and Princess Tiana, who had been living with me since my wife's abandonment in 2008, felt like a fight for my very soul. The thought of losing them, of being torn apart from the only family I had left, filled me with a sense of dread and desperation.

As I recounted the events that had led me to this moment, each word was weighed down by the pain and betrayal that had defined my marriage. Selena did not want custody of our children and certainly was not capable of raising our children on her own, and truth be told, I did not know how I would do it until it was forced upon me. Selena wanted to fight me in court out of revenge and control, it had nothing to do with our children, but since I had rejected her and gave up on her due to the extra-marital affairs, she kept this charade up and used our children as pawns. The revelation of my wife's secret pregnancies and subsequent attempts to give the children up for adoption cast a shadow over the proceedings. When the agency contacted me because Selena and I were still legally married, I knew I had to take action. These children, born out of her extramarital affairs, were legally but not biologically mine. I made the difficult decision to relinquish my legal parental rights to them, a choice I felt was in their best interest.

My wife's attempt to give them up for adoption was a tactic advised by her attorney to conceal her affairs and their births. I did not want to raise these children or be held responsible for them, and I was relieved when the judge ruled in my favor, sparing me from any obligations towards them.

As the courtroom drama unfolded, my soon-to-be ex-wife's persistent evasion of her visitation responsibilities became glaringly apparent. It was a stark reminder of the uphill battle I faced as a single parent, shouldering the weight of parenthood alone. Her erratic behavior and blatant disregard for our children's well-being only fueled my determination to fight for their safety and stability. When the judge finally rendered a decision, it felt like a small victory amidst the chaos. He ruled in my favor, granting me the divorce that would become official in 30 days. Which meant that I had legal custody of Prince Avatar and Princess Tiana, and the judge granted Selena visitation rights.

However, the battle for their well-being was far from over. As I reflected on the tumultuous journey that had brought me to this point, a sense of weariness settled over me. The road ahead would be long and fraught with challenges, but I was determined to persevere. For in the eyes of my children, I found the strength to continue, to protect and nurture them with every fiber of my being. And with that resolve burning within me, I vowed to continue fighting, to stand as a guardian against the storm, to ensure that Prince Avatar and Princess Tiana would always have a safe and loving home with me. Despite the court's ruling, my ex-wife's unwillingness to fulfill her visitation obligations loomed over us like a dark cloud, casting a shadow of uncertainty over our lives.

Post divorce, my ex-wife's visitation rights were clearly outlined in the court order, yet she consistently failed to fulfill her obligations. Over the course of three years, she neglected her visits, forcing me to continuously pursue her to adhere to the terms set by the court. Despite the specified location for visitation exchanges, she repeatedly disregarded the order, leaving me to navigate the challenges of co-parenting alone. During one particularly alarming visitation, our children returned home bed wetting, a behavior they had never exhibited before. They recounted disturbing episodes of their mother's erratic behavior, including arguments with past lovers and destructive outbursts that left them frightened and traumatized. These incidents only served to intensify my determination to fight for their safety and well-being. As if her negligence wasn't enough, my ex-wife further jeopardized our children's stability by abruptly relocating without informing me or the court.

She withdrew them from their (AMES) school without a word, leaving me in the dark about their whereabouts. When I discovered her empty apartment, I was gripped with fear and desperation, prompting me to take action to protect my children. I called the police to report that my ex-wife had absconded with our children. I demanded to file kidnapping charges, emphasizing the court order she had violated. Yet, despite my pleas and concerns for my children's safety, their response was, "She is the mother, it is not a kidnap."

The police said. They did not offer any immediate resolution. Their help as usual was inadequate, leaving me feeling helpless and vulnerable. In a desperate attempt to regain custody and ensure their safety, I scheduled an appointment with their pediatrician to have them examined for signs of abuse. While relieved when the results came back negative, I remained haunted by the possibility of harm inflicted upon them in my absence.

Despite my ex-wife's continued neglect of her visitation rights, almost four years had passed since my children returned to my care. Her absence had left a void in their lives, yet I remained steadfast in my commitment to provide them with a stable and loving home. As I reflected on the challenges we had faced and the battles yet to come, I knew that the road ahead would be fraught with obstacles. But in the eyes of my children, I found the strength to carry on, to fight for their well-being with every fiber of my being. And with that resolve burning within me, I vowed to continue the fight, to stand as their guardian against the storm, and to ensure that Prince Avatar and Princess Tiana would always have a safe and loving home with me.

* * *

Personal Life Lesson Reflections

In this chapter, I stood in the courtroom, battling through the pain and chaos of divorce while fighting for my children's well-being. Divorce is more than the legal dissolution of marriage; it tears at the emotional fabric of a family, often becoming a battleground where resentment, bitterness, and unhealed wounds surface. For me, it was not only a fight for my own peace of mind but, more importantly, a fight for the future of my children. The courtroom battles, hidden truths, and betrayals tested my resilience, but they also fueled my determination to create a safe and stable environment for Prince Avatar and Princess Tiana. As I reflect on this period, it becomes clear that despite the heart-break, there were lessons to be learned about perseverance, fatherhood, and navigating a flawed system.

Takeaways

Resilience in the Face of Adversity

Divorce can be an emotionally devastating process, but maintaining focus on the well-being of your children provides the strength to persevere. The fight for custody wasn't just about legal rights—it was a battle for my children's future, and their safety was my driving force.

The Importance of Legal Preparedness Documenting every incident, conversation, and behavior is critical when navigating custody battles. In my case, having evidence and records helped me secure sole legal custody and protect my children.

The System Isn't Always Fair

The legal system often operates with biases, particularly against fathers in custody disputes. Despite systemic hurdles, perseverance and a clear strategy can lead to success—even when the odds are stacked against you.

The Need for Self-Reflection

Divorce forces you to confront your past mistakes and short-comings. While it's important to fight for your rights and your children's safety, it's equally crucial to reflect on your own actions, ensuring that you grow and improve from the experience.

Staying Focused on Your Children

Throughout this emotional battle, it's easy to get lost in bitterness and anger. The best way to move forward is to remain focused on your children, ensuring that their needs, stability, and happiness are prioritized above all else.

This chapter serves as a reminder that while divorce and custody battles are deeply painful, they also present an opportunity to redefine family, build resilience, and become the parent your children truly need.

CHAPTER 11

Single Fatherhood

"His Dream" - Asher Roth

Fatherhood was my greatest gift but raising you on my own taught me that love is the most powerful force in the face of life's greatest challenges.

A letter to my sons and daughters

My Dearest Children,

The most challenging task a father has is protecting his children and his family. As I sit down to write this letter, my heart is filled with immense love and pride, that the love and sacrifices of our journey have shaped the remarkable individuals you are becoming. This is a letter to you, my beautifully talented and loving children. You are approaching adulthood, and I find myself reflecting on the incredible journey we've shared—a journey filled with challenges, sacrifices, and above all, love.

Becoming a father was the best thing that ever happened to me, second only to the gift of life itself. From the moment you were born, I vowed to give you the best life I could offer. I set aside my own dreams to focus on yours, and when I became a single father, I fought even harder to ensure you had everything you needed.

In 2007, and 2008 when our family dynamic shifted, and I found myself navigating the world of single fatherhood, I knew the road ahead would be tough. But nothing could have prepared me for the challenges that lay ahead—yet every single moment was worth it. As time passed I remember how you both, in your innocent and loving ways, dubbed me "Number One Dad." Even though I was your only dad, I often felt unworthy of that title because I wished I could give you more than I had to offer.

Balancing work, home, and the emotional needs of two young children was overwhelming, especially after your mother left. Yet, despite the financial strain, the long days, and the sleepless nights, I was determined to raise you myself. I refused to rely on babysitters or daycare, choosing instead to be present for you in every way possible. This decision brought its own set of challenges, but it was born out of my deep love for you both. I remember the financial strain, the loss of jobs, and the isolation I felt without reliable transportation. Turning to government assistance was a humbling experience, and using foodstamps was a mix of shame and relief.

Society's stereotypes about single fathers only added to my struggles, but I remained resolute in my mission to provide for you.

As I reflect on these times, I remember the immense challenges you faced as well. I was heartbroken by the treatment you received at school—Prince Avatar, when you were exposed to inappropriate material by a teacher, and Princess Tiana, when you were involved in that bus accident, and later, when you were placed in a chokehold by a teacher. These incidents still fill me with anger and sorrow. I did everything in my power to protect you, to advocate for you, and when necessary, to remove you from environments that didn't honor your safety and well-being. Homeschooling became our refuge, a time for us to reconnect, and for you to thrive in a loving and supportive environment.

Amidst all these challenges, I began to feel the weight of single parenthood more heavily. I questioned whether I was enough, whether I could fulfill both the roles of parent and father. But now, as I look back, I see that all I needed to be was your father—the best father I could be. Through it all, your smiles, your laughter, and your love were my anchor. You kept me going during the darkest days.

As you stand on the brink of adulthood, I want you to remember that everything I did, I did out of love for you. I encourage you to read, speak, and grow rich in knowledge every day. It will give you the freedom your heart desires. Hold on to love, learn to forgive, and never forget that you are not responsible for the divorce or the struggles that followed. You are the light of my life, and I am endlessly proud of the people you are becoming.

I will never forget the day each of you was born—you were perfect little angels. Each of you made me the humblest and most appreciative father. You changed my life for the better and taught me how to love again. Even though our interactions are now limited, and you are learning my truths through the pages of this book, know that you will always have a place in my heart and a home with me.

Please forgive me for any pain caused by the separation, for any promises I could not keep due to the circumstances beyond my control. Life may have been hard, but you are the most perfect part of my journey. Despite everything, I will always be here for you, no matter what. Remember who you are, where you come from, and who you belong to.

Looking back on our journey together, I see that fatherhood has been my greatest achievement. My hope is that you carry with you the lessons learned, the values instilled, and the love that has always been at the center of our lives. Together, we have faced challenges, and together we will continue to pursue happiness and fulfillment.

With Love,

Abba

* * *

Personal Life Lesson Reflections

In this chapter, I reflect on the immense joy and responsibility that came with becoming a father, especially after stepping into the role of a single parent. The journey has been a roller-coaster of emotions, filled with sacrifices, challenges, and love. Through my struggles, I found purpose in protecting, guiding, and nurturing my children. Single fatherhood tested my resilience, but it also deepened my bond with my children, teaching me invaluable lessons about love, perseverance, and the power of family.

Yahkhahnahn Ammi

As I wrote this letter to my children, it became clear to me that every decision I made, every battle I fought, was driven by my love for them. This chapter is a testament to the trials of single fatherhood and the profound impact that love and dedication can have on a family. Though it hasn't always been easy, the rewards have far outweighed the challenges, and my children have been my anchor through it all.

Takeaways

Love Fuels Perseverance

The love we have for our children gives us the strength to push through even the darkest times.

It is this love that drives us to fight for their future, no matter how difficult the road becomes.

Fatherhood is an Ongoing Journey

Being a father doesn't end when your children grow older. It's a lifelong commitment to guide, support, and protect them, regardless of the challenges or circumstances.

The Importance of Presence

As a single father, I chose to be present for my children rather than relying on external support systems. This decision created a deeper connection and gave my children the security they needed to thrive.

Resilience in Adversity

Single parenthood is often filled with financial strain, emotional challenges, and isolation. But resilience in the face of adversity not only strengthens us but sets an example for our children on how to navigate life's challenges.

Forgiveness and Healing

It's crucial to teach our children the power of forgiveness—both for others and themselves. Letting go of blame allows us to move forward with love and create a foundation for healing and growth. This chapter is a tribute to the enduring love a father has for his children. It underscores that, despite life's hardships, the bond between a father and his children remains unbreakable and continues to inspire strength and hope.

CHAPTER 12

Police Violence & Public Health

"Alright" - Kendrick Lamar

Every battle I've fought has taught me that true strength is born from struggle, and the most powerful victories are won within

In the heart of America's crisis, a powerful call for justice rings out: "A community's health under siege, a people's spirit unbroken amidst a racial epidemic—so-called Blacks reclaiming identity and reshaping their destiny." I could tell you the truth, but it might be hard to hear. As a survivor of the Ferguson Unrest and a passionate social justice advocate, I declare that police violence is not only an injustice; it is a public health crisis for marginalized communities. This crisis is not new—it's a continuation of violence that stretches back to the slave trade. The trauma it creates is a planned pandemic, devastating the so-called Black community and others like a slow moving disease. While many officers serve with integrity, there are those whose presence brings chaos and turmoil, especially within our communities.

When I refer to "so-called Blacks," I do so intentionally. This term reflects the imposed identity we have carried, a name rooted in colonialism and slavery meant to strip us of our heritage and humanity. To me, it's a reminder that our history, rich with kings, queens, scholars, and warriors, is far too complex to be reduced to a color or label. By rejecting the label "Black," I am not ignoring our struggles but demanding recognition for our full humanity and history—our story is deeper than skin color.

Today, police violence disproportionately claims the lives of Black men and women, youth and elders alike, exposing the systemic racism that fuels this public health emergency. This violence extends to Indigenous and Hispanic populations, revealing that the crisis is intersectional and ingrained in the very fabric of American policing. Behind prison walls, this brutality takes on a different form—hidden from public view, shielded by wardens who can impose lockdowns and mask deaths as suicides. The loss of life goes largely unnoticed until it is too late for families to intervene. My birthday, August 21st, connects me to a darker chapter in U.S. prison history—the death of George Jackson in 1971 during an escape attempt at San Quentin, which sparked the Attica Prison uprising just weeks later. The bloodshed that followed from September 9th to 13th saw 39 lives lost, including both inmates and correctional officers. These events were born out of desperation, exposing the injustices of incarceration that persist today. Fast forward to 2016, and on the 45th anniversary of Attica, prisoners across America once again rose up in protest, this time striking against forced labor, racial discrimination, and brutal conditions-the same issues we fight for in society.

Yahkhahnahn Ammi

In 2018, a prison strike, spanning from August 21st to September 9th, became one of the largest in U.S. history. This action was a direct response to the Lee Correctional Institution riot, another tragic episode in the ongoing narrative of violence, neglect, and exploitation within U.S. prisons. These strikes are linked to a long history of resistance against the system that continues to enslave and exploit.

The 13th Amendment may have abolished slavery for most, but it left an opening for forced labor within prisons, creating a modern-day plantation behind bars. During my almost decade of incarceration, I witnessed firsthand the inhumane conditions and systemic abuse that these strikes sought to address. It became clear to me that the so-called free society outside those walls was just as hostile to Black bodies and lives. Ferguson was proof of that. I remember the protests—the tear gas, the rubber bullets, and the sound of police sirens as we stood for our right to exist without fear. The violence we endured was not only physical but psychological, rooted in a deep history of systemic oppression. This pattern of police violence takes a profound toll on the health of entire communities. Living under constant threat fosters an environment of fear and trauma, undermining mental well-being and social cohesion. Entire neighborhoods are left grieving, their trust in institutions shattered. The fear of a knock on the door that never brings good news hangs over us like a cloud.

The numbers are staggering. The United States has a homicide rate seven times higher than other high-income countries, with firearms used in homicides at a rate 25 times higher. This crisis is exacerbated by the prevalence of police shootings that continue to steal the lives of unarmed Black men, women, and children. It is not just about criminal justice—it's a public health emergency that demands an urgent response. But this fight is not new. It echoes back to the earliest forms of resistance against oppression. It's the fight of the political prisoners, like Mumia Abu Jamal, who continue to call out for justice despite being silenced behind bars. It's the fight of every community that rises up in protest after another name is added to the long list of victims of police brutality. It's the fight for survival in a society where your skin color can dictate whether you live or die.

In prison, we fought too. We fought to be seen, to be treated as humans. And today, outside those walls, we continue that fight, knowing that the stakes are just as high. The police shootings of unarmed Black men, women, and youth are a reminder that the struggle for justice extends far beyond the prison gates. It's a reminder that in both places—in prison and in so-called free society—the system was never built for us.

In this chapter of my life, I see the correlation between these two worlds—inside and outside—and I see how both are locked in a cycle of systemic violence and oppression. But I also see the resilience in our communities. I see the protests, the marches, the voices that refuse to be silenced. And as long as we continue to stand together, demanding accountability, justice, and the right to live without fear, we will keep moving forward.

Citations

*Blau, Max, and Grinberg, Emanuella. "Why US inmates launched a nationwide strike." *CNN*, October 31,2016.

Yahkhahnahn Ammi

*National Center for Health Statistics. "Homicide Rates in the United States compared to other high-income countries, 2019.

NEWSPAPER ARTICLES

PRESS TV: "White Supremacists Entering US Police: Activist"

Thursday, 30 July 2015 5:44 AM [Last Update: Thursday, 30 July 2015 10:54 AM]

People protest in Staten Island on the one year anniversary of the death of Eric Garner, New York, July 17, 2015. (AFP Photo)

Press TV has conducted an interview with Yahkhahnahn Ammi, a human rights activist based in Saint Louis, and Maxine Dovere, a political analyst in New York, to discuss police brutality in the United States and the recent mysterious deaths in American jails.

Ammi says African Americans have been subject to genocide for a long time now, and the issue of police brutality is a part of that trend since some white supremacists choose law enforcement as their cover.

The fact that all the recent instances of police violence in the US involve a victim that belongs to minority groups rules out their randomness, the activist adds.

The American society is struggling with many hidden tensions, he says, that lead to these issues. Yet, in a clear double standard, the

US government goes after other nations under the pretext of human rights.

"It is hypocrisy to speak out and point the finger against other nations when we have human rights violations going on here."

He also points to the case of Sandra Bland and dismisses suicide allegations surrounding her death. Ammi says it is "*sickening*" to see how white police officers kill blacks and other minorities in the United States.

Meanwhile, Dovere says although the high number of deaths in US jails is "*a shame*," it does not entirely concern a certain race. She also argues that the issue of police brutality in the United States is brought into light because of the level of transparency in police work and the media coverage that it gets. The analyst accuses all UN countries that condemn police violence in the US of lacking transparency in their police work.

White supremacy is a "*global power system of mass oppression*": A war against people of color in general, Blacks in particular.

White supremacy is and always has been in a deep symbiotic relationship with our structures of government and with our theoretical beliefs going back to the American Revolution and even before." **#African Americans #USA #Human rights #White supremacist**

* * *

NATIONAL

First Coast: "National Guard deployed to Ferguson"

Yahkhahnahn Ammi

https://www.firstcoastnews.com/section/national

Sunday night and early Monday morning, protesters shot at police.

"About 1,000 people march peacefully in New York City's Union Square. Vigils are being held across the country for people organizers say died at the hands of police brutality. The events come in the wake of the shooting death of Michael Brown by a police officer in Ferguson, Mo., and the death of a New York City man caused by a police officer's apparent chokehold.

Author: Yamiche Alcindor

Published: 7:10 AM EDT August 18, 2014 Updated: 7:10 AM EDT August 18, 2014

FERGUSON, Mo. — Missouri Governor Jay Nixon early Monday ordered the National Guard into Ferguson hours after police said escalating violence led to shootings, arrests, and "pre-planned" acts of aggression by protesters.

Nixon made the announcement following another night of clashes between police and protesters in the suburb of St. Louis.

Sunday night and early Monday morning, protesters shot at police, threw Molotov cocktails at officers, looted local businesses, and carried out a "coordinated attempt" to block roads and overrun the police's command center. The National Guard will "help restore peace and order and to protect the citizens of Ferguson," the governor's office said.

"Tonight, a day of hope, prayers, and peaceful protests, was marred by the violent criminal acts of an organized and growing number of individuals, many from outside the community and state, whose actions are putting the residents and businesses of Ferguson at risk," a statement from Nixon's office said. "These violent acts are a disservice to the family of Michael Brown and his memory, and to the people of this community who yearn for justice to be served and to feel safe in their own homes."

The shooting death in Ferguson of unarmed 18-year-old black teenager Michael Brown has led to a week of protests that have sometimes turned violent.

Late Sunday, more than two hours before a second midnight curfew was set to begin, police fired tear gas at hundreds of angry protesters who were marching down the town's main thoroughfare toward a police command center.

Authorities said they were responding to reports of gunfire, looting, vandalism, and protesters who hurled Molotov cocktails.

"Based on the conditions, I had no alternative but to elevate the level of our response," said Capt. Ron Johnson of the Missouri Highway Patrol, who is in command in Ferguson. "We had to act to protect lives and property."

At least two people were injured—including one person who was shot, Johnson said. Seven or eight people were arrested and will be charged with failure to disperse, police said.

Johnson also offered specific scenes from the night that illustrated the intensifying violence: At 8:25 p.m. local time, a person was shot on West Florissant. On this street, protesting has been centered. At 8:26 p.m., shots were fired at a nearby location. At 8:27 p.m., police learned that a "subject was down." At 8:28 p.m., police received a report of eight people with guns, and authorities' tactical teams responded.

By 8:56 p.m., hundreds of protesters marched toward the shopping center where police had set up their command post. In response, police officers lobbed tear gas at the group and asked other local police departments in the area to come to Ferguson.

And even more, at 9:20 p.m., Johnson said McDonald's employees were forced to lock themselves in a storage room after being "overrun" by protesters.

"Police were shot at, makeshift barricades were set up to block police, bottles and rocks were thrown at police," Johnson said.

He added that officials are looking into additional steps to restore calm to the city.

But some protesters said no one threw Molotov cocktails. Renita Lamkin, 43, the pastor of St. John African Methodist Episcopal Church in St. Charles, Mo., has been acting as a peacekeeper, urging people to remain calm.

"That is not true," she said when asked about claims that protesters threw Molotov cocktails.

Yah Ammi, 30, agreed, saying protesters did nothing to provoke officers. He did however say protesters planned a march to the police's command post. In the middle of marching there, officers threw tear gas at the group.

"They cut us off and they began shooting without warning," Ammi said. "They began shooting into the crowd with women, children, and the peaceful, innocent protesters who were here exercising our constitutional rights."

The situation became particularly intense and confusing when protesters were trapped between officers firing tear gas on one side and shots of gunshots on the other side. Dozens of people ran onto side streets, ducked behind cars and hid behind buildings in fear.

One protester, Keshonda James, 35, was driving away from police when a canister of tear gas shattered her windshield. The exploding glass hit her left arm, which was later bandaged by a fellow protester.

"Glass exploded everywhere. This isn't cool. I'm not down here looting," James said.

Bryan Jones, 23, was among those running. He said he felt more comfortable running toward the sound of gunshots than fleeing back toward police. He said he has been harassed by police his entire life.

"It's horrible that I feel like I'm better off running away from the tear gas and running toward the people that are busting at the cops," Jones, 23, said.

The unrest also led officials to close all schools in the Ferguson-Florissant School District on Monday, according to KSDK TV.

The school district received information late Sunday evening that has contributed to safety concerns for students walking to school or waiting for buses on the impacted streets, the station said.

Yahkhahnahn Ammi

Meanwhile, a preliminary autopsy found that Brown was shot at least six times, but the circumstances of his death remain unclear.

Several years later, Michael Brown Jr. was murdered, an unarmed black youth, and I feared for my children's safety. I feared that either of them could fall victim to police brutality."

* * *

I felt that I could be murdered at the hands of the police at any given moment. I never thought I would live to see 18, 21, 25, or 30. I did because prison preserved me; had I been out in society, my life could have been cut short. I never thought I'd make it to live that long, but I did, and my journey hasn't been easy.

It's been far from easy. All my life, I've had to fight—to protect my life, my reputation, my image, my character, my position in this world.

Before I was a teenager, I attended more than several of my cousins' funerals who died at the hands of gun violence. One of them was a double funeral—two male cousins lost to gun violence. I lost my cousin Sophia, who was the youngest, about 13, when she was murdered in the streets of Philadelphia. I lost my little cousin Dion, who did not make it past 22. I also lost friends to gun violence over the years. Why is it that every time we turn on the news here in America, we see more victims of gun violence? It is disheartening to hear that a particular city has the highest murder rate, only for the news to later announce that a separate city now holds that grim title. We must not become desensitized to these murders. Innocent lives should never be taken, especially those who are unarmed.

My children and I rode through the streets of Ferguson. They took part in "Stop the Violence" rallies and protests with me. From the time they were born, they witnessed my activism. Though always protective of them during my activism, I taught my children at a very young age to look out for each other, take care of each other, protect each other, always stick together, and always love each other. As a single father, I instilled these values in them. I had to give them everything that I failed at as a youth. I wanted to provide them with every tool I could. Imagine growing up in this wicked, God forsaken world filled with uncertainties. As they got older, they began to see the violence, the police murdering unarmed men, women, and children. They saw it on the news, heard about it, and went to these protests with me. They saw me dressing up every day in a bulletproof vest, and a tear gas mask.

When Michael Brown Jr. was murdered, for my safety I had to put on a bulletproof vest. I purchased it from a fellow co-worker at a part time night club security gig I worked on the weekends, in St. Louis. I had to wear it every single day because I did not know who I could trust, I confronted people like Jesse Jackson in a YouTube video that went viral, and I confronted organizations that I felt did not have our communities best interest.

My life was also threatened by the police. I had to put earplugs in my ears, a tear gas mask over my face, and other protective gear because we were living in a war zone. It was horrific. My children and I saw militarized tanks, the National Guard, and militarized police oppressing peaceful demonstrators, including myself and my family. I had to protect them at all costs. No child should see their father putting on a bulletproof vest and tear gas mask to go outside because an 18-year-old unarmed black boy was murdered by the cops. Any sign of unity was an opportunity for law enforcement to disunify, to disperse us for coming together as a community.

Michael Brown Jr. was the spark that set this nation on fire, bringing millions around the world together to stand up against injustice. Police violence and gun violence are public health and safety issues, and are a crisis at best. Those who perpetuate it often have mental illnesses. If you're on that side of the fence, I challenge you to get help. See a counselor or a therapist for help. When a community is predominantly black, the police department should reflect that demographic. More black officers should patrol black neighborhoods.

Conversely, if a community is predominantly white, more white officers should patrol those areas. This isn't about segregation; it's about cultural familiarity and effective community policing. Let me tell you a story about the police department in Brooklyn "Lovejoy" (Illinois).

The police force in Brooklyn "Lovejoy" had always been predominantly black, reflecting the community it served. Over the years, they incorporated white cops who were not familiar with our community or its residents. These officers began writing excessive traffic tickets, conducting stop and frisks, and engaging in other forms of harassment, usually targeting residents for driving while black to meet their quotas. This led to increased tension and distrust between the community and the police. Now, today under the new leadership that town has achieved something no one ever thought was possible, it has an all-White police force in the center of an all-Black community. Officers unfamiliar with the culture and lives of the community they serve are more likely to engage in discriminatory practices, especially if they harbor racist attitudes. These officers do not understand the nuances of the community and often view residents with suspicion, leading to unnecessary confrontations and harassment. As a father and an activist, I continue to fight for a world where my children can live without fear. A world where they don't have to witness their father gearing up for battle just to protest or walk the streets peacefully. A world where justice is not a distant dream but a tangible reality.

I am not anti-police; I am anti-racism, anti-hate, anti-white supremacy. I stand firm that every individual has the right to defend themselves against all acts of violence and oppression. As Malcolm X once said, "*I don't even call it violence when it's in self-defense; I call it intelligence.*"

In his famous speech "The Ballot or the Bullet," Malcolm X said, "I don't mean go out and get violent; but at the same time, you should never be nonviolent unless you run into some violence. I'm nonviolent with those who are nonviolent with me. But when you drop that violence on me, then you've made me go insane, and I'm not responsible for what I do."

Police should always be held accountable, especially for any life they take, and they must maintain transparency. An outside, unbiased entity should investigate them, as law enforcement should never investigate their own, particularly after causing a homicide.

This ensures fairness and justice in every investigation. The melanated, or so-called black, community needs to not only feel protected but actually be protected against acts of violence. Every other race, including the homosexual community, is protected, except the so-called blacks. There should be laws to protect our endangered "Black" species against "Black hate," violence, and genocide.

Police officers want to go home every day, and they should, just as every melanated man, woman, and child has that same right. No parent should ever have to worry about whether their family member will be murdered or return home in the same manner they left.

Everyone deserves the right to life, liberty and happiness. People should have safety and security in their own communities. It is a fundamental right that transcends race and status. This is not just about enforcing laws; it's about creating an environment where everyone, regardless of their skin color, can live without fear. For true reform, we must ensure that law enforcement is held to the highest standards of accountability and transparency. Only then can we begin to rebuild trust between the police and the communities they serve. This is not an attack on the police; it is a call for justice, equality, and the protection of all citizens.

In standing against racism and hate, we affirm the value of every human life. We demand a system where accountability is paramount, and transparency is the norm. By doing so, we pave the way for a future where everyone can live without fear and with the assurance that justice will be served. To my readers, the time for change is now. We cannot stand by as our communities are torn apart by violence and injustice. We must hold our law enforcement accountable and demand transparency and reform from the police stations to the White House. Advocate for policies that promote community-based policing, mental health support for affected communities, and stricter gun control measures.

Get involved in local activism, support organizations working towards police reform, and use your voice to amplify the stories of those who have been silenced. Together, we can create a safer, more just society for all. When I was 11, I visited friends and family whom I hadn't seen in a few years. Late one night, I found myself inside what we colloquially call the China-men, or more commonly known as the Rice House—a Chinese restaurant— ordering some Chinese food. The curfew sirens in the town I was visiting, the town where I grew up, had just come on, and the police were patrolling the area, casting an ominous presence over the night.

As I exited the Chinese restaurant, my baseball cap flew off and fell to the ground. As I bent down to retrieve it, I suddenly felt a yank on my T-shirt, and before I knew it, Officer Boone was hitting me, slapping me upside my head. The shock and pain were overwhelming. A group of men, women, and youth from the community stood frozen, watching the brutality unfold.

Boone threatened that if anyone tried to interfere, he would shoot me and anyone else who approached. In that moment, my fear turned into a deep, burning hatred for the police. I was utterly terrified and thought I was going to die that night. The terror of that night is seared into my memory. The helplessness I felt as a young boy being brutalized by someone who was supposed to protect and serve remains a scar that has shaped my view on police violence.

The sight of the uniform, the feel of his grip, and the sting of his blows are memories that have never faded. After the assault, I ran to my mama's (Grandmother Jackie's) house, my heart pounding and tears streaming down my face. I told my family what had happened, and they were immediately outraged.

My mother, stepfather Goliath, grandmother Jackie, and other relatives sprang into action. We drove to the police station, our car filled with a mix of anger and fear.

The police chief Jerome, who happened to be an uncle of mine on my father's side of the family through marriage, met with us and addressed our concerns directly. Apparently, Boone didn't realize who my family was. I never found out the details of the conversation between the police chief and Boone, but I never had any more issues with him or that police department.

This incident was a defining moment in my life, one that shattered my childhood innocence and opened my eyes to the harsh realities of police violence and the systemic issues plaguing our law enforcement. It was then that I realized, for many in our community, the police are not protectors but oppressors. This stark revelation has stayed with me, shaping my worldview and fueling my determination to advocate for change. As I reflect on this experience, I see it as a microcosm of the broader struggle faced by Black communities across America. The fear, anger, and trauma I felt that night are emotions shared by countless others who have endured police brutality. This personal encounter was not an isolated event but part of a larger pattern of systemic racism and violence that continues to affect our lives. The night Boone assaulted me, I felt a visceral fear that I might not survive. This fear is a constant reality for many so-called Black individuals when encountering law enforcement. The anger that burned within me was not just personal but collective, a response to the ongoing injustice faced by our community. This trauma, while deeply

145

personal, connects me to a larger narrative of resilience and resistance. This incident ignited a fire within me to fight for justice and reform. It made me acutely aware of the urgent need for systemic change in my hometown and across the nation. The realization that our lives are undervalued, and our voices often silenced has driven my activism and commitment to advocacy.

Understanding that my experience is shared by many others has strengthened my resolve. I see myself as part of a larger movement striving for justice, equality, and the end of police brutality. The journey has been fraught with challenges, but each step forward is a step toward a more just and fair society. The fight for justice is not just about addressing individual incidents but dismantling the systems that allow such violence to persist. It's about creating a world where Black lives are truly valued and protected, where our children can grow up without the fear of becoming the next hashtag. My advocacy is fueled by the hope for a future where we no longer have to march, protest, or plead for our basic human rights.

As I continue to reflect on my past, I draw strength from the collective power of our community. Our shared experiences of injustice and our unwavering resilience are what drive us forward.

Together, we can create the change we so desperately need and ensure that the next generation can live in a world where justice prevails. Since that harrowing incident with Boone, my commitment to advocating for social justice has been unwavering.

I have consistently spoken out against injustices, rallied to defund the police, and fought against excessive force and brutality. My fight for human rights stems from the belief that everyone deserves freedom from oppression and abuse. I acknowledge that not all cops are bad, just as I vehemently oppose criminalizing and ostracizing innocent Black men. Growing up in the 1990s was a tough time for melanated American youths. The following year, the world watched in horror as Rodney King was brutally beaten by police officers in Los Angeles. I vividly remember seeing the footage on the news—each blow, each cry of pain etched into my memory.

The sheer brutality of the officers' actions was undeniable. Though the assault I endured a year prior was traumatic, it paled in comparison to what Rodney King experienced. The city erupted in outrage and flames, a visceral response to the relentless oppression.

I prayed fervently for Rodney King's survival, hoping that justice would prevail, and the officers involved would be held accountable. As the trial dragged on, my outrage grew. The verdict, which acquitted the officers, felt like a profound betrayal. The excessive force used against an unarmed Black man underscored the pervasive issue of police violence. It gave real, tangible meaning to the hashtags **#DrivingWhileBlack and #PoliceViolence**.

Reflecting on these pivotal events, I see how they have profoundly shaped my path to advocacy. The visceral fear and seething anger I felt during my own assault, coupled with the collective outrage that swept the nation after Rodney King's brutal beating, ignited a deep-seated determination within me to fight for change. These experiences have not only underscored the urgent need for systemic reform and justice but have also become the driving force behind my relentless pursuit of equality.

Each memory, as painful and vivid as it is, serves as a stark reminder of the battles we've fought and the resilience we've shown. They are the wellspring of my strength, fueling my unwavering commitment to speaking out against injustice. The path to advocacy is often fraught with challenges—moments of despair, disheartening setbacks, and seemingly insurmountable obstacles. Yet, it is a path I am resolutely committed to walking, driven by the vision of a better future for generations to come.

As I navigate this journey, I carry with me the weight of these memories, not as a burden, but as a testament to our collective struggle and our indomitable spirit. They remind me why I fight— why we must persevere and push forward.

The road ahead may be long and arduous, but it is a road worth traveling. For in our struggle lies the promise of a brighter, more just world, a world where future generations can thrive free from the oppression and abuse that have marred our past.

These reflections are more than personal musings; they are a call to action, a plea for others to join in the fight for justice. By sharing my story, I hope to inspire others to see the importance of standing up against injustice and to understand that our voices, when united, can bring about profound change. Together, we can build a future where equity, and equality is not just an ideal, but a reality.

In the aftermath of that fateful year emerged a tragic pattern of police brutality and systemic racism relentlessly against marginalized communities and claiming the lives of countless Black men, women, and children. The frequency and severity of these incidents exposed a deep-rooted crisis within our society. This pattern of violence and injustice is starkly highlighted in the

Yahkhahnahn Ammi

"List of unarmed African Americans killed by law enforcement officers in the United States" on Wikipedia. This list includes names like Malice Green, Amadou Diallo, Ronald Madison, James Brissette, Sean Bell, Oscar Grant, Carey Ball Jr., Eric Garner, Michael Brown Jr., Kajieme Powell, Vonderrit Myers Jr., Korryn Gaines, Freddie Gray, Philando Castile, Atatiana Jefferson, Breonna Taylor, George Floyd, Kendra Boyd, Sandra Bland, Tyrone West, Trayvon Martin, Tamir Rice, Aiyana Stanley-Jones, and many others.

Each of these names represents a life unjustly cut short, a family shattered, and a community plunged into grief and anger. These senseless deaths, broadcasted on the news and shared across social media, have profoundly affected me as both an advocate against domestic violence and a protective father.

The sheer inability to offer solace to grieving parents who have lost their children to excessive force and unnecessary gun violence is a weighty burden on the psyche. It's a trauma that reverberates not only through those directly involved but also through those of us who witness these tragedies from afar.

As an advocate, I am constantly reminded of the fragility of Black lives in a society that often views us as expendable. The images of these lost lives haunt me, driving home the urgency of our fight for justice. Each name on that list is a stark reminder of the work that remains to be done and the systemic changes that are desperately needed. The weight of these tragedies fuels my resolve to speak out, to march, to advocate, and to demand accountability. For those of us indirectly affected, these tragedies create a persistent sense of vulnerability and fear. They challenge us to confront uncomfortable truths about our society and our place within it. The ongoing struggle for justice, equity and equality becomes personal, a call to action that we cannot ignore. These deaths are not just statistics; they are poignant reminders of the human cost of systemic racism and police brutality.

In reflecting on this tragic pattern, I find renewed strength in the collective efforts of those who continue to fight for change. Our voices, when united, have the power to break this cycle of violence and create a society where so-called Black and Melanated lives are truly valued and protected. The path to justice is long and fraught with challenges, but it is a path we must walk together, fueled by the memory of those we've lost and the hope for a better future.

The tension was palpable as we gathered in the streets of Ferguson, our voices united in a call for justice. I was a frequent leader of the protests, standing at the forefront, demanding accountability and an end to the systemic brutality that plagued our melanated communities. The unrest that followed Michael Brown Jr's tragic death was a turning point, a moment that would change the course of my life forever. I survived the Ferguson unrest, but not without consequence.

In the years since, I've been vocal about the militarization of the police during Ferguson. The sight of police snipers, armored vehicles and heavily armed officers descending on peaceful protestors is etched in my memory. It was a war zone, and we were the enemy. This stark reality fueled my rallying cry to defund the police, to redirect resources away from a system that perpetuates violence against us.

Our movement faced not only external opposition but also internal challenges. I spoke out against the national Black Lives Matter

Movement, which infiltrated Ferguson with outside money influencers and agendas that diverged from our original purpose. We sought to protect Black lives, to uphold our human and civil rights. Yet, ulterior motives were at play, diverting our struggle into channels that did not serve our community's needs. This stance upset many, including my ex-wife and her co-conspirators painting a target on my back.

In an article published by the St. Louis American Newspaper titled "Harris-Stowe forum looks at Ferguson from varying black perspectives" by Chris King on August 9, 2015, I was quoted saying, "Media-hungry people were paid under, over and across the table," claiming that outside money was responsible for "dismantling the movement."

This quote encapsulates the betrayal we felt as the movement we started to protect our community was co-opted by those with other agendas. I saw provocateurs, members of law enforcement, and paid protesters hijacking our cause, exploiting the movement for personal gain. It was disheartening to see our genuine efforts manipulated. Activists were being targeted, and I feared I could be next. The death threats against my life were real and terrifying.

Each day, I wondered if I would face the same fate as the protesting sister in Ferguson, who survived an attempted assassination by police snipers. Would I be silenced for daring to speak truth to power?

While I escaped physical harm, the character assassination I endured was a death sentence in its own right. In our society, to destroy a Melanated or so-called Black man's reputation is to destroy his very essence, often leading to physical harm or worse.

Despite these challenges, I continue to fight for my freedom. "Demand Human Rights Now!"

I often say, reflecting on the ongoing harassment, intimidation, and attempts on my life. These experiences have only strengthened my resolve. The fight for justice is far from over, and I remain committed to ensuring that our voices are heard, and our rights are upheld.

Facebook has restricted access to my intellectual property, including another page of mine they canceled: facebook.com /groups/humanrightsjc/. I have been censored and silenced for speaking truth to power. The emotional toll of being targeted and living under constant threat is immense. The fear of being the next name on a tragic list of martyrs haunts me. But it is this fear that fuels my determination to keep fighting. I continue to speak out, to stand up, and to lead, knowing that my survival and the survival of my community depend on it.

The lessons I have learned from the Ferguson unrest are profound. I have learned the importance of unity, of standing together in the face of oppression. I have learned that our fight is not just against the visible forces of violence, but also against the insidious forces that seek to undermine our movements from within. And most importantly, I have learned that the struggle for justice is a lifelong commitment, one that requires unwavering resolve and resilience. To my readers, I offer this advice: never underestimate the power of your voice.

Stand firm in your convictions, even when the path is fraught with danger. Remember that true change comes from within our communities, and we must remain vigilant against those who look to co-opt our movements for their gain. Above all, keep fighting for justice, freedom, and the rights of all people to live with dignity and respect. During that period, I hosted my television show on a local public access channel in East St. Louis, Illinois. Each report of murder or brutality against our people stoked the flames of my outrage, but it was the senseless killings of unarmed youth that pushed me to action. I founded SWIP, the Stop the Violence campaign, leveraging my platform to collaborate with international artists and musicians, launching a community-driven violence prevention initiative.

The deaths of Trayvon Martin, Tamir Rice, Michael Brown Jr., and others reignited the fire within me, compelling me to do more. I spearheaded the production of several "Stop the Violence" mix-tape albums featuring tracks from international artists, amplifying our message and uniting voices against the epidemic of violence. This action wasn't just about raising awareness; it was a call to arms, a rallying cry for change. Through SWIP and our mix-tape albums, we sparked conversations, challenged perceptions, and empowered our community to stand up against injustice. Each song, each lyric, was a testament to our resilience and our commitment to a better future.

However, our work was far from over. As the list of names of those lost to violence grew longer, so did our resolve. We continued to produce music, host events, and engage with our community, determined to make a difference. The fight against violence was not just a campaign; it was a movement that united people from all walks of life in a common goal: to stop the violence and create a safer, more just world for all.

Through SWIP and our music, we were able to reach people far and wide, spreading our message of peace and unity.

We may have started small, but our impact was undeniable. We showed the world that change is possible, that by coming together and raising our voices, we can make a difference. As I look back on those days, I am filled with pride for what we accomplished. Our journey was not easy, and the road ahead is still long, but we proved that even in the face of adversity, we can rise up and make our voices heard. The fight against violence is far from over, but with determination, passion, and unity, we can create a world where everyone can live free from fear.

Initiatives: Stop the Violence Advocacy Awareness Projects

At the heart of our mission is a commitment to raising awareness and taking action against violence in all its forms. Our *Stop the Violence* advocacy projects aim to inspire change, foster dialogue, and promote peace within our communities. Below are some of our key initiatives:

STOP THE VIOLENCE VOL. NO. 1: GENOCIDE

1. https://swippoetry.bandcamp.com/album/stop-the-violence-vol-no-1-genocide

This powerful compilation brings together voices from across the community to address the devastating impact of violence, particularly focusing on the theme of genocide. Through spoken word and music, this project seeks to educate and motivate listeners to take a stand against violence.

Yahkhahnahn Ammi

STOP THE VIOLENCE VOL. 2

2. https://swippoetry.bandcamp.com/album/stop-the-violence-vol-2

Building on the momentum of the first volume, *Stop the Violence Vol. 2* continues the conversation by exploring different aspects of violence and its impact on society. This album features a diverse array of artists who use their talents to advocate for peace and nonviolence.

*STOP THE VIOLENCE: SWIP POETRY CHAPTER (FORMERLY)

https://www.facebook.com/yahkhahnahnammi/about

Our initiative, formerly known as the *SWIP Poetry Chapter*, has been at the forefront of using poetry and spoken word as tools for advocacy. This platform provides a space for artists and activists to share their experiences, raise awareness about the consequences of violence, and encourage community action. Through these initiatives, we strive to make a meaningful impact in the fight against violence. Each project is a call to action, urging individuals to come together, speak out, and work towards a future free from violence. We invite you to explore these resources, engage with our content, and join us in our ongoing efforts to Stop the Violence.

My advocacy extended beyond music and media. I took to the streets, organizing and taking part in peaceful protests and rallies across Illinois and Missouri. These demonstrations were more than just shows of solidarity; they were a call to action, a demand for justice and accountability. My efforts weren't confined to the streets. I took my message to the halls of academia, sitting on a panel at Harris-Stowe State University, a historically Black college. Here, I engaged in critical discussions about the Ferguson unrest, shedding light on the fraud and external influences that looked to undermine our movement. It was a platform to expose the truth, to challenge the narratives that sought to silence us.

However, I didn't stop there. I realized the power of storytelling and the importance of amplifying marginalized voices. I began reporting and conducting my interviews, becoming the host of several podcasts that gave a voice to community members on social justice matters.

These podcasts were a platform for truth, a space where our stories could be heard, unfiltered and unapologetic.

My efforts caught the attention of media outlets, and I gave interviews with Press TV and was quoted in several newspapers about my experiences in Ferguson. These interviews were not just about me; they were about shining a light on the realities of police violence and systemic racism. They were about challenging the status quo and demanding change. Through my advocacy, I looked to inspire others to join the fight for justice.

I wanted to show that change is possible, but it requires courage, determination, and unity. My journey is far from over, but I am committed to continuing the fight and using my voice and platform to create a better, more just world for all.

* * *

Yahkhahnahn Ammi

Personal Life Lesson Reflections

In this chapter, as I look back on my journey, from being a father fighting for custody to an activist on the front lines of social justice, to a man who's had to put on a bulletproof vest just to peacefully protest—I realize that my life has been a continuous battle against the injustices that seek to break us down. But through these experiences, I've learned some of the most profound lessons that I hope will resonate with you, my readers.

Resilience is born from adversity. Life will throw you into battles you never asked to fight. Whether it's the struggle to protect your children, the fight against systemic oppression, or the personal demons you face within—adversity is inevitable. But it's in these moments that resilience is forged. I've been knocked down more times than I can count, but every time, I got back up. Not because it was easy, but because it was necessary. Resilience isn't about never falling; it's about refusing to stay down.

The importance of standing up, even when you stand alone, cannot be overstated. There will be times when you are the only voice in a room, the only one willing to challenge the status quo. I stood up in Ferguson, in front of community leaders, and even in the face of death threats, because I knew that if I didn't, the silence would be deafening.

Standing up for what's right, even when you stand alone, is a testament to your character and your commitment to justice. Don't be afraid to be that voice, even if it trembles. Love is the most powerful weapon. In all my battles, the one thing that has kept me going is love. The love I have for my children, for my community, and for justice is what drives me forward. Love isn't just an emotion; it's an action, a commitment to protect, to nurture, and to fight for what is right. When you act out of love, you act with a power that no amount of hate or violence can ever destroy.

Your story is your power. We all have a story, a narrative that shapes who we are and what we stand for. My story of losing and regaining custody, of fighting for justice in the streets of Ferguson, of confronting the injustices in our society—these experiences are my power. They are my testimony. Don't be afraid to share your story. Your experiences, your pain, your triumphs—they are what make you unique, and they have the power to inspire, to heal, and to create change.

Change is a marathon, not a sprint. The fight for justice, for equality, for a better world—it's a long, often exhausting journey. There will be setbacks, moments of despair, and times when it feels like progress is impossible. But remember, change doesn't happen overnight. It's a marathon, not a sprint. Pace yourself, stay committed, and never lose sight of the goal. Every small step forward is a victory.

Protect your peace, even in chaos. The world can be chaotic, filled with violence, hate, and injustice. But amidst the chaos, it's crucial to protect your peace.

Whether it's through prayer, meditation, spending time with loved ones, or simply finding moments of solitude—take time to center yourself. You cannot pour from an empty cup. By protecting your peace, you ensure that you have the strength to continue the fight.

The power of community is undeniable. No one fights alone. Throughout my journey, I've seen the incredible power of community—people coming together to support one another, to fight for a common cause, to lift each other up in times of need. Whether it's your family, your friends, or your neighbors, lean on your community. There is strength in numbers, and together, we can achieve more than we ever could alone.

Takeaways

Resilience is your greatest ally in the face of adversity.

Keep getting up, no matter how many times you fall. Stand firm in your convictions, even when it feels like you're the only one. Your courage can inspire others to find their own voice.

Love fiercely and let it guide your actions. It's the most powerful force in the world.

Own your story and share it. Your experiences hold the power to transform lives, including your own.

Commit to the long haul in the fight for justice and change. It's a marathon worth running.

Protect your inner peace, even in the midst of turmoil. It's essential for your well-being and your effectiveness in the fight. Lean on your community and recognize the strength that comes from unity. Together, we are unstoppable.

CHAPTER 13

Momma's Baby, Daddy's Maybe

"Diamond & Wood" – UGK

The line between trust and betrayal was about to be redrawn in ways I never imagined

Meeting Robin – a situationship begins. Three years later after my divorce from Selena finalized in 2013. I navigated the chaos of single fatherhood in St. Louis, balancing my responsibilities as a father and the demands of my job as a taxi driver. I had no idea that a seemingly ordinary encounter would lead to one of the most complicated chapters of my life. This is the story of how I met Robin, a woman who would challenge my understanding of love, loyalty, and fatherhood in ways I never imagined. Our first meeting was unremarkable on the surface—Robin was a passenger in my taxi. She had a charm about her, a dual nature that intrigued me. Around me, she was sweet, calm, and almost vulnerable, but I quickly learned that she had a wild side, especially when she was with her friends. This contrast ironically drew me in overtime, I was told that I was too tight, and needed to live a little because apparently, I took life too seriously and before long, we found ourselves in what I can only describe as a "Situationship."

There was a connection, but it wasn't rooted in deep commitment or love. It was casual, undefined, and lacking the structure of a traditional relationship.

As our interactions became more frequent, I tried to keep things light, avoiding any serious entanglements. But life has a way of steering us in unexpected directions. Robin and I had sex once, and the condom broke. She claimed to have been on birth control and could not get pregnant. She suffered more than several miscarriages with previous lovers. Robin soon discovered she was allegedly pregnant with our first child together, and our casual situationship took a sudden turn. Faced with the reality of an unplanned pregnancy, we decided to move in together. She moved into a two bedroom apartment with me and my two children Prince Avatar and Princess Tiana, rent free. I was in the process of finding a small house on Humphrey Street where we hoped to build a stable environment for our new growing family of almost five. The birth of our son, Prince four months later, was both a joy and a struggle. His arrival into the world was marked by an emergency C-section, and seeing him for the first time was an emotional experience I will never forget. But our happiness was short lived as Prince faced serious health challenges, spending his first days in the NICU. Those days were grueling, with daily hospital visits and a constant worry for his survival. As Prince fought for his life, the dynamics within our family began to shift. My older children were affected by the new addition, and Robin's behavior grew increasingly erratic. Her dual nature became more pronounced—sweet and caring one moment, distant and wild the next. I began to notice her complicated relationship with Marco, a friend whose presence was unsettling. My suspicions grew, and the tension in our home became palpable.

The situation took a devastating turn when I uncovered Robin's long-term affair with Marco. The betrayal was profound, not just because of the affair, but because it raised painful questions about Prince's paternity.

Confronting Robin and Marco only deepened the rift between us, leading to a strained and hostile relationship that felt beyond repair. The betrayal didn't just shatter my trust; it also led to a fierce legal and emotional battle.

Robin manipulated the situation, making it increasingly difficult for me to see my son. The heartache of being kept away from Prince was unbearable, and I found myself in a constant struggle to be part of his life. Ultimately, I faced a painful decision—whether to continue fighting in a battle that seemed unwinnable or to step back for the sake of my own peace and stability. This chapter of my life taught me hard lessons about love, trust, and the complexities of relationships. It forced me to reassess what it means to be a father and to find strength in the face of overwhelming challenges. While the experience left deep scars, it also provided me with valuable insights that I carry with me today. As I look to the future, my commitment to being a present and loving father remains unwavering. I share this story not only as a reflection of my journey but as a message to others who may be facing similar struggles. Life's challenges can be relentless, but with resilience and determination, we can find a way forward.

Yahkhahnahn Ammi

I was a single father and taxicab driver in the City of St. Louis during this time. I worked for two cab companies, Laclede Cab Company, where I started during the Michael Brown Jr. uprisings, and later for St. Louis American Cab. Robin was a passenger I picked up on three occasions. We exchanged numbers, and she agreed to show me around St. Louis since I was still learning the area. Robin worked as a hostess at a downtown hotel in St. Louis. We talked on the phone and sometimes hung out.

She seemed sweet and reserved around me, but she was different around her friends and family. She was a little spicy and ghetto and loved to drink and party every weekend when she wasn't at work. That was a turn off for me. She was cool, just not my type. Romantically, I was not attracted to her. She did have a nice body. We began exploring a friendship and told each other that we were not in a relationship; what we had was a situationship. One night, Robin invited me over to her apartment. We had sex one time, the condom broke and she became pregnant, allegedly by me. Robin's lease on her one-bedroom downtown apartment was ending, and it was not renewed. After finding out she was pregnant, I invited her to share my two-bedroom apartment. We dated for a while prior to living together and continued dating while living together. I did not allow her to pay any bills. My intention was for her to save her money and for my children to all live under one roof, a point I emphasized.

I had a growing family, and a new son on the way. We needed more space. I contacted a realtor, and he showed me a three-bedroom house in the south city on Humphrey Street. It was undergoing renovation. He agreed to lease the home to me and said, "If you can show me consistent on time monthly payments, this house could be yours." I loved the house and agreed. He gave me the keys, and we moved into the three-bedroom home at 3400 Humphrey Street.

I was at work when I received a call from Robin's chain smoking aunt informing me that Robin was in the hospital and the doctors needed to perform an emergency C-section. As a cab driver, I quickly ended my shift and drove to BJC, Barnes-Jewish Hospital, located in Midtown. Upon arrival, I meticulously washed my hands up to my elbows and put on scrubs and booties over my shoes before being buzzed into the surgery room.

I arrived just in time to witness my son's birth via C-section. I watched as his tiny body was suctioned, wrapped up, placed on a breathing machine, and settled into a glass ventilation crib. He was born prematurely, and I assumed the role of his personal photographer, feeling the responsibility to document the experience. My mind was filled with countless questions, unsure of where to start or what to say. Despite seeing Robin on the table, seemingly fine, and observing our son Prince in the care of doctors and nurses, the reason for his premature birth eluded me. There was some type of breach, but my focus was clear—I had to be there for him. While I was happy to witness the joyous occasion of our son's birth, I couldn't shake the complex emotions, especially as Robin referred to our child as her "miracle baby," claiming she had previously struggled to conceive with other partners.

Because Prince was born prematurely, weighing less than four pounds, he could not immediately come home with us. The doctors worked to ensure his survival while our families were in constant prayer and concern for our little "Prince", fighting for his life. It was heart-wrenching to see him in the breathing machine, which essentially had to breathe for him. Every day for several months, Robin and I were at the hospital from sunup to sundown, facing this challenging time together. It was not just challenging for us but also for my two children, Prince Avatar and Princess Tiana, who watched their brother fight for survival. We were restricted to two visitors at a time, and Robin's grandmother and aunt from her side of the family were frequent visitors, providing support and driving Robin to and from the hospital on days I was working.

We all stood by Prince's side month after month, witnessing his progress. We tried to limit visitors to immediate family to maintain a calm environment for our son. After about three months, Prince was making significant progress. One day, when I went to visit him in the NICU, I found Robin with a man I had never seen before.

They were about to visit Prince together. When I asked who he was, Robin said he was a friend. I sat in the NICU waiting area, waiting for Robin and the man to emerge from visiting our son.

I couldn't shake my curiosity about this stranger, especially since Robin's family seemed so familiar with him. However, I did not know his name or identity until Robin introduced him as Marco. It wasn't until after their visit with our son that Robin revealed more about him. Her demeanor towards me suddenly changed, and she snapped, "He's just a friend," rolling her eyes. It was a side of her I had never seen before. "Prince" was doing good health wise and the doctors said he would be released from the NICU in a few months. Robin and I thought prayerfully.

Before Prince was released from the hospital, Robin listed her mother and aunt as proxies for WIC (Women Infants and Children) "WIC" pick up vouchers, that included baby food vouchers for our son Prince, excluding me from accessing the government issued food or voucher assistance for our child. I Thought this was extremely odd. Why would she hide this from me, and not list me as a proxy for our son?

We were incredibly thankful and grateful that God had allowed our son to live and overcome his struggles. He was now able to breathe on his own and had almost gained enough weight to be discharged. Everything looked good; he was healthy and growing strong. Several months later, Robin and I got good news from the doctors at the NICU. They were confident in releasing Prince. I told my children who were also overjoyed. We all got dressed to drive to the hospital. It was an exciting day and the moment we had all predicted. After Robin and I completed paperwork, the hospital cleared Prince, and we drove home with our little bundle of joy. Our little Prince was released from the NICU to come home in our care. Once we arrived home, everyone piled in my bedroom and sat on my bed waiting to take turns holding their little brother Prince. I took a nap after getting all settled in our home.

Selena Returns. Meanwhile, during this time Selena called my cell phone asking, "Will you allow "my babies" to come stay the weekend with me?" First of all, 'her babies?' I was shocked that she had called unexpectedly and was astounded by her requests. Selena had done absolutely nothing for our children, and at the time owed more than $10,000 in child support arrears. I immediately said, No! But, we can meet in a public place. Maybe at the park, or the Synagogue. I would not jeopardize the safety of our children or allow them to stay the weekend at her house. I thought. The nerves. How could she? Especially, since we have not spoken in years, and I had no idea where she lived. The last

Yahkhahnahn Ammi

time I trusted her with our children and followed the court order she absconded with them anyway. She demanded to speak to "her babies." I told her to call them on their cellphones, and I reminded her that their phone numbers had not changed. I told Selena that our children needed consistency, and that she could not keep running in and out of our children's lives. I said, "Before you begin visiting our children again, you're gonna have to be consistent, and it is up to our children and their comfort. If you wanna be around our children it is gonna be on our terms. Selena, agreed. I spoke with our children and told them their mom had called for them. I asked them if they wanted to speak with her, and began visitation again. They agreed.

Selena, called almost daily for about two weeks before we allowed her into our physical space. She asked where we could meet. I told her at Tower Grove Park. The children had a good time at the park. I saw from a distance. We met there a second time. She asked for my home address. Reluctantly, I gave her our home address and hoped it would not be a mistake. I told her we could do the next visit at our home. I discussed this with Robin. We arranged a day and time. One week later, my phone rang. It was Selena. She arrived. I told our children that their mother was waiting outside to see them, and they were happy.

Robin was in bed. She breast fed Prince until he fell asleep. I told her Selena had arrived. Robin and Prince remained in our bedroom with the door closed at the time. Robin would return to work on the morning shift. She needed to rest that evening. I left our bedroom. I asked Prince Avatar and Princess Tiana to give their mom a tour of their bedrooms after I let her inside. The doorbell rang. I met her downstairs. I explained our house rules: during your visit, our children's bedroom doors must remain open, no shoes could be worn inside our home, and there would be no yelling, or profanity.

I also told her that my newborn was asleep in my bedroom and I was not to be disturbed. I asked her to have our children come get me when she was ready to leave. More than several hours had passed. I gave them private space to catch up and bond. Our children showed Selena their toys, and they played games together. I heard their laughter as I laid in bed with Robin and our newborn son Prince. Princess Tiana knocked on my door and entered. She said, *"Abba, mommy is ready to leave now."* Thank you Princess. I got out of bed. I walked Selena downstairs and locked the door behind her. Several days later, Selena called my phone announcing that she was outside. She demanded to see our children. I told her to leave. The next day Robin told me that she had noticed a woman sitting inside a car outside our home. I did not think anything of it. I brushed it off. I thought it was probably a parent awaiting the school bus to arrive to watch their children off to school. Several days later, Robin shared her concerns about the woman who parked outside of our home as she left for work in the morning. The woman in the car turned out to be Selena. My phone rang. I realized Selena was the stalker the moment she called my phone letting me know that she was outside. I told her we have to make plans for her to see our children. One week later, I made plans to have Selena visit our home once again. Once Selena arrived, she demanded to speak with me aggressively downstairs. *"I won't fight with you concerning my babies if you take me off child support."* She said. What do you mean fight with me? I asked. I have no idea what you are talking about. You have the nerves to blackmail me? I walked her upstairs to see our children. Robin and our son Prince were both inside the bedroom. I told Robin about the conversation Selena, and I had downstairs.

It was too much to deal with and I would not have our peace disturbed inside our home. After Selena left and the visitation concluded, Robin and I decided it would be her last visit inside of our home. I would only allow future visits in a public setting. Shortly after that verbal altercation with Selena about her stalking and showing up at my home unannounced, demanding to visit our children, things took a turn for the worse. I told Selena, This will be your last visit with our children inside of my home. All future visits will be somewhere in public. For several months, Prince was at home with us, and we had to adjust our schedules around our newborn son. Selena had threatened the sanctity of our home, and it was my job to protect our peace. Prince Avatar and Princess Tiana always called me their "Number One Dad." While it's true that I was their only dad, hearing them say it often left me feeling unworthy. I was riddled with self-doubt, unsure if I was truly enough for them. I wanted to give them the world, to provide them with more than I ever had.

Single fatherhood was a constant challenge, but every moment I spent with them reminded me it was worth it. We savored the simplest joys—sitting around the dinner table, laughing together over stories and games, and just being present with each other.

That bond was everything. I really miss those sacred moments. At that time, my children were attending a public charter school because they had faced too many hurdles in the traditional St. Louis Public School system. As an involved parent and active member of the PTO, I noticed something troubling early on: one of the schools they attended had a habit of using excessive timeouts for the kids. It felt like every minor misstep earned my daughter hours of isolation, more punishment than guidance.

I wasn't one to stay silent when it came to the well-being of my children. I raised the issue repeatedly with the teachers and even brought it up at PTO meetings. But the school refused to listen, brushing aside my concerns as if they didn't matter. Even when I went to the superintendent of the district, hoping to find a sympathetic ear, I hit a brick wall. He said, *"They should not be putting preschoolers in excessive timeouts."* After that meeting, nothing changed.

That was just the beginning of the problems. One afternoon, Prince Avatar came home with a story that chilled me to the core. His teacher—an openly homosexual Black man—had exposed him and the other students to inappropriate pornography on a classroom computer. My blood boiled with anger. How could something like that happen in a school, a supposed safe space for learning? I immediately stormed back to the school, demanding action. I insisted that the teacher be fired on the spot. But nothing happened—no suspension, no consequences, I did get an apology from the principal. However, they protected that teacher, leaving me feeling powerless and furious. Before I could even wrap my head around that situation, another nightmare struck. Princess Tiana came home one day with tears in her eyes. She told me that she had been involved in a bus accident.

Her front teeth had been chipped in the incident, but the school and the bus company had failed to inform me about it. They had labeled the accident an "incident," as if that softened the blow. They didn't call me, didn't send a note—nothing. I found out from my own daughter, who arrived home 3 hours late from school and stood there shaken up with a smile marred by chipped teeth. I was livid. I marched back to the superintendent's office and demanded answers.

I brought all the evidence with me—pictures of her chipped teeth, her dental records, witness statements from Tiana's doctors, and proof of the accident. Still, the school and the bus company continued to minimize the incident. My frustrations mounted by the day. I couldn't believe how little they seemed to care about the children's safety, let alone their education.

That was it for me. I wasn't going to let my kids be collateral damage in a system that didn't value them. Furious, I pulled Prince Avatar and Princess Tiana out of that school immediately. I enrolled them in a different public charter school on the other side of town, hoping for a fresh start, praying they would be safe and treated with the care they deserved. The constant shifting from school to school took a toll on all of us. I knew they needed stability, but no matter where we went, something always seemed to go wrong. As much as I tried to shield them from the chaos, it wasn't enough. I could not afford private school.

I wanted to be their "Number One Dad"—the dad who protected them, who kept them safe. But every failure, every moment when the system let them down, felt like my own personal failure as a father. Those experiences hardened my resolve. I realized that I couldn't just rely on others to ensure my children's safety and well-being. I had to step up in every way possible, even when it meant taking on battles that no father should have to fight alone.

I wasn't perfect, and I certainly wasn't the superhero they believed I was, but I was their dad—and that was enough reason to keep fighting. After the trauma my children experienced at the new school, my decision to homeschool them became inevitable. Princess Tiana came home one day, trembling and scared. She told me through tears that her teacher—a white man, who happened to be homosexual—had placed her in a chokehold when she couldn't stop crying in class. My heart shattered. I knew I had to act. This was the same teacher, another parent also accused of choking her son, fortunately her son came home with visible bruises on his neck and face. We couldn't stay silent. The other parent and I took immediate action—we called 911, reached out to an attorney, and contacted the local news. We wanted an investigation, we demanded accountability. Yet, despite our efforts, the teacher was never fired. He quietly resigned, only to be hired as a principal at another school. Our case never went to court. It was like justice was slipping through our fingers. I couldn't let this go on. My children had already been through enough, and I wasn't going to put them through any more of the school system's failures.

As a family, we sat down and decided—it was time to take their education into our own hands. They were already enrolled in Hebrew school on the weekends, and they loved it. Homeschooling wasn't something I had ever considered before, but it felt like the best way to protect them from further harm. It turned out to be one of the best decisions we ever made. Homeschooling wasn't just about education; it was about healing. It gave us time to reconnect, to spend time together, and to focus on what truly mattered. The stress of unsafe classrooms and unchecked teachers faded away, replaced by an environment of love and learning.

Yahkhahnahn Ammi

We rediscovered joy in the little things—whether it was making breakfast together in the mornings or turning everyday activities into life lessons. What's more, my children didn't lose out on the enrichment they needed.

We found a school nearby that offered ancillary classes in music, art, and physical education. I would drive them there after our homeschooling sessions, and they thrived in these creative outlets. Prince Avatar and Princess Tiana fell in love with music. They excelled in their classes, mastering their instruments with enthusiasm and dedication. The teachers at this school were different—caring, supportive, and invested in their growth.

Looking back now, I realize that homeschooling wasn't just an escape from a broken system; it was an opportunity to rebuild our family's foundation. We grew closer, and I could see the confidence and happiness return to my children's faces. I may not have felt worthy of the "Number One Dad" title before, but watching my children flourish made me believe that maybe, just maybe, I was living up to it after all. Homeschooling wasn't the path I expected to take, but it became the path we needed. We reclaimed control over our lives and found a way to give my children the safety, love, and education they deserved.

As difficult as the journey had been, the decision to homeschool gave us something no school could ever provide—peace. July, August, September of 2016 passed. My older children enjoyed homeschool, and Robin continued to work downtown as a hostess. I was still driving a taxi, and things were going well. However, Robin had been exposing our newborn son to her entire family, including an aunt who was a chain smoker. I asked her repeatedly not to have him around second-hand smoke, knowing it could develop into asthma or worse, and I asked her not to have everyone all in his face. "He is gonna become cross-eyed," I warned. Despite my concerns, she continued to do so. We had previously discussed plans for our son to spend time with my side of the family, but this had not yet happened. "Truth has the inherent power to produce the promised effects." (Bhaktisiddhanta Sarasvati)

Robin out of the blue, had falsely accused me of having sexual relations with Selena behind her back. "I ain't stupid, ya'll fucking, that's why she always parked outside when I leave in the morning for work." Of course, I denied the allegations, because they were simply not true. How had we gotten here? I thought. I prayed for the truth. As I wondered, what results or consequences brought Robin to this conclusion? The concept that Selena and I had anything going on was completely absurd. Reality set in when I discovered Robin who projected her guilt on me was the person who had been having a secret and ongoing love affair with Marco. She revealed that Marco was a married, bisexual man who co-parents with his wife. I had only been with Robin for almost two years and was shocked to learn that the affair had been going on between her and Marco for eight years at that time, raising the unsettling possibility that Marco might be our child's actual father.

[Reflecting]

It all made sense why I noticed a change in her attitude. At the NICU visits after I saw her and Marco together. She became very irritated whenever I was around. We didn't talk as often as we used to before our son was brought into this world. There were days when Robin didn't want me to accompany her to the hospital to see our son. She claimed her aunt and mother would pick her up after work, or she would get a ride from work with a coworker. I found this strange since I had always been the one to pick her up from work ever since I'd met her years ago as a cab driver. Now, there were times when we would arrive separately at the NICU. I asked for the truth and it led me to the outcome. Damn. The truth does hurt. It was the reason why the dynamics between Robin and I shifted drastically after that. I questioned her loyalty and her morals when we finally got home that day.

We were both exhausted and didn't talk much. After dinner that evening, we all went to sleep. The next morning, after getting my children off to school for ancillary, upon returning I tried to have a conversation with Robin about her shift in attitude, and I asked, how did we get here? You previously praised me as a single father to members of your family, and friends boasting about my single-parenting skills. You mentioned that you had never had a father present in your life while growing up. How do we resolve this? Robin stood there with her arms folded, with an attitude while flaring her nose. She never responded. I left.

She lost respect for me because I questioned her entanglement and the secrets she had kept from me. She wanted to have her cake and eat it, too. Six months after Prince was released from the hospital, that weekend Robin and I agreed that I was going to introduce him to my side of the family as we had previously agreed upon. Especially since her side of the family had seen him every day since he was born. My mother had not yet met him, and my sister April, who was dying of cancer, had only seen him once before she passed away from stage four pancreatic cancer. This weekend was an important opportunity for my family to meet our new addition. While at work, I called Robin to ensure that she had packed our son's clothes and diapers, as I planned to take all my children to spend time with my family. When I arrived, Robin had not packed his bags, which frustrated me. Despite this, I remained hopeful for a positive weekend with my son and my family. When I arrived home to pick up my children and take them to their grandmother's house for the weekend, Robin dropped a bombshell. She wouldn't let me take Prince and threatened to call the police and have me arrested. Her reason? My name wasn't on the birth certificate, and she claimed I wasn't the father. I was stunned.

"You are so fucking evil," I snapped, the first time I had ever used such strong language directed towards a woman. I couldn't recognize the woman standing before me.

Who was she? It was true; I hadn't signed the birth certificate at the hospital because I wanted a DNA test done, especially after meeting Marco, the man Robin claimed was just a friend but who seemed to have a significant presence at the hospital. I grew more suspicious of his involvement and the probability that he was Prince's father. Despite not signing the birth certificate, I signed other documents at the hospital including his discharge documents and I signed off on those as Prince's father.

She immediately made a phone call and packed up our son and her belongings. She moved in with her aunt, the chain smoker. Months later, she and her mother, (who had nothing to do with Robin until Prince was born) who had her own apartment, moved into Robin's apartment. I thought it was weird. From that time on, Robin prevented me from spending time alone with our son or taking him to see my family. It wasn't until he was eight months old that she finally agreed. I took Robin and all three of my children to see my family for the first time. Marco started showing up more frequently at Robin's apartment, often coinciding with my visits to Robin's apartment. She became more furious when I approached Marco about getting a paternity test done during one of our frequent interactions. He verbally agreed to it, but Robin immediately said, "He don't have to get shit."

I was shocked and confused. She had never acted like this around me before. I found it weird that all of a sudden He was either coming over or leaving as I arrived. I told her this was uncomfortable, unacceptable, disrespectful, and confusing to our son Prince. It was odd, unsettling even, how quickly things changed. The home I once felt secure in began to feel foreign, like a place where I no longer belonged.

Just when I thought I had seen the worst, the rug was pulled out from under me. For a time, I had everything a man could dream of—children, a house, a car, and a newborn son. Life seemed perfect, until it all began to unravel. I found myself in court once again, this time fighting to protect my family and our property without an attorney. The Realtors were determined to sell the property quickly, and to avoid any legal delays, they decided to evict me immediately. A ten-day notice to vacate was posted on my front door. It was the week of Thanksgiving, November 2016 the courts would be closed for the Holidays. I had to move quickly if I planned to keep our property, with no money for an attorney on such short notice. Besides, I had just paid the realtor my monthly rent, I also paid the water and electricity bills too. After arriving at court, I contested the notice in front of a White male judge in St. Louis City civil courts. His words still haunt me: "We protect property, not people." I lost the case that day. The next morning, I filed an emergency appeal in an appeals court.

The receptionist told me, "The judge will rule on it, and you'll be notified." I waited for hours, only to be told to leave and that they would contact me with the decision. When I returned home, my life was turned upside down. Strangers were in our home. My children and I were suddenly thrown out of our home. The sheriff arrived and callously ordered men to throw all our belongings into a construction dumpster. Despite my desperate pleas, he refused to let us salvage anything. He warned me, "Leave or I will arrest you for trespassing." My children cried and I stood helplessly, watching as our possessions were discarded without a shred of remorse.

I drove away, feeling utterly defeated. Later, I discovered that the Realtor, a White man who had given me the keys to that house, had scammed me. I had always paid my rent on time and kept meticulous records, I even presented this evidence in court.

So, the ten-day notice was a devastating shock. I couldn't understand why this was happening to us. Even though I presented all my records and receipts in court, I lost the battle against the scam. The legal system had failed us, leaving my children and me homeless, stripped of everything we owned. I lost the case because, in the eyes of that court, I was just a Black, illiterate (about the law) man without an attorney. I wasn't ashamed to admit that I didn't know the law. I had never gone to law school, never practiced law. I was simply struggling financially and too poor to hire an attorney. I represent many fathers like me, fighting to protect the rights of my family and our property. That day in court, it became painfully clear that they didn't care about us at all. I was a nervous wreck, but I had to be strong for my children. I reassured them that we would rebuild our lives. I had saved some money

Yahkhahnahn Ammi

from my taxicab job, but it wasn't enough. To supplement our income, I worked as a food delivery driver, often with my oldest children by my side. We turned it into a game, betting on who would get the biggest tip from customers. Losing our home was devastating, and I fell into a deep depression.

However, I knew I had to stay strong for my children. We stayed with family, in hotels, and even lived out of my SUV for a while. It was not a Happy Thanksgiving for us. This experience propelled me forward, and I was determined to make a fresh start in Kansas City, Missouri. Through all of this, I kept my children with me, homeschooling and caring for them as best as I could. Despite our homelessness, I was determined to be the best parent I could. Despite the Lack of Support system in St. Louis, I refused to be separated from my children. I found creative ways to keep my family engaged in daily events, trying to maintain a sense of normalcy. Most nights, I stayed awake, watching and protecting my family from the harsh realities of city life as my children slept soundly in our black SUV.

In the midst of all of this Robin wished me and my children a Happy Thanksgiving. I did not tell her what happened. While she was settled in her new apartment, with a full-fledged bar and daily drinks, often with Marco. We were forced to live or die tryin'. One day, during a visit to see Prince, I discovered she had been smoking weed with Marco in the house while our son was in the other room, this was prior to marijuana being made legal in Missouri. This behavior was alarming, and it made me realize I didn't truly know the woman I had been dating all those years. I did not smoke cigarettes or marijuana and as a rule I did not date women that did.

I confronted her about this, and was told, "*I do what the fuck I want in my house.*" You are right. I took my two children who stood by my side with me and left. Ninety days before all this transpired, Robin and I had a discussion that centered around my decision to temporarily relocate my family to Kansas City, Missouri to work as an Uber driver. I asked if she wanted to come, and she said, "No."

I later informed Selena of my plans to take our children with me before we left St. Louis; she agreed and thought it would be a good idea. She was really struggling financially, and receiving government assistance. I told her that I had a career opportunity to become an Uber driver and that I would let her know once we got settled in. I told her that I would not provide my home address, but I would let her know the hotels we were staying at and the area we would move to in Kansas City once that had finalized. She agreed. In the meantime, I encouraged both her and our children to communicate via our children's cell phones because they both had cell phones since they were ages three and four. Selena rarely communicated with any of us on a consistent basis, and when she did, it was a shock to us all. After all of this drama, I decided that now was as good a time as any to make the move. It sure beat house-hopping, living in a tent, and staying in temporary shelters.

The potential move to Kansas City could offer us a chance to start afresh and improve our situation. The decision wasn't easy; I had to save every penny I made from DoorDash and Postmates and really budget if we were going to make a move this month, as I had planned and discussed with my family.

I also received some financial help from friends and some family members, which made the intended move more feasible.

Additionally, I saved some money from my previous taxicab job, which helped cover some unexpected expenses. Despite the challenges, the thought of a new beginning filled me with hope and determination. I was ready to leave the hardships behind and embrace the opportunities that lay ahead. This experience has taught me the importance of resilience and adaptability, and I am grateful for the strength it has given me. I look forward to the future with optimism and excitement, knowing that we have overcome so much and are now on the path to a brighter tomorrow in Kansas City. We would leave the morning of December 25th, 2016.

They say that history has a tendency of repeating itself. I questioned why I attracted two women who wanted to keep me out of our children's lives. I fought Robin to be an active father in our son Prince's life, but she consistently pushed me away, refusing to let me be more involved. I went from being a great father to not having a role in my son's life. But when confronted by my parents, she claimed that she wanted me to have an active role in his life. In reality, she made excuses every weekend, claiming he was busy or with her family. She would go weeks and months without communication, ignoring my calls and preventing me from seeing our son. When I gave her money, everything seemed fine, but if I wasn't giving her cash, it was a problem. Robin labeled me as a, 'no-good-for-nothing-ass daddy and a deadbeat dad.' I was sick of it.

She needed to get her act together because I wasn't going to be used only when it was convenient for her. It was sickening. I missed my son and wanted quality time with him, not just when it suited her. She refused to listen, insisting I was only interested when it was convenient for me. She often used and twisted my words to fit her narrative. Especially when she was in the wrong. For the record, it was never convenient for me; I wanted to be there for my son. I agreed to take him on weekends because she had taken my weekdays away, always having him at her chain smoking aunt's house, where smoking was allowed.

Robin knew that we were moving to Kansas City, she hated the idea and wanted me to stay, but did not even offer sanctuary when I revealed that my children and I became homeless and lost everything due to the Realtor's scam.

Robin refused to acknowledge my role as a father to our son Prince, often cropping my image out of pictures of me with our son Prince and claiming she was a single mom on social media. She contacted my dad and stepmom, asked them for money, and claimed I wasn't doing anything for Prince. Meanwhile, I was buying our son expensive gifts, custom made shoes and toys, only for her to give them away to her lil cousins and then ask my dad and stepmom to buy more. She would even send back money I sent her via CashApp as financial support for our son Prince, she insisted on cash instead. I was sick of dealing with her excuses and games. I never got the chance to have that paternity test done because she always had an excuse as she reasoned why our son could not spend the weekend with me. I love our little Prince, and part of the delay with getting the paternity test was my fear that he may very well not be my son and that would forever crush me. It was terrifying, but I knew it would have to be done eventually. It was a constant battle. I grew tired of her constant threats to call the police to have me arrested for bullshit lies she made up to control and blackmail me. So, I had to do the most devastating thing a father could do, walk away from the situation, and the drama for peace sake. I allowed all of the stress from these women to consume me. I had to take control over my failing health concerns. It was killing me.

Through the pain and turmoil of betrayal and legal battles, I learned valuable lessons that have shaped my perspective on life and relationships. I learned the importance of trust and communication in a relationship and the devastating consequences of betrayal. I learned that sometimes, the people we trust the most are capable of hurting us the deepest. My advice to anyone going through a similar situation is to stay strong, to fight for what is right, and to never lose hope. Betrayal may shake your faith in humanity, but it is possible to heal and find peace. Surround yourself with supportive people who uplift and encourage you, and never be afraid to seek help when you need it. The journey to healing may be long and difficult, but it is worth it in the end.

* * *

Personal Life Lesson Reflections

In this chapter, "Momma's Baby, Daddy's Maybe," is a heart breaking chapter in my memoir that encapsulates a period of intense personal growth and painful self-discovery. The trials I faced during this time—ranging from betrayal and legal battles to the struggle for stability—forced me to confront deep truths about relationships, fatherhood, and my own resilience. Through the emotional whirlwind of this chapter, I gleaned invaluable lessons that reshaped my understanding of love, trust, and personal strength.

My relationship with Robin began with ambiguous boundaries and casual intentions, which seemed manageable until it took a significant turn with the birth of our son, Prince. This transition from a casual situationship to a deeply entangled one illuminated a crucial lesson: even relationships that start without clear direction can evolve into complex and impactful connections.

The consequences of our situationship dynamics revealed that casual or undefined connections can have profound and lasting effects. This experience taught me the importance of being mindful and intentional about the relationships I enter, understanding that even seemingly trivial interactions can lead to significant changes and challenges in life.

Trust, once broken, is challenging to repair. Robin's betrayal—particularly regarding the paternity of our child—was a painful reminder of how fragile trust can be. The emotional turmoil that followed her infidelity highlighted the critical need for open and honest communication. Trust must be built and maintained through transparency and consistent actions. When communication falters, it can create a breeding ground for misunderstanding and betrayal. This chapter underscored that in any relationship, whether romantic, familial, or otherwise, maintaining trust requires vigilant and honest dialogue. Addressing issues directly and truthfully is essential to prevent the erosion of trust and the next fallout.

Fatherhood evaluated my limits in ways I never anticipated. The challenges I faced—from dealing with Prince's health issues to navigating the emotional fallout of Robin's actions—highlighted the immense resilience needed in parenting. Being a father is not solely about providing material support but about being a steady, loving presence through life's trials. This chapter reinforced that true fatherhood involves unwavering commitment and the ability to face adversity head on. It's about showing up for your children, advocating for their well-being, and providing stability and love regardless of the obstacles. There comes a point when fighting for a relationship or situation can become detrimental to your well-being.

My experience with Robin revealed the importance of knowing when to step back and prioritize my mental and emotional health. Deciding to distance myself from a toxic situation was a difficult but necessary step for self-preservation. This lesson taught me that self-care is not a form of weakness but a vital aspect of supporting overall health and well-being. Sometimes, the most courageous decision is to let go of situations that cause harm, even if it means enduring short-term pain for long-term peace.

The journey through this tumultuous period reaffirmed the power of resilience and faith. Life's challenges can be relentless, and finding a way forward can seem daunting. However, my experience showed me that resilience—along with faith in oneself and in a higher power—can guide you through even the darkest times. This chapter highlighted that no matter how deep the pain or how uncertain the path, holding onto resilience and faith can provide hope and strength. These qualities were crucial in helping me navigate the difficulties and rebuild my life.

In reflecting on this chapter, I recognize that the challenges I faced were not just obstacles but opportunities for profound personal growth. The lessons learned during this period have shaped my understanding of relationships, fatherhood, and personal strength.

By sharing these insights, I hope to offer guidance and encouragement to others navigating similar struggles.

Life's most significant lessons often come from the hardest experiences, and embracing these lessons can lead to greater wisdom and resilience.

Takeaways

Be Mindful of Relationships

Recognize that even seemingly casual relationships can have significant impacts. Enter every connection with clear intentions and be aware of its potential consequences.

Prioritize Trust and Communication

Build and keep trust through honest and open communication. These elements are essential for healthy and enduring relationships.

Commit to Fatherhood

Being a father goes beyond financial support. It involves being a constant, loving presence in your child's life, especially during challenging times.

Know When to Let Go

Sometimes, letting go of harmful situations is necessary for your peace of mind and well-being. Prioritize your mental and emotional health when making tough decisions.

Yahkhahnahn Ammi

Hold on to Resilience and Faith

Use resilience and faith as tools to navigate life's challenges. These qualities will help you find hope and strength even when the journey is difficult.

By sharing this chapter, I hope to offer guidance and hope to those facing similar struggles. Life's lessons, though often hard earned, shape us into stronger and wiser individuals. Embrace the journey, learn from the challenges, and remember that you are not alone.

CHAPTER 14

The Altercation

"Heartless" - Kanye West

Francine's phone call that day would set off a chain of events, drawing me into a storm of violence, lies, and betrayal, testing my limits and revealing dark truths buried beneath the surface of my life.

Francine Coldburn, an actress deeply involved in both the conscious community and the Black Lives Matter movement in St. Louis, was a woman I had first met during the Ferguson protests two years earlier. She was a force of nature—marked by a constant swirl of chaos, her life a blend of passion and unpredictability. She often confided in me about her troubled past—her father's abuse, losing custody of her children, and a series of violent relationships. Though I listened and offered advice, I kept my distance, unaware that she had secretly been stalking me during and after the unrest for at least two years. Even more shocking, I had no idea at the time that Francine was both a friend and lover to my ex-wife. When she reappeared in my life, it wasn't just to reconnect. Her return sparked a web of lies that would smear my name and pull me into her storm of deceit.

Francine, entrenched in an abusive relationship with her boyfriend Teddy, who had been assaulting her for years, decided to shield him by accusing me of attacking her. She fabricated this narrative to protect her secret of cheating with Teddy for five years, concealing their abuse because Teddy was a married man, and she didn't want their affair exposed. Hiding her long history of destructive relationships, which had already cost her custody of her children, Francine dragged my name through the mud. As her lies unfolded, I was left fighting to clear my name while the painful truths of her life—and her hidden connections—came to light. What began as a simple phone call soon became a battle against lies, betrayal, and the toxic secrets she had kept hidden for years.

Little did I know that Francine's phone call would unravel a web of deceit and danger, pulling me into a conspiracy that would test my resilience and uncover dark secrets lurking in the shadows of my past. The phone buzzed in my pocket, pulling me from my thoughts. I glanced at the screen. It was Francine Coldburn, the actress I had met two years ago during the Ferguson Unrest. Our paths had crossed multiple times, and she often poured out her heart to me. Her father had molested her numerous times as a child. She lost custody of her children because of violent relationships. She felt like she didn't fit social norms. She was fed up with her current boyfriend, who constantly mistreated her. I listened and offered advice where I could, but it was overwhelming. I hadn't told anyone about my wrongful eviction or that my family had lost everything. My pride kept me silent.

Today felt different. The weight of the world pressed on my shoulders. I needed more money fast and had set a goal I didn't want to fall short of. I spent days delivering food until I was exhausted. Mama (Jackie) agreed to watch my children during the daytime while I worked. If I could work as hard as I did in my activism, this should be a piece of cake. My thoughts were interrupted by the phone. It was Francine. Her number wasn't saved in my phone, so I hesitated before answering. Despite her persistent advances and my repeated rejections, she kept reaching out. I was about to hang up when she said, *"Have you heard of a vegan restaurant called Sweet Arts?"* "No, I haven't," I replied.

"Can you meet me there? I'm buying you lunch, and I want to introduce you to the owners. They're pretty dope, artists, too!"

I figured, why not? I agreed to meet her.

When I arrived, the rain was a light drizzle. Francine was waiting, parked outside. I opened her car door, and she teased, *"I guess chivalry isn't dead."* Smiling, I held the door to the restaurant open for her, prompting her playful response, *"Oh my, I am not used to this."* "The men don't do this here?" I asked. All I did was open a few doors, it was common courtesy I was taught as a child. What was the big deal? I thought.

"Not usually," she replied.

Inside, Francine introduced me to the vibrant and Melanated married, vegan owners. Francine guided me through the restaurant, showcasing its beautiful decor and prime location. The place was enchanting, resonating with artistry and culinary delights.

Yahkhahnahn Ammi

As we settled at a cozy table, we perused the menu, exploring a variety of vegan options. The conversation flowed effortlessly, connecting over shared interests in art, protesting, and our personal experiences.

The ambiance of Sweet Art's created the perfect backdrop for our discussion about community initiatives. While ordering food and desserts, I appreciated the restaurant's charm and the company I was in. The evening unfolded with laughter, delightful flavors, and the promise of something new. Sweet Art quickly became my favorite vegan restaurant.

As we waited for our food, I asked Francine to point me to the restroom. With a subtle look, she guided me and asked, "*Do you need a hand?*" I grabbed her hand teasingly and said, "As a matter of fact, I do." She took me seriously, and held my hand tightly. She followed me into the restroom, locking the door behind her. Adrenaline rushed through me. Standing face to face, she danced and quickly turned around, lifting her dress to reveal her nakedness. We had sex. I had never done anything like that before, certainly not in public. After our unexpected encounter, our vegan burgers and desserts were ready.

We sat down to eat, sharing flavors and conversation. I told her about my upcoming move to Kansas City, Missouri. She frowned and said, "*Hopefully, this won't be the last time I see you.*" I thought, oh shit, here we go.

As the meal concluded, it began to rain outside. I walked Francine to her car and opened her car door. She embraced me warmly and said, "*Yah, I had an amazing time with you.*" "Me too. Thank you for inviting me to lunch," I replied.

She rolled down her window as I stepped away and teased, *"I'll call you later."* The air was charged with a promise that seemed to grow stronger with each moment. What the fuck did I just do? I thought. Did I just open Pandora's box?

Three days later, while at Mama's (Jackie's) house, I woke early to make a vegan breakfast for my children before work. Just as I was leaving, Francine called, crying hysterically.

"Hey, what's up? Why are you crying?" I asked. "I am sick and tired of this motherfucker. Teddy put his hands on me again. Can you please come over and change the locks to my four-family flat? I am done, and I want him out of my house and away from me."

"I'm calling the police, and then I'm on my way," I said. I hung up and called 911, but I couldn't reach the St. Louis 911 center since I was in Illinois. I drove across the McKinley Bridge which adjoined both Illinois and Missouri and called again, finally reaching the right dispatch.

I explained the situation and informed them that I was on my way, driving a black Ford Expedition with my emergency flashers on. I arrived at Francine's building, and the police pulled up shortly after. I explained the situation to the officers, and they followed me up the narrow stairs to her apartment. The door hung ajar as Francine stood motionless in the doorway, the faint scent of marijuana and cigarettes clinging to her clothes. She made a feeble attempt to mask the marijuana's pungency, but it lingered in the cold air. Her face was pale, eyes swollen from crying, with dark circles beneath them. A sharp draft whispered through the gap, hinting at the chill of the apartment behind her, as if no heat had touched it for days.

Yahkhahnahn Ammi

"He's gone," she said, her voice trembling. She glanced nervously at the officers, then back at me.

"Do you want to press charges?" one of the officers asked. Francine shook her head vigorously. *"No, I just want him out of my life!"* She exclaimed.

The officers exchanged glances but didn't push further. They took down some details and left, leaving us standing in the dimly lit hallway.

Seeking Safety. She turned to me, her eyes pleading. "Can you change all the locks and stay here for a few days? I need to feel safe."

Hesitantly, I nodded. "I'll help, but you'll need to pay for my time and for the tools or supplies. I need the money for my services, and I'm here only as a friend."

She agreed. "I can pay for the tools now and pay you the rest when I get paid on Friday."

Inside her two-bedroom apartment, the stale smell of cigarettes and marijuana hit me immediately. The living room was cluttered with ashtrays overflowing with cigarette butts and the remnant of smoked blunts.

Seeing my discomfort, Francine quickly began to tidy up. "I'll cook us dinner," she offered, forcing a smile.

Looking around her apartment, I said, "I'd prefer to order out," trying to keep my tone light. Francine sighed and nodded. She then listed the repairs she needed: changing the locks to the building she owned, including her apartment unit, the main front and back doors, and the basement lock. Additionally, her furnace needed to be lit, and she wanted me to mount a television on the wall.

I started with the locks, making several trips to the hardware store for supplies. The bitter cold from the unheated apartment bit at my fingers as I worked. I replaced the locks on the front and back doors, the basement, and her apartment unit. I gave her both sets of keys. Each turn of the screwdriver felt like a small victory, bringing a sense of security back to her home.

Next, I tackled the furnace. The pilot light was out, and the air inside was frigid. After some fiddling and a few failed attempts, the furnace roared to life, sending warmth through the vents. Francine let out a sigh of relief, and I could see some of the tension leave her shoulders.

I noticed that after each completed repair, she added more tasks, extending to other apartments in the four family flat that she owned. I didn't mind as long as she paid for my services as agreed upon by Friday.

As I stood there, watching the furnace hum and feeling the warmth spread through the apartment, I couldn't help but reflect on the past few hours. They had been intense, filled with unexpected tasks and emotional conversations. But there was a sense of accomplishment, too, in having helped a friend in need. Francine looked at me, her eyes softer now. *"Thank you so much, Yah. I don't know what I would have done without you."*

I nodded, feeling a mix of exhaustion and satisfaction. "Just take care of yourself, Francine. And remember, I'm here as a friend."

Yahkhahnahn Ammi

As I gathered my tools and prepared to leave, I realized that despite the chaos and discomfort, there was a deeper connection forming. Helping Francine brought a sense of purpose and fulfillment that went beyond the immediate tasks at hand.

I was ready for dinner to arrive from Lulu's so we could eat. Francine and I talked while we waited, or rather, she did most of the talking. She recounted her five year relationship with Teddy, a married man who had promised to leave his wife for her. I had always told Francine that he wouldn't leave his wife; he was using her for money and convenience. I listened more than I spoke, absorbing her words and trying to offer support where I could. The conversation continued through dinner, filled with her laughter and sighs of frustration.

After dinner, we discussed my eviction and the sleeping arrangements.

"I'll sleep on the couch," I said.

"And I'll sleep in my bedroom once I return. I am going dancing," *she said.*

"Be safe and have fun. I'll leave in the morning to check on my children. I'll be back tomorrow evening after work to finish the tasks," I said.

Francine nodded. "Thank you, Yah. Oh, and by the way, I invite *you and your children to stay here as long as you need to."*

I was not ready for my children to meet her or any woman for that matter. I did not want to blur the lines. Hesitantly I said, "Thank you, I'll only need a few days before we leave for Kansas City. I

195

know it's your apartment, but you have to promise not to smoke if I agree to stay because we are asthmatic."

"I can agree to that," she said.

We said goodnight, and I eventually fell asleep, the weight of the day pressing down on me. Francine returned. While I was asleep, she performed oral sex on me. I thought I was having a wet dream until I opened my eyes and saw her head bobbing between my legs. Too exhausted, I laid there until I fell back to sleep.

The early morning bird chirps and the brightness of the rising sun woke me. I stretched, feeling the stiffness from the couch, and then showered to prepare for the day. It felt like I was in a new place, because Francine cleaned her house while I was asleep.

Francine greeted me with a surprise: hot tea, scrambled vegan tofu eggs, and maple vegan breakfast sausages. The aroma filled the kitchen, making my stomach rumble. It was delicious, down to the very last bite.

"Thank you, Francine. This was unexpected, kind of like last night," I said, savoring the flavors. She smiled. "I wanted to show my appreciation." She handed me a set of spare keys to her apartment and to the front door of her building. *"Keep these, just in case I am not here."*

I pocketed the keys and left to check on my children. Though it had only been one night away from them, I missed them dearly. I brought them breakfast from Burger King, our favorite fast-food spot, and spent quality time with them before heading out for my food delivery shifts. The day flew by in a blur of orders and deliveries. That night, I returned to Francine's place. She was eagerly expecting my arrival, excited to get the television mounted.

"*Are you ready to tackle this project?*" she asked, her eyes sparkling with enthusiasm. I nodded. "Let's get to it."

The concrete wall required a heavy-duty power drill, so I made another trip to Home Depot. The drill roared to life, each vibration sending tremors up my arms.

It was tough working through the solid concrete, but I managed to secure the mount and connect the television. Sweat trickled down my forehead, and my muscles ached from the effort. Francine watched every movement I made until it was time for her to leave. There was no time to show pain or exhaustion. Francine left for work while I continued completing the tasks before me. She came home on her lunch break and stood back, admiring the finished product. "It looks perfect. Thank you so much, Yah."

I wiped my brow and smiled. "I'm glad I could help. It was quite the challenge, but we got it done." As we stood there, the television finally mounted and her home feeling more secure, I couldn't help but reflect on the past couple of days. They had been intense, filled with unexpected tasks and emotional conversations. But there was a sense of accomplishment, too, in having helped a friend in need. Francine left. I assumed she would be back after she got off work with the money she owed me for the repairs to her unit. I set mouse traps throughout her building and completed the repairs to the other unit. I waited for the inspector to arrive; everything went well, and I communicated the outcome with Francine.

I left for the day, spent time with my children, and decided to bring them over to Francine's that night. We would stay there for two days and leave on Christmas morning to see their mother and pick up the gifts she claimed she had for them before we left town. Francine left me a voicemail asking, "Why did you leave here without telling me?" I must have missed that call; it had gone straight to voicemail, and I was glad I did because I did not owe her an explanation. She still had not paid me for all of the tasks that I completed. I did not know what her obsession was with me or why it was driven by a desire to control and possess me, but it had reached a boiling point.

My children and I had a great time together, spending time with Mama (Jackie) and visiting other family members before we left town. Afterwards, we drove to and arrived at Francine's later in the evening, closer to their bedtime. I introduced my children to Francine by their nicknames, and then I put them to bed. They both slept in the guest room of Francine's apartment.

We all ate vegan breakfast the next morning and shared laughs. We put cartoons on the mounted flat screen that I had installed. After a few hours had passed, I asked Francine if she didn't mind watching them as I ran a few errands. She agreed. I talked to my children before I left and told them to use their cell phones to call me if they needed to.

I left, bought outfits from the store, and then I picked up food from Burger King and returned to Francine's. We all ate lunch. Afterwards, I took my children to a park so they could play and run around. Before you knew it, it was dinner time, so we sat inside an all you can eat Indian buffet restaurant and returned to Francine's. We all talked, played card games, watched television, and I put them to bed. Francine asked me to come into her bedroom after putting my children to sleep. We both sat on her bed. She gave me $50 and promised to pay me the rest before I left. She wanted to talk more about her relationship with Teddy and getting him out of her life. I listened as she expressed herself. It was late, and I was tired. I didn't really want to hear any of this right now, but I kept my composure. We discussed other topics, including her getting a new car, because Teddy placed a lien on it. She wanted a new career, because she claimed to hate her current job as an insurance agent, and wanted to start her own company. After talking, or rather listening to her we had sex, and I fell asleep.

I woke up coughing and sneezing to the foul smell of marijuana and cigarettes. Francine had gotten up while I was asleep and had been smoking in the living room. I reminded her of our agreement and confronted her about this. She had an attitude, so I went to check on my children and then back to the bedroom. I reached out to Alicia, our mutual friend and one of Francine's accountability sisters, and thought I texted Alicia the concerns that I had regarding Francine. Instead, I accidentally sent the text to Francine's phone... I could not believe that I sent the text to the wrong number. Damn. I later forwarded the text to the correct number. I had hoped that her sister could help the situation; I later found out that it infuriated Francine even more. When I woke up, I took my children to the St. Louis Science Center and the History museum. I spoke with Alicia that morning; she told me the talk with Francine was successful. I was glad to hear that.

However, Francine sent me several text messages while I was sleeping asking when we were leaving because she wanted us out of her house. I did not read them until later that day. We stayed the night at Mama's (Jackie, their grandmother) who was happy to see them.

When we arrived back at Francine's house that morning, apparently, Teddy and she had an argument, which led to a physical altercation outside of her apartment building before my children and I arrived. Her downstairs neighbor had already called the police, unbeknownst to me at the time. Once inside the apartment, my children sat on the couch in the living room. Francine, whose face was swollen, asked me to come into her bedroom to talk. I instructed my children to sit in the living room and watch television before I closed Francine's bedroom door.

That's when Francine yelled, *"You don't have to leave, I am tired of men leaving me!"* She immediately lashed out at me.

She punched me on the top of my head with a closed fist and in the face. As she unleashed her frustration on me in her bedroom, I found myself once again caught in the crossfire of her obsession. Each blow and scratch inflicted upon me was a testament to her unwillingness to accept my decision to leave.

Despite my efforts to defend myself and reason with her, the physical altercation left me bruised and battered, a reluctant victim of her relentless pursuit. I grabbed her and held her down on the floor until she was calm enough to stop attacking me. She yelled to her downstairs neighbor to call the police. I could hear my children's knocks on the door asking "Is everything okay Abba?" as they cried. I told them that everything is fine. Francine got up and went to her basement to smoke some weed and cigarettes to cover up the marijuana smell before the cops arrived. I called Alicia and told her what had just happened. By this time, the police had arrived. She exited the apartment and walked downstairs to speak with the two white male officers as I waited upstairs with my children. I comforted them. The police wanted to speak with me because Francine had lied to them, claiming that I had attacked her. At that time, the downstairs neighbor opened her door and told them she was the person that called and that Teddy was the person that assaulted Francine but had driven off before they arrived. I told them that I was unaware of what happened before I arrived, but that my children and I had just arrived recently when she lashed out at me. The scars on my wrists and the bleeding scratch she left on the side of my face from her fingernails were evident enough for the police, who asked if I wanted to press charges. I declined, and they told me that I was fine to stay if I wanted to or that I could leave for a few hours until she calmed down. I decided to do the latter.

Our plan was to leave Christmas morning after bidding farewell to our families. Despite the setbacks and the unexpected altercation with Francine, I called Alicia back and asked if I could come pick her up so I could take the children to see their mother. She said, "Yes." We set off to pick Alicia up; she would act as my witness and ensure peace amidst the tension between Selena and me. We arrived at Alicia's house.

My children played with hers as she made me some of that ginger tea that I love so much. Alicia sat in the front passenger seat, while my children enjoyed their own space in a separate row of the SUV. Alicia and I discussed what had transpired before she arrived. I thanked Alicia for accompanying us and acting as a witness to maintain peace, despite the initial scorn she endured from my ex-wife. Despite being granted visitation rights and placed on child support, Selena did not exercise her visitation privileges until September-October 2016.

With our temporary move to Kansas City looming, I almost begged Selena to see the children before our departure. She agreed to meet us, claiming to be armed with gifts for our kids.

Upon arrival at the apartment complex off Cole and Carr Street, I parked on the side Carr street near the entrance of her gated apartment complex.

Accompanied by Alicia, I waited for Selena. Eventually, she emerged, offering hugs and kisses but conspicuously empty-handed. She confessed to having no gifts and promised to provide them later—a familiar pattern of empty promises that had disappointed and disillusioned our children. Despite my repeated pleas to her not to make such promises, Selena was not reliable. As we drove away, the tears in my children's eyes tore at my heartstrings.

They looked to me for solace, and I did my best to lift their spirits with promises of happy meals with toys from Burger King. It hurt me to see my children's tears and disappointment.

After this disheartening reunion, I dropped Alicia back home and spent just enough time at her place to share a cup of ginger tea and for the children to play with her kids. Soon after, we hit the road, gearing up for the four-hour drive ahead. The brief stops at Alicia's home had set a positive tone for the road trip that lay ahead. During the journey to Kansas City, the emotional turmoil of the day weighed heavily on my mind. Despite the challenges and disappointments, the camaraderie with Alicia and the brief stop at her home had set a positive tone for the road trip ahead. As we traveled, I couldn't help but reflect on the importance of this move for our future.

Arriving in Kansas City, I found myself in geographically and emotionally unfamiliar territory. The decision to uproot our lives for the sake of work and a fresh start weighed heavily on me, but I was determined to make the best of it. With my children by my side, I saw this move as an opportunity for growth and new experiences. As we settled into our temporary accommodations, the weight of responsibility settled on my shoulders. Everyone back home was counting on me, my children relied on me, and I, most importantly, counted on me. Even if it meant enduring temporary hardship in a hotel until our apartment became available, I was committed to making this new chapter in our lives work.

In the midst of uncertainty, I found solace in the resilience of my children and the prospect of a brighter future in Kansas City. Despite the challenges ahead, I was determined to embrace this opportunity for change and build a better life for us all. It was then that the court had granted me custody of our children after six years of single-handedly raising them after she abandoned our marital home. After we left for Kansas City, Francine and Selena began publicly posting drama and lies about me on Facebook. The online attacks were relentless and filled with accusations designed to ruin my reputation. I responded by announcing that Francine was deliberately exposing men to sexually transmitted diseases, and was having an affair with a married man who was the actual abuser. When I revealed this truth, she really flipped out and, in an effort to shut me up, she lied on me and used her political connections to have me falsely arrested several months later for a crime I did not commit.

The situation escalated to the point where Facebook blocked, censored, and permanently banned me. It was a messy and unnecessary spectacle that only added stress to an already tense situation. As I tried to navigate this chaos, I couldn't shake the feeling that there was more to the story.

I began to notice disturbing patterns and connections between Francine and Selena's actions. It wasn't just random drama; it felt orchestrated, as if they were working together to bring me down. The online attacks were just the beginning. Memories of strange occurrences at my home before the eviction started to resurface. The unsettling feeling of being watched, the anonymous threats, and the inexplicable incidents—all seemed to point to a deeper conspiracy.

It became clear that Selena wasn't acting alone. Francine had played a significant role in stalking me and making my life a living hell. My determination to move forward was now fueled by the need to uncover the truth. A web of deceit and betrayal needed to be untangled, and I was prepared to face whatever challenges lay ahead. As we settled into our new life in Kansas City, I knew that this was just the beginning of a long journey. The full extent of Francine and Selena's conspiracy would be revealed in the coming chapters, and I was ready to confront it head-on.

It was a new beginning despite the challenges and the ominous signs, I stayed hopeful. Kansas City represented a fresh start, a chance to rebuild and find clarity. My focus was on my children, their happiness, and our future. But I couldn't ignore the lingering shadows of the past.

The truth about Francine and Selena's collusion would come to light, and I was determined to expose it. Stay tuned as the story unfolds, revealing the depths of deception and the strength it takes to rise above it all. There is much more to this tale of resilience, betrayal, and the relentless pursuit of truth.

* * *

Personal Life Lesson Reflections

In this chapter, I was drawn into a complex and painful series of events that unraveled before me, revealing deceit, betrayal, and a darker conspiracy than I had initially realized. Through the encounter with Francine and her toxic relationships, I experienced an emotional and physical confrontation that tested my boundaries, patience, and ultimately my resolve to move forward with my life. I found myself entangled in a difficult situation that challenged my character and forced me to reassess the people I allow into my life. Despite the chaos and pain, there were valuable lessons learned, teaching me the importance of self-respect, boundaries, and focusing on the future for the sake of my children.

Takeaways

Establish Boundaries

It is crucial to maintain clear boundaries in any relationship, especially when dealing with people who may take advantage of your kindness. Failing to establish boundaries early can lead to unhealthy attachments and difficult situations, as I learned from my interactions with Francine.

Trust Your Instincts

When something feels off, it often is. My instincts warned me about Francine's behavior long before the situation escalated. It's important to listen to those gut feelings, as they can protect you from harm.

Control Your Environment

Your environment deeply affects your well-being. From the smoky, chaotic apartment to Francine's unstable behavior, I realized the importance of protecting me and my children from toxic environments.

Resilience in Adversity

Life will throw challenges at you, sometimes from unexpected sources. Staying resilient and focusing on the bigger picture—my children and our future—helped me push through the chaos and keep moving forward.

Self-Care and Responsibility

Taking care of yourself is just as important as taking care of others. Amidst all the drama, I had to remember that my own health and safety mattered. It's easy to get caught up in helping others, but self-care must be a priority to avoid burnout and danger.

This chapter serves as a reminder that we must stand firm in our values, guard our personal space, and remain resilient even when

Yahkhahnahn Ammi

faced with adversity. Life's challenges, while often painful, help us grow stronger and more focused on what truly matters.

CHAPTER 15

Bitter Baby Mama

"Baby Mama" – Three 6 Mafia

Co-parenting with Robin wasn't just a struggle—it was an exhausting battle of manipulation and obstacles, where my love for our son was the only thing keeping me from walking away.

T he air in my apartment was thick with the kind of silence that presses down on your chest, making it hard to breathe.

I sat on the couch, staring at my phone, willing it to vibrate, to flash with some sort of message. But there was nothing. Days had passed since I last heard from Robin, and the absence of any response was gnawing at me.

Parenthood wasn't supposed to be this way—cold, distant, full of unanswered questions and closed doors. I had always imagined raising Prince together, the two of us working as a team despite the fact that our relationship had ended. But what had once been a shared dream of co-parenting had turned into a battlefield where every interaction with Robin felt like another skirmish. And I was growing tired of the war.

Yahkhahnahn Ammi

Co-parenting with Robin wasn't just a struggle—it was an exhausting battle of manipulation and obstacles, where my love for our son was the only thing keeping me from walking away.

When Prince was born, I thought our split wouldn't change the love we both had for him. I was wrong. From the moment our relationship fell apart, Robin's bitterness grew, hardening her responses to my every attempt at cooperation. The woman I once knew became someone unrecognizable—hostile, dismissive, unwilling to meet me halfway. Every day felt like a test of patience, with Prince caught in the middle.

It started with the missed calls. Then came the unanswered texts. Days, sometimes weeks, would pass with no word from Robin, leaving me in a state of limbo. I knew she was upset with me, but it felt like she was punishing me by keeping me from our son.

I remember one evening, after days of silence, I sent her a message: *"Robin, I miss our son. When are you going to let me and his siblings see him?"* The words felt like I'd sent them a hundred times before, falling into the same abyss of unanswered pleas. The silence was deafening, but I couldn't stop trying. I had to be there for Prince, no matter how many walls Robin put between us.

When she finally responded, her replies were as cold as the silence had been. Short, vague texts that said nothing, left me with more questions than answers. Sometimes she wouldn't respond at all. But the worst part wasn't the silence—it was the feeling of being excluded, like I was shouting into a void while my son was slipping further away with each unanswered call. I'd try again. *"Is everything okay? Where have you moved to? I just want to see Prince."* But my texts were met with more deflection, more

209

coldness. And when Robin did respond, her words lacked any warmth or interest in co-parenting. It wasn't about Prince anymore—it was about control, about keeping me at a distance.

One night, fed up with the constant strain, I sent a blunt message: *"Are you keeping Prince from me and my side of the family? Is Marco his father? What's going on?"* I could no longer ignore the growing suspicion that Robin's new relationship was affecting her willingness to let me be a part of Prince's life.

Thanksgiving was approaching, and I hadn't seen Prince in weeks. The weight of not having him for the holiday hurt more than I could admit. Still, I reached out again, hoping that maybe, just maybe, this time would be different. *"How are you and Prince doing? Will he be coming over for Thanksgiving?"* But once again, my message was met with silence.

Then, on Thanksgiving Day, **Robin finally responded,** but her message felt hollow. *"Happy Thanksgiving to you, Princess Tiana, and Prince Avatar from Prince."* No mention of him coming over, no acknowledgment of the holiday I desperately wanted to spend with him—just a cold greeting.

"Happy Thanksgiving to you too," (Even though she knew we did not celebrate pagan holidays) I replied, refusing to let her sidestep the real issue. *"But why haven't you let me see or talk to Prince? What's going on, Robin?"* My questions felt like they were bouncing off a wall, as her responses always deflected, never addressing the heart of what I was asking.

Yahkhahnahn Ammi

In an attempt to lighten the mood, I texted her: *"Your song 'Juju on That Beat' is playing on the radio."* I hoped that maybe a touch of nostalgia would soften her, remind her of the good times.

"That's my baby's song," **she replied.** *"Our baby's song,"* I corrected, reminding her that, no matter what had happened between us, we still shared a child. But the distance between us had grown too vast. Robin was lost in her bitterness, and Prince was caught in the crossfire.

Co-parenting with Robin wasn't just about handling a difficult relationship; it was about survival. It was about staying strong in the face of constant resistance, about trying to be there for my son despite every obstacle Robin placed in my way. The impact on Prince was evident—he was stuck in the middle, dragged into a war he never asked to be part of. And that's what hurt the most.

I knew if I gave up, it wouldn't just be me who suffered—it would be Prince. I couldn't let that happen. No matter how many roadblocks Robin threw up, no matter how bitter she became, I had to be there for my son. I had to show him that I was still fighting, still present, still his father.

Robin's bitterness may have turned our co-parenting journey into a nightmare, but it taught me invaluable lessons about resilience, patience, and the unbreakable bond between a father and his child. I couldn't change Robin's behavior, but I could remain steady in my commitment to Prince. I had to be his anchor, even when the storms of co-parenting threatened to tear us apart.

As difficult as it was, I held onto the hope that one day, Prince would see the truth. That one day, he'd understand that I never stopped fighting for him, never stopped loving him.

And through every unanswered message, every missed moment, I stayed focused on that belief—that the love I had for my son would outlast the bitterness.

The fight was far from over, but I knew one thing for sure: it was a fight worth having. Co-parenting with Robin may have been one of the hardest battles of my life, but it was one I couldn't afford to lose. For Prince's sake, I would keep fighting.

It was Thanksgiving Day, November 24, 2016, when I texted her again.

"Where is Prince? What are you doing?" I typed, my patience thinning. I had been calling her repeatedly, trying to figure out why I hadn't seen our son.

Robin finally replied, "I am at work. I get off at 12."

I felt a wave of irritation wash over me. "You mean that's OUR baby's song," I texted, responding to a previous message where she had claimed Prince's favorite song.

I was determined. "I'm coming to see Prince today. Please text or give me the address."

After a long pause, **she responded,** "*You know...*" followed by a reluctant, "*Okay.*"

Yahkhahnahn Ammi

November 26, 2016

The back-and-forth continued two days later. I tried again: "Are you going to let me come see Prince after you get off work? I called you."

She responded vaguely, "I am in a meeting," as if that explained the silence.

Hours later, she texted, "I was at work. Today was my last day. I'm on vacation until December 14th."

I took a deep breath. She was always on the move, and I had to carefully navigate the cracks in her schedule just to have a chance at seeing my son.

November 27, 2016

I asked her directly the next morning, "You never answered my question. When can I see Prince?" (No response)

The days were turning into weeks, and I couldn't shake the feeling that she was intentionally dragging things out.

December 4, 2016

Finally, Robin texted, offering a brief opening. *"Incredible Pizza at 3 if y'all wanna do it."*

I jumped on the opportunity. "Okay, thank you. We'll be there," I replied, grateful for the chance to spend some time with Prince.

Later, I texted her, "He is a classic man! Very beautiful. Thank you!" Seeing Prince again was bittersweet; these small moments meant everything, but the inconsistency in our co-parenting was taking a toll on all of us.

December 9, 2016

As practical matters arose, our conversations continued in fragments. I asked her, "Huggies size 4, right?" and **she confirmed,** *"Yeah."* The daily grind of parenting seeped through the texts, but meaningful discussions about our son were always on the periphery, dodged or delayed.

February 23, 2018

Nearly a year later, the tension had barely eased. I texted Robin again. "When are you going to let me spend time with Prince?"

Her response was sharp: "Aww, my number hasn't changed. So do not come at me with that. You stopped calling and texting."

I couldn't believe her words. I had been trying for months to see him. "It has been months since you allowed me to have him over. You keep telling me he is sick, etc. But you claim you want me in his life. Your actions haven't shown that. When can I come pick him up?"

Her answer was defensive. "Because he was sick. And I didn't want him on the bus with a cold. And when you got your truck fixed, you stopped coming around. I called you numerous times about his eye surgery, and you blocked me."

I hadn't blocked her, and I told her as much. "You're lying, Robin. I've been asking to see Prince for months." It felt like she was rewriting the narrative, making me out to be the absent parent

214

when in reality, I was doing everything in my power to stay connected.

February 24, 2018

The next day, I made one last push: "Are you at home? Can I come get Prince?"

She replied, "I'm not home. I'll be there by 5. But yeah. How long are you going to have him so I can pack his things?"

This was my life—constantly navigating through excuses, negotiating for time with my own child. Each message was a battle, and it seemed Robin was always ready with a reason to delay or deny. But I wasn't going to give up. Despite her bitterness and all the roadblocks she put in my way, my commitment to Prince remained unshakeable.

Through all of this, I learned that co-parenting with a bitter ex wasn't just about surviving the arguments—it was about persistence, resilience, and never losing sight of what mattered most: my son.

Each text, each message, was a small victory in a larger war I was determined to win, for Prince's sake.

The ongoing tension between Robin and me reached new heights as we exchanged more heated messages, each filled with frustration and unresolved issues. Despite our differences, I was determined to see my son, Prince, and make co-parenting work.

February 24, 2018

At 4:32 PM, I texted Robin, "3-4 days." I wanted to keep Prince for a few days and spend some real time with him, but I knew she'd have concerns.

She replied at 4:41 PM, "Okay, but if he starts crying, making himself throw up, bring him home."

Her lack of trust in my ability to care for our son was clear in every word, and it irritated me. I wasn't a rookie parent.

At 5:17 PM, I texted her, "What time should I come pick him up from your house? Please meet me outside. Thanks."

She responded at 5:27 PM, "I am getting his things together now."

Then, at 5:28 PM, *"He should be ready by 5:45."*

I told her at 5:29 PM, "I will be outside by 6. Please pack two of his favorite toys and his bike I got him." Then I added, "I will not be reachable on this phone when I leave out." I was embarrassed, because I had to use a Google Voice internet number that only worked via a WiFi connection.

Robin quickly fired back, clearly agitated, "So how am I going to get in touch with you? I need a number unless he will not be going."

At 5:34 PM, **she texted**, *"Do not worry about picking him up since you are not reachable."* Her reply was meant to derail everything at the last minute, as usual.

Yahkhahnahn Ammi

February 25, 2018

The next morning, at 10:11 AM, I sent her a message. "You did not pack his wash soap, etc." I wasn't trying to nitpick, but these little things mattered when caring for a child.

Robin responded at 10:20 AM, "Which number do you want me to use? Because yesterday you said it was not reachable. And I forgot his soap."

At 10:56 AM, I texted, "This one."

She quickly shot back at 11:01 AM, "*Just making sure because I promise you said this number was unreachable.*" She was always quick to find a reason to escalate things.

February 26, 2018

By Monday morning, the situation had hardly improved. Robin texted me at 8:54 AM, "Good morning. How is Prince doing? Are you bringing him home today or tomorrow?"

At 10:24 AM, she followed up again, "I do not know what number you want me to call or text, but I am trying to see how my son is doing." Her tone felt accusatory, as if she was implying I wasn't caring for Prince properly.

Finally, at 11:08 AM, I responded, "If you stop blocking my number when you get agitated with the concerns I have regarding our son, then I wouldn't have to call you from other people's phones." I was tired of playing these games. "Also, Prince is too old for a bottle now. You need to have him only use sippy cups."

I could almost feel her frustration building through the phone when she replied at 11:21 AM, "Quit fronting, man. I don't know what you're on or who you're fronting for, but don't come at me like that." Her words were harsh. "Just because you made kids doesn't mean anything to me. And as long as my son is with anybody, I am going to call and check on him, point blank, period."

At 11:36 AM, I texted back calmly, "I'm getting his hair braided today."

Then, at 11:37 AM, I added, "He needs a sippy cup, no more bottles. Have a good day at work. I'm trying to enjoy my time with Prince. I don't need any drama from you or your side."

Later that Day

At 1:00 PM, I let her know, "Prince will return home today. What time will you be home? "Robin replied at 1:01 PM, "3:00."

I clarified, "As you know, I didn't have him for 3 or 4 days as I requested. I picked him up from your house Sunday at 6 PM. I didn't get him Saturday, as you indicated because I was at a funeral, in case you forgot."

Robin wasn't having it. At 2:10 PM, she texted, "You got Prince on Saturday. You were supposed to get him Friday. But it was short notice. So, I said you can get him Saturday at 6." She always twisted the narrative. "But you would know that if you quit playing games and changing your number every time I call or text."

The back-and-forth was exhausting, and I was done with her games. But at the end of the day, my focus was on my son. As much as Robin tried to block my time with Prince, I stayed committed to being present for him.

At 3:22 PM, Robin texted, "I'm home. You can bring Prince home. My phone was dead."

March 2, 2018

The following Thursday, at 8:39 AM, I reminded her, "His items are not missing. I explained they were in the washing machine. I'll return his items along with his new outfits that you can keep at your house for him." Then, with a touch of hope, I asked, "When can Prince come back over?"

This was my reality—constantly negotiating, constantly hoping for cooperation that often never came. But no matter how many obstacles Robin placed in my way, I remained steadfast in my determination to stay connected with Prince. I wasn't just fighting for time with my son—I was fighting for a father's right to be present in his child's life.

The back-and-forth with Robin felt endless. Every time we had a plan to meet, it seemed like she had a reason to complicate things. But no matter how frustrating it got, my priority remained the same—spending time with Prince.

Saturday, March 24, 2018

At 12:40 PM, Robin texted, "We're super busy so if you decide to take Prince, he's at my aunt's already ready. Just text or call me and I'll have her bring him downstairs. Thanks."

I couldn't shake the feeling that she was brushing me off again. But I was committed to seeing my son, so I texted her again the next day.

Sunday, March 25, 2018

At 8:48 AM, I asked, "Are you off work today? I would like to pick Prince up from you. What time will you be home and have him ready?"

Hours passed without a response. By 11:23 AM, I was getting impatient, so I texted again, "???" Still nothing.

At 2:46 PM, frustration building, I asked, "Did you block me from calling you again? I've been calling and texting you since yesterday. So, you're not gonna let me get Prince?"

Finally, Robin responded at 4:07 PM, **"So, are you taking Prince to the circus or not before I get him ready like yesterday?"**

Her response was casual, as if she hadn't been ignoring my calls all day. I replied, "I am on my way. I asked you yesterday to have him ready. You did not acknowledge my calls or texts yesterday…"

I sent the same message again at 4:10 PM to make sure she got it. "I am on my way."

Sunday, April 8, 2018

After several more instances of her avoiding communication, I had reached my breaking point. At 7:26 PM, I texted her in anger, "You on some straight bullshit Robin!!! I can't believe you would stoop so low…"

Yahkhahnahn Ammi

I was beyond frustrated. "You already know what it is… May God have mercy on you for this. If you had no intention of letting me pick him up, why tell me you had him ready and that I could come get him? You got me wasting gas and my time for nothing."

Robin's response was shocking, but typical of how far things had escalated. At 7:27 PM, she replied, "You shouldn't wish bad on no one. You know it goes back to you. Keep it up and I will call the police on your ass and tell them you tried to rape me too."

Her words hit me like a punch to the gut. I was furious but kept my composure. At 7:37 PM, I responded, "Yeah, wait till it's your turn. You think what you are doing is cute? Enjoy your date tonight."

Sunday, April 22, 2018

Robin texted me again at 3:16 PM, *"I'm off work now."* It was always like this—she'd go silent for days, then expect me to jump at her convenience. Wednesday, April 25, 2018

By mid-week, I had enough of the games. At 9:01 AM, I texted her, "I am not about to keep playing these games with you about Prince. You tell me to come get him and don't have him ready, or you block my number while I am enroute. Grow up!"

Thursday, May 3, 2018

I wanted to keep things civil, but it seemed impossible. At 6:46 AM, **Robin texted**, *"I didn't call you. Prince had my phone this morning."* It was another excuse, and I wasn't buying it.

I responded a few minutes later, trying to move past it. "Is it okay if Prince spends the weekend with me? I can pick him up this evening after you get off work."

To my surprise, Robin seemed willing. "It's always okay. But I can't be playing these games with you... When you're mad at me, you take it out on him... Like last week he was ready to go, and you just left him... He's getting older and asks for you now... So, I hope we can put our differences aside and do what's best for him."

Her words stung, but I knew it wasn't the full truth. "That is not the truth! You know that's not what happened, but okay." I wasn't going to argue about the past. *"What time will you be home?"*

At 7:30 AM, she replied, *"I'll be home at 3."* I thought things might finally be settling down.

Friday, May 4, 2018

Robin's constant checking in on Prince always came with a tone of suspicion. At 9:32 PM, she texted, "So, this is what I'm talking about. I don't care about you having Prince. But when I check on him, I want a response. It's your fault you don't check on him when he's with me."

I had enough of the accusations. The next day, I responded at 4:05 PM, "I am not going to feed into your delusional nonsense. I do not have our son around any woman that I may or may not be sleeping with. He is, however, around some of his relatives on my side of the family and some of them are women. What time will you be home? So, I can bring Prince."

Yahkhahnahn Ammi

At 4:24 PM, Robin shot back, "I'm not at home. I'm out in the county and you said the weekend. So, that's till Sunday. I already have plans."

Her lack of communication about these "plans" was infuriating. "Oh well, you said weekend, and I already had plans. So do what you want." She said.

Saturday, May 5, 2018

The games continued. After trying to coordinate all day, Robin told me to drop Prince off at her aunt's house. I did as she asked, but when I arrived, no one was there.

At 6:02 PM, I texted her in disbelief, "You had me drive all the way over to your aunt's house to drop him off. No one is even here. Now you're playing games. You need to come meet me and come get Prince. He does not have his medicine. I have to go to work. I told you I would keep him until Saturday, which is why I got him on Thursday!!! You have responsibilities to him as a mother."

Robin's response was cold. "Get off my phone. You didn't give me a day, so weekend to me means till Sunday... Keep it up, imma have your ass arrested...I'll tell the police that you tried to rape me too, then your ass will go to jail!"

This constant battle drained me. I was doing everything I could to be a present father, but Robin seemed intent on making things harder at every turn. Despite her threats and the endless games, I stayed committed to Prince. He was my son, and no amount of manipulation would keep me from being the father he deserved.

The rollercoaster of co-parenting with Robin seemed to have no end. Every interaction was filled with accusations, threats, and manipulation. But through it all, my goal stayed the same—being present for my son, Prince.

Saturday, May 26, 2018

After spending several days with Prince starting May 19, I returned him to Robin. The silence that followed wasn't unfamiliar. As usual, Robin kept Prince from me for weeks, using him as a pawn. I didn't hear from her again until she needed me for babysitting.

Saturday, July 28, 2018

Out of the blue, Robin messaged me: "GM. What time was you picking Prince up tomorrow so I can have him ready? In the morning or when I get off work?" It was typical for her to reach out only when it was convenient for her, not for the sake of our son. I replied, "I'll come by this evening and discuss it with you."

The next day, I waited for her reply, but none came. Frustrated, I texted her: "No reply? No call, etc.?"

Finally, at 4:30 AM, she responded: "I didn't understand why you had to come by and discuss the time you were coming to pick him up. You already told me Friday you were getting him Sunday. I just wanted to know the time so he could have been ready. You could have just texted me that."

It was another example of her twisting the narrative and avoiding any real coordination.

Yahkhahnahn Ammi

Thursday, August 2, 2018

A few days later, Robin messaged me again: "Hey, I'm off this weekend. Did you want to get Prince?"

I seized the opportunity and picked him up, keeping him for a week. For a brief moment, things felt calm. But as usual, the peace was short-lived. Shortly after I returned Prince, Robin blocked my number again, preventing me from seeing him for years.

Friday, April 14, 2023

After years of silence, **Robin reached out:** *"Good morning, is this your new number? I was seeing what time you was picking Prince up tomorrow so I can let my aunt know."* Her message felt hollow, and by now, I knew that Robin only reached out when she needed something or when it was convenient for her, not because she truly wanted to co-parent.

Saturday, November 18, 2023

Months passed, and I decided to check in again: "What time are you off work today?" I wanted to see Prince and spend some time with him.

Robin responded, "I'm getting off now. Prince is sick."

Trying to keep things cordial, I asked, "Can you have him video call me?" Communication between us had always been strained, but I kept trying for Prince's sake.

Sunday, November 19, 2023

The next day, I texted her again: "What time can you have Prince's clothes packed up today? He's gonna stay with me for a few days." I wanted to plan everything properly.

Later, I texted her about a small issue: "His feet stink. You gonna have to send him with another pair of shoes and keep his shoes washed. I'm going to wash them now."

As always, Robin's response was defensive: "Every time you get him, you always have something to say."

I tried to deescalate the situation: "Stop taking it personal, it's not an attack." But deep down, I knew every interaction with Robin would be met with resistance.

Tuesday, November 21, 2023

Things flared up again. I texted, "I see you and Marco have been having fun these past few days. I'll bring Prince back when he leaves. So, you can have your privacy."

Robin's response was dismissive: "First off, me and Marco ain't been having fun for a few days. He just picked me up from work today. I went to the concert Sunday. But you can bring Prince now if you want. Me and Marco are just talking like we always do. Have a great day."

I responded, determined to keep things civil but clear: "Take the gloves off. What concert? We were in your area the past few days and noticed you had company, so we kept it moving. That's all. Do you. We are good. Keep the gloves off."

Yahkhahnahn Ammi

It was another exhausting exchange, a continuation of the same pattern. Robin was always trying to divert the conversation, pushing me away when all I wanted was to be involved in Prince's life.

Monday, November 27, 2023

By the end of November, I was still trying to make arrangements. I texted Robin: "I want to take Prince to get a pair of shoes Friday. Can you have him ready?"

But as expected, the conversation was met with more delays and avoidance. Each time I tried to make plans, I faced the same wall of resistance from Robin. Her excuses and accusations never stopped, and the toxic cycle continued.

By December 2023, it was clear to me that co-parenting with Robin would never be easy. Her constant interference, emotional manipulation, and use of Prince as a pawn were exhausting. I had spent years trying to be an active father, yet each effort was met with resistance. Still, I refused to be deterred.

The cycle with Robin never seemed to end. Every interaction followed a frustrating pattern—she only reached out when it was convenient for her, avoided communication when it mattered, and used Prince as a pawn. Despite all of this, I remained committed to being an active father in Prince's life.

Co-parenting in high-conflict situations is never easy. It's about more than balancing schedules; it's about navigating emotional barriers and ensuring that the child knows both parents care. Though Robin's manipulation created distance between me and my son, I continued to hold on to hope for a future where Prince knows I was always there, fighting to be part of his life. No matter how many obstacles I faced, one thing remains clear: Prince deserves a stable, loving, and consistent relationship with his father, and that's something I will never stop fighting for.

This journey has taught me resilience, patience, and the true meaning of love for my child. Co-parenting isn't about winning battles with an ex—it's about making sure the child has access to both parents, no matter the hurdles. While I couldn't control Robin's behavior, I could control how I showed up for Prince. I have learned that I'll always be there for him, no matter how challenging the situation becomes.

* * *

Personal Life Lesson Reflections

In this chapter, Navigating the turbulent waters of co-parenting has been one of the most challenging experiences of my life. The constant back-and-forth, the emotional manipulation, and the sheer frustration of trying to maintain a relationship with my son, Prince, in the face of relentless obstacles tested me in ways I never imagined. Through this difficult chapter, I learned that co-parenting isn't just about sharing time; it's about resilience, patience, and unwavering love for my child. Despite the bitterness that Robin often directed toward me, I realized that my role as a father was to rise above the conflict. It was easy to get caught up in the anger and frustration, but that would have only hurt Prince in the end. Instead, I focused on what truly mattered—being there for my son, showing up consistently, and ensuring he knew that I was always fighting to be a part of his life.

Yahkhahnahn Ammi

This experience taught me the importance of perseverance in the face of adversity. Even when it felt like Robin was trying to push me out of Prince's life, I refused to give up. I learned that love is more powerful than any bitterness or conflict, and it is that love that will ultimately provide Prince with the stability and support he needs. While I couldn't change Robin's behavior, I could control my response to it, and I chose to stay strong for my son.

Takeaways

Resilience is Key

In high-conflict co-parenting situations, your resilience and determination are your greatest assets. Never let someone else's bitterness deter you from being present in your child's life.

Focus on the Child, Not the Conflict

It's easy to get lost in the anger and frustration of dealing with a difficult co-parent. Always remember that the most important thing is your child's well-being. Keep your focus on providing them with love, stability, and consistency.

Control What You Can

You can't control how your ex-partner behaves, but you can control how you respond. Choose to respond with patience and love, for the sake of your child. Your actions will speak louder than any words.

Never Give Up

Even when it feels like you're fighting a losing battle, remember that your persistence matters. Your child will one day understand the lengths you went to be a part of their life, and that will mean everything to them.

Love is Stronger Than Conflict

Ultimately, love is what will guide you through the toughest times. When faced with adversity, let your love for your child be the driving force that keeps you going. Your love can overcome any obstacle and will be the foundation of your relationship with your child.

CHAPTER 16

Kansas City, Uber Driver

"Breezin"- George Benson

In the whirlwind of Kansas City nights, where Uber shifts collided with fatherhood, I found that every ride was a lesson, and every mile brought me closer to balancing love, work, and the art of perseverance.

In the whirlwind of Kansas City, balancing fatherhood and Uber driving, I found unexpected connections and profound lessons. I met with the Uber team at their headquarters in Kansas City, submitted all my background documentation, and registered my SUV for ride-sharing. Now, all I had to do was wait for them to activate my account, and then I would be an authorized driver for Uber. I had my schedule all planned: I would work during the night while my children slept and spent the day being a father, educator, and chauffeur. After several trips to the office, my account was finally activated, and it was time to get paid.

More than three years after ending an eight-year marriage, I decided to download a dating app that had been popping up on my phone for a couple of weeks. With a hectic work and family schedule, online dating seemed like the way to meet new people. Hoping to find the woman of my dreams, I created a profile, added photos, got verified, and started swiping left for those who seemed incompatible and right for those who caught my interest. The app began matching me with potential partners, but my initial experiences were a bit of a mess. I encountered people in situationships, secretly married or in relationships, and even received messages from individuals not aligned with my dating preferences. Just as I was considering deleting the profile and app altogether, she caught my eye—Ayanna Leeché. Beautiful and sharing many things in common, I thought, "Oh my God, maybe we can hit it off."

We exchanged numbers, and from that moment on, we hit it off instantly. Daily conversations and video chats became our routine—mornings before she headed to the University of Missouri-Kansas City (UMKC), evenings after school, and even on weekends. Ayanna was a dental school student studying to become a dentist at UMKC, and our connection felt promising. As our conversations continued, I tried to name her cultural background because of a slight accent I heard. She later revealed that her father is Jamaican and her mother is a Black woman. The more we talked, the more we discovered shared interests, dreams, and a genuine understanding of each other's values.

Gradually, our interactions shifted from the digital realm to real-life moments. We decided to meet in person, transitioning from the virtual connection that had sparked our interest to the prospect of building something tangible. Little did I know that this chance encounter on a dating app would lead to a chapter in my life filled with unexpected joy and connection. Ayanna, with her curvy silhouette, naturally long black hair, and well-endowed figure, stood about 5'1". Her pearly white teeth framed a drop-dead smile, complemented by a sexy professional voice that added charm to our conversations.

I opted for a laid-back, casual dining experience at a restaurant before my Uber shift to ensure a smooth date. Ayanna was even more beautiful in person. We hugged and sat at the bar, talking, laughing, enjoying a bite to eat, and sharing a glass of wine—an ideal setting for our first meeting. The date was a success. The following week, on a cool and sunny Tuesday, Ayanna and I discussed meeting on January 27th.

Excited, I agreed without realizing that it was a Friday night, one of the busiest nights for an Uber driver. She said, "I have a UMKC social event to attend, but I will not be there for very long." Nevertheless, we agreed to meet up after her event and my Uber shift. I told Ayanna that I had a really nice time with her and would like to do this again. She smiled and said, "I had a great time also. Yes, we can do this again."

I juggled DoorDash and Postmates during the daytime with my children. I wanted their homeschooling education to be fun, structured, and eventful. We had field trips, and I rewarded them for completing their homework assignments. I taught them about the importance of having open communication and always keeping the lines of communication open with my children, in person or over the phone. I bought a cell phone for my son and daughter when they were three and four years old. I had a personal phone line but also had to invest in a second phone for Uber. I now have two cell phones with me: my personal phone and a business phone that I use for Uber customers, and occasionally for calls when my personal line has reception issues.

My children and I had checked into a hotel room, and within two weeks after arriving in Kansas City, we were finally able to move into our new apartment in Raytown. Glad to finally be out of that hotel room and living in our new apartment, I enjoyed spending every moment with my daughter, who was eight, and my son, who was nine at the time. They had access to my personal line to talk or video chat, as well as my business number for emergencies. My children are highly creative and excel at everything, especially music and art. We had a long day. My children were in the back seat, enjoying movies and games on their tablets. They loved drawing, painting, and everything art and music related, and I encouraged their creativity, which they shared with me each day.

After spending the day making food deliveries with my children, taking them to the playground, and treating them to a meal at a restaurant, after getting my children settled in for the evening, I made sure they knew they could video chat or call me if they needed anything. To ensure their safety, I kept a monitor and security system handy in case of emergencies. While they slept, I worked overnight as an Uber driver to support us. I was in the parking lot about to begin my Uber shift when I received several text messages from my children, who had fun creating digital arts. My daughter created her first video collage and sent me an amazing video. My son sent me some cartoon-like images, too. Their thoughtful talent brought tears to my eyes. My daughter would often send these little emoji images, too.

They were so cute, except I did not know what some of the facial emoji expressions meant. My children depend on me; they deserve to have a good father in their life. I am everything that they have; they need me. Although single fatherhood has not always been easy, I would not trade it for anything in the world. I love my children so much, and that is why I have fought so hard for them.

* * *

Personal Life Lesson Reflections

In this chapter, I found myself in the midst of balancing the many demands of single fatherhood, work, and the pursuit of love and connection. Navigating the role of a father, educator, and Uber driver, I encountered unexpected challenges and heartwarming moments that reinforced the importance of perseverance, love, and self-discovery. As I moved through the days and nights—homeschooling my children, managing delivery jobs, and working the night shift for Uber—I learned valuable lessons about the essence of fatherhood, flexibility, and the joy of newfound connections. Ayanna's presence in my life added another dimension, offering me hope and excitement as we built a relationship amidst the chaos of daily responsibilities.

Takeaways

Balance is Key

Balancing work, parenthood, and personal life is never easy, but it's essential to prioritize what's most important. My children's needs and happiness came first, even as I pursued my own goals and relationships.

Open Communication

Whether with my children or Ayanna, keeping the lines of communication open fostered trust and understanding. This lesson applies to all relationships—communication helps build strong connections and avoids misunderstandings.

Embrace Flexibility

Life will not always follow the plan. Being adaptable—whether it's changing schedules or managing new relationships—allows for growth, new experiences, and ultimately, more meaningful moments.

Cherish Small Moments

The small gestures, like my children's artwork or video collages, brought immense joy to my heart. It's the little things that often remind us why we work so hard and why we must stay resilient.

Perseverance in Parenting

Single fatherhood taught me the value of perseverance. The journey isn't always smooth, but the love and commitment to my children push me forward every day.

This chapter serves as a reminder that even amidst the hustle of life, there are profound lessons to be learned. By staying flexible, cherishing small moments, and keeping communication at the forefront, we create a foundation for love, success, and personal growth.

CHAPTER 17

Money, Power & Light District

"Big Rich Town"- 50 Cent

"You don't even like Black girls," Ayanna said, setting off a chain of unexpected events that would challenge my night and my understanding of friendship.

A simple night of Uber driving turns into a whirlwind of unexpected encounters, deep conversations, and surprising revelations about friendship and love. It was Friday, January 27th. Ayanna and I had plans to meet later that night, and I looked forward to seeing her. I eventually logged out of the DoorDash and Postmates apps and logged into Uber. I had a few pickups, one of which was at the Kansas City International Airport heading to downtown Kansas City. I also picked up a few other passengers in the downtown area, all going short distances. After taking a quick break to eat and drink a Sprite, the Uber app notified me of another passenger pickup at 7:16 p.m. I arrived in front of a brownstone apartment building in the downtown neighborhood at 7:21 p.m., only to find Ayanna waiting there. We both laughed at the coincidence, and I got out of the driver's seat to greet her with a warm embrace. She chose to sit in the front passenger seat and shared her plans for the evening, including a social fraternity meeting her school was hosting. "What are the odds?" she asked.

"I know, right? Crazy coincidence," I laughed.

"I'm so happy to see you! Just so you know, our plans haven't changed. We're still on for tonight, but it might be later because I have a social meeting I need you to take me to now. Can you be close by when it's over? And can you pick up my friend Desireé Shady afterwards?" "Sure, not a problem," I agreed.

Driving from her apartment to the social event only took about nine minutes. After dropping her off, I continued with Uber, picking up additional fares until it was time to check in with my children. Time flew by, and soon, it was time to pick up Ayanna. I repeated my normal routine, got out, and ran over to the front passenger door. She hopped in again, directing me back to her apartment. Ayanna said, "I need to change into some different shoes, and Desireé is waiting."

When we arrived, 'Shady'(Desireé) was standing outside. She had ordered an Uber before we arrived, but Ayanna said, "Girl, you can just cancel that Uber ride. We're here now. Get in." Desireé tried to cancel her other scheduled Uber ride and wanted to pair an Uber ride with us instead. After a brief wait, she joined us, sliding into the back seat.

Yahkhahnahn Ammi

"So, you're the man Ayanna's been talking about nonstop!" she (Shady) exclaimed. I laughed and replied, "It appears so."

"It's nice to finally meet you. You better take good care of my girl and thank you for doing this. I will pay you and tip you well." She asked about coordinating a ride through the Uber app. "No problem, happy to help," I reassured her, suggesting not to worry about it as it was just a friendly favor. She insisted on paying.

Ayanna ran inside for a change of shoes and returned, looking stunning in a different outfit. We sat for a moment before driving away. Conversation flowed as the three of us talked about various topics, including some more serious discussions about my intentions regarding Ayanna. Shady asked personal questions from the back seat, trying to gauge whether I was a good fit for her friend.

She blurted out, "Girl, doesn't he remind you of Malik?" Ayanna was silent.

As we were on our way to the Power & Light District, Ayanna suddenly remembered she had forgotten to change into the shoes she wanted to wear. We turned around and drove back to her apartment to get them. I had not logged into the Uber app, so I was driving them around as a friend. They both insisted on paying me for my time and wanted to tip me through the Uber app. I reminded them that I was not logged into the Uber app, but if they insisted on putting gas in my SUV, they could pay me through the Square App. When we got to Ayanna's apartment for the second time, Shady and Ayanna both went inside while I waited in the SUV. About ten minutes later, they returned, apologized for the delay, and we headed back towards the Power & Light District downtown.

Ayanna asked, "Can you pick us up from the Power & Light District once we're finished?"

I assured them that I would pick them up at the front door of the building. Shady expressed concerns about affecting my earnings on a busy night. I reassured them that I was there as a friend, not as an Uber driver. Throughout the night, Ayanna and I stayed in contact, exchanging texts to coordinate pickup times.

Ayanna called me a few hours later and asked if I could come pick up Shady because she was ready to leave. I told her I would be there shortly. Ayanna called again, saying, "Shady is on her way downstairs to you; she is trying to pair an Uber ride with you now." Around 12:30 a.m., I called Shady to see if she was ready. She came downstairs, and I asked her to call Ayanna and put her on speakerphone. I wanted to confirm that Ayanna was okay with me taking Shady home without her being present. Ayanna said she was fine with it.

I told Ayanna that I would return to pick her up after dropping off Shady. She said, "That's fine. I'll be ready by then. Thank you so much for understanding." I reassured her that everything was fine and that I would pick up a few more passengers before returning.

I wanted her to enjoy herself with her friends. I reminded Shady that I was picking her up as a friend, and she canceled the Uber ride. Still, she insisted on paying $30, including tips, through my Square App. We settled on $28.75. As I drove from the Power & Light District towards her apartment, we talked about my relationship with Ayanna. Shady also discussed her struggles with classes at UMKC and contemplated dropping out and returning to her family out of state. I provided a safe, polite, and professional ride as a friend, just as I did with everyone, including my own children. It was a lifestyle for me. She was one of my 'girlfriend's' best friends. As the night came to an end, I reflected on the unexpected events and the conversations that had taken place. It was a night filled with surprises, deep connections, and valuable lessons about friendship and relationships.

* * *

Personal Life Lesson Reflections

In this chapter, friendship and trust are powerful pillars in relationships. The events of the night reminded me of how vital these qualities are. Ayanna's trust in me to safely oversee her and her friend's transportation highlighted the foundation of mutual respect and reliability that defines true friendship. Flexibility and adaptability became necessary companions that night, reminding me of life's unpredictability. Being able to shift plans without resistance allowed for new experiences and deeper connections to form.

The importance of boundaries and communication also surfaced. By checking with Ayanna before taking Shady home, I demonstrated respect for her comfort and boundaries, a vital ingredient for nurturing trust in any relationship. Small gestures carry significant weight. Offering help, like driving friends around without expecting anything in return, can strengthen relationships and create lasting bonds that are often formed in simple, thoughtful acts.

Lastly, feeling versus reality can often cause misunderstandings. Conversations with Shady revealed how different perspectives shape how people view your actions and intentions. It reinforced the value of clear communication and staying true to your values to ensure your actions are always aligned with your integrity.

Takeaways

Value of Genuine Connections

The night illustrates the value of genuine human connections. Whether it's a friend or a partner, maintaining honesty and showing up for others can foster deep and meaningful relationships.

Importance of Empathy

Being empathetic, as shown in my interactions with Ayanna and Shady, can help others feel supported and understood, which is key to any successful relationship.

Navigating Friendship and Romance

The chapter provides insight into balancing friendships and romantic relationships, highlighting the importance of clear communication and respecting each other's needs.

Adapting to Life's Curveballs

Life rarely goes as planned. Being adaptable not only helps you manage unexpected situations but also opens the door to unexpected and enriching experiences.

Yahkhahnahn Ammi

Learning Through Experience

The events of the night underscore that every situation, no matter how mundane, offers an opportunity to learn and grow. It's a reminder to reflect on daily experiences for personal growth.

CHAPTER 18

The Client: Taken and Rescued

"Hero"- Mariah Carey

What started as a routine Uber ride quickly turned into a race against fear and danger, where the promise to rescue a stranger would test the limits of my courage and compassion.

It started raining as I arrived and greeted my passenger. I held a red umbrella over her head to prevent her from getting wet, and she thanked me as I opened the rear passenger door. Her smile was warm and sweet. Before driving off, I asked my passenger if she preferred to listen to music or a ride in silence. She didn't have a preference, so we spoke, and she shared that she was visiting from Spain. We talked until we reached her destination. I exited the vehicle, grabbed the umbrella, and held it over the rear passenger door as she exited. She thanked me once again, and I gave her my business card. We said our goodbyes.

Yahkhahnahn Ammi

I received another notification, a ping to my next passenger pickup location. I was seven minutes away from Kansas City Kansas. When I arrived in this beautiful rich and gated neighborhood, something about being there felt strange. I felt a slight chill on the back of my neck going down my spine. The client did not provide an exact pickup address, only a location. I parked on high alert and waited for five minutes. It was dark and quiet. There was no soul in sight. Is this a setup? I thought. I was about to pull off when I got the call. The client was a woman who said that she did not know where she was but needed a ride home. She sounded young, maybe sixteen years old or even in her early twenties. She was whispering. Was it a prank? Then, she disconnected the call. I waited for her to come outside. I called her back, but I could not reach her. I drove away.

She called back. She said, *"Please don't leave me here. I don't know where I am, but I really need your help. They drugged and raped me; put me in the trunk of their car, and now they have me in a room. I just really wanna go home!"* She cried. It all made sense why she could not give me an address to pick her up from, but it became frustrating to me at first because it seemed as if she was playing with me on the phone. I drove back and told the client that I would be in a black SUV, flashing my emergency lights, and told her to stay on the phone with me if she could. "I am coming to get you." I said. I had an urgent sense of responsibility to this client. I would find her and take her home.

I told her that if she saw my lights flashing to let me know. I got back there fast and entered through the gates. I drove through and around the apartment complex at five mph, circling the entire neighborhood. I could not give up. I had made a promise to myself and to that woman, and I planned to keep that promise. She said, *"I can see the lights now, they are flashing in the bedroom window, but I am afraid. I'm not sure how I am going to leave because I hear them talking in the other room. I don't know how many men are out there."*

I instructed her to remain calm, advising her to listen closely to the sound of their voices, discerning whether they were close to the door or not. I assured her of my commitment to help and emphasized the importance of following my instructions. When she told me that the voices seemed distant, I directed her to open the door cautiously, watch and feel her surroundings, and then quietly sneak out. Inquiring about the available entrances, she mentioned access to the back door, with the men in another room, the kitchen. I asked her if she could see a way out, and she said there was a back door and that the men were in another room. I told her to escape quietly and quickly, assuring her that I was waiting for her outside.

When the opportunity arose, she snuck out of the room, fled through the back door, down a flight of wooden stairs, and into the night around the building.

I waited in my parked black SUV, driving slightly further from the building in the direction of her pinned location while keeping my lights flashing. Following my guidance, she circumvented the building to avoid detection. Moments later, I spotted her in the shadows.

Suddenly, a four-door maroon car approached, driven by a man with short, straight black hair, olive skin, and of an undetermined ethnicity. Attempting to document the situation, I pointed my cellphone at his face to take a picture and video. He noticed and sped away before I could capture his photo.

With the client approaching, carrying her shoes in one hand and her cell phone in the other, I ran to her side, opened the front passenger door, and ushered her inside. She was a young white woman with blondish-brown hair past her shoulders and baby-blue eyes.

I could tell she had been crying because the tears watered through her mascara and makeup. We exited the apartment complex. I recommended that she contact the police right away. I contacted Uber and told them what was going on. Her cell phone battery had died, so I handed her an extra phone charger to use. I gave her my other cell phone to use to make the 911 phone call. She handed the phone to me, and the police asked me all types of questions. It felt like an interrogation. I was not the suspect. Frustrated, I gave the phone back to my client. The police said, "Stay there. We are dispatching a police car now." My client said she did not feel safe waiting there. We were somewhere in Kansas City, Kansas, and my client lived in Kansas City, Missouri. I told the police, "We are not waiting here. My client's safety is my priority, I must take her home." She stayed on the phone with the police until we reached her apartment complex. I noticed the unmarked cars because one of them had been trailing me for some time. As we parked, unmarked cars turned their emergency lights on. As officers and detectives approached my vehicle, my client looked over at me, disconnected her cellphone from the charger, and said, "Thank you!"

The police began asking her questions, and they thanked me for getting her home safely. I told them that the other police department my client had spoken to wanted us to stay there until they got there, and I did not feel comfortable doing that. They said, "*You made the right decision; those guys were being idiots, we got it from here.*" Relieved that she was safe, I drove away. This had been one hell of a night. I had to get back to Ayanna.

* * *

Personal Life Lesson Reflections

In this chapter, I found myself thrust into an unexpected, high stakes situation that reminded me of the unpredictability of life and the immense weight of responsibility we sometimes carry for others. What began as an ordinary night of work quickly transformed into something far more harrowing. This experience taught me profound lessons about courage, instinct, and empathy in the face of danger.

One of the most impactful takeaways for me was the realization that even in seemingly mundane moments, we can be called to rise to the occasion and act as protectors or guardians for someone else. I had no prior relationship with this young woman, yet her life and safety suddenly rested in my hands. It was a moment that demanded not only quick thinking but also deep compassion and a willingness to confront fear. The decision to return to help her, despite not knowing the full extent of the danger, was driven by an instinctual commitment to another human being. I couldn't abandon her because doing so would have meant betraying the principles of kindness and decency that guide my actions. It also illustrated the importance of trusting our inner voice and allowing it to guide us when logic and certainty are lacking.

Yahkhahnahn Ammi

Another lesson I drew from this experience is the power of empathy in moments of crisis. The young woman was scared and vulnerable, and while I couldn't fully comprehend her trauma, I could offer her safety and reassurance. I could listen, guide, and, ultimately, be the support she needed to escape a potentially life-threatening situation. This taught me that sometimes, the most important thing we can do is to simply be there for others—to offer a sense of hope in the darkest moments.

This experience also deepened my understanding of responsibility. As I drove through that neighborhood with a promise to this woman in mind, I realized that promises aren't just words.

They are commitments that bind us to action, especially when someone's well-being is at stake. In fulfilling that promise, I was reminded of the personal power we all hold—the power to change lives, even if only for a moment.

Lastly, I was reminded that life isn't always about grand heroics; it's about small, brave acts of service. Whether it's holding an umbrella for a stranger or helping someone escape a dangerous situation, these acts have the potential to leave lasting imprints on both our own lives and the lives of those we help.

Takeaways

Trust Your Instincts

In times of uncertainty, your instincts can be your greatest ally. They may push you toward acts of bravery that surprise even yourself.

Empathy in Crisis

When others are in danger or distress, often the greatest gift you can give them is your presence, a listening ear, and calm guidance.

Commitment to Promises

Promises should be taken seriously, especially when they concern the safety or well-being of others. Following through can make all the difference in someone's life.

Courage is Contagious

Courage isn't the absence of fear, but the determination to act despite it. When we act with courage, we inspire others to find their own strength.

CHAPTER 19

Misunderstandings and Reconciliation

"Money, Power, & Respect" - DMX & Lil Kim

One misunderstood text set off a spiral of confusion, but through patience and open communication, Ayanna and I managed to turn a moment of tension into a deeper connection and understanding.

Ayanna's words echoed in my mind, a stark reminder of the misunderstandings that can arise from incomplete conversations. After dropping off Shady, I resumed driving for Uber, expecting to meet Ayanna later that night. We stayed in touch over the phone as I picked up and dropped off passengers, eventually finding myself at the Power & Light District, where I dropped off Ayanna and Shady at one of the nightclubs. As the night progressed, I texted Ayanna to let her know I'd be heading back to pick her up. However, Ayanna's response left me perplexed. Her message read, "You don't even like black girls." Confused and taken aback, I sought clarification, unsure if the message was intended for me. It turned out that Ayanna had misunderstood our previous conversations about Francine, mistakenly believing she was white.

Despite the initial confusion, Ayanna eventually found me, explaining that she had taken off her shoes because her feet hurt. We hugged, and she apologized for any inconvenience, concerned that I might have missed out on other fares. As we drove to her apartment, she explained that she needed to tidy up before letting me in. Despite the misunderstanding, our bond remained strong, and we talked and held hands as I drove.

Once we arrived in the parking lot at Ayanna's place, I dropped her off. Ayanna promised to call me in a little while once she tidied up her apartment. She said, "*It won't take long.*" Meanwhile, I headed off to my next passenger, reflecting on the evening's events and the importance of clear communication in relationships. As I dropped off my last passenger for Uber.

[Reflecting]

I wondered how the client I had rescued was doing and if the police had found the guys who drugged, kidnapped, and raped her. I couldn't imagine what she was going through.

My thoughts were interrupted by a phone call I got from Ayanna. She said, "*It's okay for you to come back over now, my apartment is clean and I have showered.*" I am on my way. I looked forward to spending some quality time with Ayanna. We stayed in touch over the phone between passengers I picked up and dropped off that night. Finally, my shift was over, and I was happy to drive back downtown to Ayanna's apartment. I pulled back up to

Yahkhahnahn Ammi

Ayanna's gated parking lot and called her. I had forgotten that she had given me the white key card to enter the parking lot. She waited for me in her pink terry cloth robe and slippers and chuckled as I struggled to find the parking key. Amused, she warned, "*I hope you didn't lose it because I don't have a spare.*" I continued rummaging through my pockets and scanning the SUV for the elusive swipe card key until I finally found it. With a sigh of relief, I used the key to enter the parking lot.

Unbeknownst to me, it was the same key that granted access to her apartment building, eliciting more laughter from her. The irony of the situation dawned on me, and we shared a light-hearted moment. She greeted me with a big hug before we went inside. We held hands and kissed, then talked.

After a brief period, Ayanna suggested that we go inside. I agreed, mentioning that I needed to use the bathroom badly. We held hands while walking to her apartment building. She laughed and said, "*You could have peed outside in the parking lot.*" I said, "I would not dare."

We walked up two flights of stairs to her second-floor apartment. She opened the door to her cozy one-bedroom apartment, with a quaint kitchen to the right. We took our shoes off at the front door. She sat on the couch next to a small square living room table lit with a lavender scented candle. I used the bathroom, and when I came out, she hugged me, and we kissed. We walked back towards the couch, where she pushed me against the living room wall and kissed me passionately. She slid her hand over my crotch, found my zipper, and performed fellatio on me. Ayanna then took off her shirt and bra. I took off my shirt and pants. We walked into her bedroom, shedding our clothes. The room was lit by candles, and

Ayanna's perfume smelled heavenly. Her queen sized bed was soft yet firm. I logged out of the Uber app, officially off the clock. (Uber continued to track my location from the app).

We kissed continuously, and the foreplay was amazing. We made love passionately in various positions. She rode me slow and then fast, until we were both well spent and exhausted. She laid her head on my chest, our legs intertwined. We slept. The next morning, we pillow talked and did it all over again. We discussed the text she sent about my dating preferences, *"You don't even like Black girls."* I made it clear that black women were all I had ever dated as an adult. Our discussion got deep, and she opened up about failing some of her classes at UMKC. She was not doing well in school and confirmed what Shady had told me: both she and Ayanna were struggling financially and academically. We talked until it was time for me to leave. As I tried to get out of bed, she grabbed my arm and said, *"Please stay."* I told her I had to go; it was daddy duty time. She insisted I stay. We had sex again and then she made breakfast and apologized for not having much food in the house because she had not gone grocery shopping yet. I told her it was fine. I ate, and then Ayanna walked me to the front apartment door. I thanked her for breakfast and told her I had to check in with my children and then get back to work. We kissed goodbye. As I walked out, she said, *"I promise to call you after I get some rest."* I said, "I looked forward to it."

* * *

Yahkhahnahn Ammi

Personal Life Lesson Reflections

In this chapter, misunderstandings are often the root of conflict in relationships, and how we navigate them can either strengthen or weaken our bonds. I learned this lesson first-hand.

The evening started with a seemingly innocent mix-up—a text message from Ayanna that left me confused and questioning her intentions.

What unfolded was a journey through miscommunication, clarity, and ultimately, reconciliation, which taught me the importance of clear communication and the power of addressing misunderstandings directly. Ayanna's text, *"You don't even like black girls,"* threw me off. It was a statement that seemed to come out of nowhere, based on a misunderstanding about my past conversations. Ayanna had misinterpreted my previous comments about Francine, assuming I was not attracted to black women. The truth was, black women had always been my preference, and I needed to clarify that to her. This moment high-lighted how easily miscommunication can lead to unnecessary tension, even when the intentions behind the words are innocent.

As the night went on, we managed to reconnect. Ayanna explained her first confusion, and we both acknowledged the importance of being more transparent in our conversations. This experience reinforced the idea that relationships thrive on open dialogue. We cannot assume that the other person understands our perspective without expressing it clearly. It's easy for misunderstandings to fester when we don't take the time to clarify our thoughts and intentions.

Our reconciliation was a turning point in our relationship, emphasizing the value of patience, understanding, and forgiveness. By addressing the misunderstanding head on, we were able to move past it and strengthen our connection. The night ended on a positive note, as we spent time together, deepening our bond and reaffirming our mutual respect.

This chapter taught me that misunderstandings are inevitable, but they don't have to be destructive. When handled with care, they can lead to greater understanding and intimacy. It's a reminder that clear communication and empathy are essential in any relationship, especially when things become unclear or confusing.

Takeaways

Effective Communication is Key

Misunderstandings often arise from unclear or incomplete communication. It's important to express your thoughts and intentions clearly to avoid confusion and potential conflict.

Address Misunderstandings Directly When a misunderstanding occurs, don't let it fester. Address it as soon as possible to prevent it from escalating into a bigger issue.

Empathy in Relationships

Try to see things from the other person's perspective. Understanding where they are coming from can help in resolving conflicts and building a stronger connection.

Yahkhahnahn Ammi

Patience and Forgiveness

Relationships require patience and the willingness to forgive. Misunderstandings are a natural part of any relationship, but how you handle them can make all the difference.

Strengthening Bonds Through Reconciliation Every conflict or misunderstanding presents an opportunity to gain experience closer. Use these moments to deepen your understanding of each other and reinforce the bond you share.

In reflecting on this chapter, I hope my readers take away the importance of communication and empathy in their own relationships. By addressing misunderstandings with patience and understanding, we can all work toward healthier and more fulfilling connections with the people we care about.

CHAPTER 20

The Conversation and The Accusation

"Survivor" - Destiny's Child

A single phone call revealed a web of betrayal, and with every whisper and accusation, the foundation of trust I had built with Ayanna began to crumble.

F rancine Coldburn had reemerged in my life with malicious intent. This time, she wasn't working alone. Joining forces with my ex-wife, Selena, the two escalated their conspiracy, determined to have me arrested for the false narrative of domestic assault they had been spreading. It all stemmed from the December 25, 2016, incident in St. Louis, Missouri—an event where I was the true victim of Francine's assaults. Back then, I chose not to press charges, hoping to leave the toxicity behind. But Francine, months later, twisted the story, accusing me of being the aggressor, all while concealing the abuse she was enduring from her lover, Teddy. She was desperate to protect him, as their relationship for the past five years was built on infidelity and violence. Suddenly, it had been falling apart once Teddy (the cheater) discovered Francine had been cheating on him with other men.

What made it worse was when Francine and Selena found out I was dating Ayanna in Kansas City, Missouri. Together, they conspired to poison Ayanna's mind, feeding her fabricated lies about my past. Their goal was simple—destroy any happiness I found, by turning Ayanna against me. In the end, Ayanna, convinced by their manipulations, joined the conspiracy, believing the false stories they had woven. What had started as a vendetta between two women became a coordinated effort to ruin my life, with every lie they told tightening the grip of their toxic web around me.

The greatest weapon you have against hate is love. Forgiving through your pain is the answer. When whispers turn to accusations, life can unravel in an instant. Among a whirlwind of false accusations and shattered trust, I discovered the true strength of resilience and the liberating power of forgiveness.

Trust is a fragile thing—easily shattered, yet so difficult to rebuild. The greatest weapon you have against hate is love. And forgiveness, though difficult, is its most potent form. But when whispers turn into accusations, life can unravel in an instant, leaving you questioning everything you thought you knew.

It was a regular day for me. I was parked in the Uber driver's designated lot near the airport, waiting to pair with my next passenger. My mind was elsewhere, preoccupied with thoughts of Ayanna and how things between us were slowly, but surely, beginning to feel real.

Suddenly, my phone rang. Alicia's name flashed on the screen. She was more like a younger sister than a friend, so when I answered, I could already sense something was off. The conversation that followed left me reeling.

"You're being set up," "It's really messy, King Yah." Alicia blurted out. Her voice carried a tone of urgency that immediately had me on edge. She went on to explain that Anita—yes, *that* Anita—had been stirring up trouble, contacting Ayanna and even dragging Francine and Selena into it. On Facebook, Selena is using an alias, 'Angie Simms.' "I am so sorry King." Alicia Said.

I could barely keep up with the names and the web of betrayal being spun around me. "Anita?" I asked, incredulous. Anita was supposed to file my taxes from her work computer at the Hollywood Casino in St. Louis. None of this made any sense. How could someone I trusted with something as important as my taxes be involved in this mess? "What the fuck!" I blurted, shocked.

As Alicia continued to speak, the puzzle pieces began falling into place. Anita wasn't just anyone. She was someone Alicia had introduced me to, a supposed paralegal and IRS tax preparer, someone who came into my life at a time when I needed help. But Anita, it seemed, had more layers to her than I initially realized.

We had met in the lobby of the Holiday Inn. She had driven all the way from St. Louis to meet me halfway in Jefferson City so we could go over my tax situation. I needed someone I could trust, and Alicia had vouched for her. But Anita, with her questions and a sharp mind, had more in mind than just taxes. I had no idea that a simple professional arrangement would lead us down the path it did. By the time we moved from the lobby to my hotel room to discuss things more privately, Anita had steered the conversation toward personal topics—topics that led to an intimate encounter. What I didn't know, and what she would later reveal, was that Anita was still legally married. By the time she confessed, it was too late. I felt bad that I cheated on Ayanna. I was tricked, and misled, But I should have known better. My golden rule had been broken: "Do not sleep with a married woman." Besides all of that, I was dating Ayanna in Kansas City, and she cannot find out. I thought. I could have kicked myself in the ass right then.

Now, Anita wasn't just a tax preparer; she held my fate in her hands. She had filed my returns, and I was relying on that money to take care of my family. But now, she was entangled in a plot I couldn't fully grasp, a plot that threatened to pull me under. It wasn't just a tax return anymore—it was leverage. I absolutely knew that Anita was up to no good that day at the hotel. I just could not quite put my finger on what she was up to, how could she go behind my back and contact Ayanna though? I thought. Even though she said I did not owe her, I paid her $200 for filing my tax return.

I stared at the screen of my cellphone in the SUV that morning, my mind spinning with what Alicia had told me. The web of lies that Anita had spun was far more complex than I had anticipated. It wasn't just about my taxes anymore—this was about my life, my relationships, my name. The silence in the SUV felt heavy as reality sank in.

Every decision I had made with Anita was now coming back to haunt me. I felt trapped, cornered, and confused by how quickly things had spiraled. I had always tried to live by my principles— honesty, respect, and a commitment to doing right by the people in my life. Yet here I was, caught in a situation I never saw coming. Anita had taken what was supposed to be a simple transaction—my tax returns—and twisted it into something far more sinister. And now, Ayanna, Francine, and Selena were all conspiring in this mess because of my poor choices. I had to figure out a way to untangle myself before the damage became irreversible.

I couldn't let these women destroy everything I had worked so hard to build. I had already been through so much—false accusations, legal battles, fighting to be in my children's lives. And now this. But there was something deeper at play here. It wasn't just about my reputation—it was about how betrayal cuts deep, deeper than any physical wound. It was the lies, the manipulation, the deceit. It was how easily trust could be shattered by the people you thought you could rely on.

A week passed, and Anita's shadow continued to loom large over my life. After Ayanna contacted Francine and Selena on Facebook, the phone calls between Ayanna, Francine, and Selena intensified, and whispers of accusations grew louder. I could feel the weight of their judgment, even from a distance. My mind kept replaying that one moment when Anita had confessed she was married, and I kept asking myself the same question: How could I have been so blind? How could I let this happen?

I reached out to Ayanna, hoping for some clarity, some resolution. When we finally spoke, I could hear the hurt and betrayal in her voice. "*I trusted you*," she said. "*I thought you were different.*" Her words cut through me, deeper than any accusation could. I had tried to be different, to be a man of integrity, but now everything felt compromised. She wasn't just angry—she was disappointed. Disappointment was worse than anger. It lingered, it seeped into the cracks of the relationship, and it stayed. I am sorry, please forgive me, I said. There was silence, and then without notice she hung up the phone.

Damn. I fucked things up with Ayanna. I found myself reflecting on that day at the Holiday Inn, replaying every moment with Anita, trying to figure out where it had all gone wrong. I wanted to believe that it was just a mistake—a moment of weakness that could be forgiven. But the reality was more complicated than that. Anita had made a choice to deceive me, and in doing so, she had set off a chain reaction that was now affecting everyone around me. There was no going back, no undoing what had been done. I knew what I had to do next. I had to confront Anita, to put an end to her manipulation once and for all. I couldn't allow her to continue to control my narrative. It wasn't just about getting my taxes done anymore—it was about reclaiming my life and my truth.

When I finally called Anita, I was met with more deflection and excuses. She tried to downplay the situation, but I could hear the guilt in her voice. "It's not what you think," she insisted.

But I wasn't interested in her excuses. I had heard enough lies. What I needed now was honesty, clarity, and closure.

"You've caused enough damage," I told her, my voice steady but firm. "You've played your games, but it ends here."

She didn't argue. There was a long silence on the other end of the line. I could feel the weight of everything that had happened, pressing down on both of us. But this time, I wasn't going to let her have the last word.

"I'll be taking care of my taxes myself from now on," I said, cutting off any chance of further discussion. "And I don't want to hear from you again."

With that, I hung up the phone. For the first time in weeks, I felt a sense of relief. It wasn't a resolution, not by a long shot, but it was a start. I had taken back control of my life, at least in this small way. And now, I could begin to focus on the larger battles ahead.

The accusations and the fallout from Anita's betrayal were still far from over. But I knew one thing for sure—I wasn't going to let this break me. I had been through worse, and I had come out stronger every time. This was just another chapter in my story, another trial that I would survive.

As I sat in that Uber parking lot, waiting for my next ride, I realized that this experience had taught me something important. Betrayal, lies, accusations—none of them could define who I was. I was stronger than that. I had been forged in the fire of adversity, and no matter what came next, I knew I would emerge on the other side.

Anita may have tried to tear me down, but I wasn't going to let her win. I was a survivor, and I would continue to fight, not just for myself, but for the people I loved, for the life I had built, and for the truth.

No matter how many lies they told, I would always have the truth on my side. And in the end, that was what mattered most.

* * *

Yahkhahnahn Ammi

Personal Life Lesson Reflections

In this chapter, I came face to face with the power of betrayal not just from one person, but from multiple sources—Anita, Ayanna, Francine, and Selena. Each of these individuals played a part in a larger scheme that nearly destroyed the foundation I had built for myself, my family, and my relationships. What I realized through this ordeal is how fragile trust truly is. A single moment of weakness, a single poor decision, can spiral into something far larger and more damaging than you ever imagined.

But with every betrayal, there's also an opportunity for growth. As painful as it is to be deceived, it forces you to look inward. It makes you reassess the people you allow into your life and the choices you've made.

I had to confront the uncomfortable truth that some of the pain I was experiencing was a result of my own decisions—my choice to trust the wrong people and my failure to address issues before they got out of hand.

This chapter of my life was a powerful reminder that love, forgiveness, and resilience are the strongest tools we have when facing hate and betrayal. Forgiveness isn't easy. It's a process, and sometimes it takes forgiving yourself before you can forgive others. But it's the only way forward. Holding onto anger or seeking revenge will only destroy you from the inside. I had to learn that letting go of my anger toward Anita, Ayanna, and the others was the only way I could move on and reclaim my life.

Moreover, this chapter taught me that we are always stronger than we think. No matter how deep the betrayal, no matter how painful the accusations, we have the ability to survive and rise above it. It's not about never being hurt—it's about never letting that hurt define you.

I realized that while I can't control what others do or say, I can control how I respond. I can choose to be resilient, to stand firm in my truth, and to keep moving forward. I made mistakes, yes, but they don't define who I am. I am stronger, wiser, and more determined because of them.

Takeaways

Trust Is Fragile, Guard It Carefully

Trust, once broken, is difficult to rebuild. Be mindful of who you allow into your life, and don't take trust lightly. People you think you know can sometimes surprise you, and not always in the best way. Protect your boundaries and your heart by ensuring that the people around you have earned your trust.

Own Your Mistakes

It's easy to blame others when things go wrong, but part of growing is owning up to your own mistakes. I made poor choices, and they came back to haunt me. But instead of running from them, I had to face them head on. Learn to recognize where you've gone wrong, but don't let those mistakes define your entire life.

Forgiveness Is a Form of Freedom

Forgiving someone who has betrayed you is not about excusing their actions, but about freeing yourself from the burden of resentment. Holding onto anger will only poison you. Forgive not because they deserve it, but because *you* deserve peace.

Resilience Comes from Facing the Fire

Adversity is inevitable, but how you face it defines your character. When accusations and betrayal strike, it's easy to fall into despair. But those moments are also opportunities to develop resilience. You are stronger than you think, and every challenge you overcome only adds to your strength.

Speak Up and Take Control of Your Life

When Anita, Ayanna, and others began to weave a web of lies, I realized that staying silent wasn't an option. Silence allows false narratives to grow. Take control of your own life, speak your truth, and don't allow others to dictate your story.

Learn to Forgive Yourself

In the midst of all the chaos, I had to learn to forgive me. We all make mistakes, but we must not let those mistakes consume us. Self-forgiveness is essential for healing and moving forward.

The Truth Will Always Matter Most

Lies may temporarily cause damage, but the truth has a way of shining through in the end. Stay rooted in your truth, and don't be swayed by the false accusations or betrayals of others. In the end, what matters most is that you know who you are and what you stand for.

Don't Let Betrayal Define You

Betrayal cuts deep, but it doesn't have to define your future. You may feel like the ground has shifted beneath you, but as long as you stay true to yourself and refuse to let bitterness consume you, you can rebuild. No one's actions or words can determine your worth—only you have that power.

Final Thoughts

In the face of betrayal, I learned some of the hardest, yet most important, lessons of my life. Trust can be shattered, but love and forgiveness are the only ways to heal. I made mistakes, and I was deceived by people I trusted. But instead of letting their lies break me, I chose to rise above. I confronted my pain, forgave where I needed to, and reclaimed control over my life.

No matter how many lies people tell or how deeply they betray you, they can never take away your truth. At the end of the day, the most important thing is how you choose to respond. You have the power to rise above the challenges, and in doing so, you will discover just how resilient and strong you truly are.

CHAPTER 21

Confessions of an Uber Driver

"S&M" – Rihanna

In a world where lies and betrayal nearly destroyed me, I refuse to let their false accusations define my story—now, I will speak my truth and reclaim my life.

It all began with Ayanna's betrayal. Ayanna Washington Leeché, a dental student at UMKC, and her friend Desireé Shady joined forces with my ex-wife, Selena, and her friends in a calculated effort to ruin me. They accused me of domestic assault against Francine, one of Selena's lovers. The charges were false, but the betrayal was all too real. These women, who once played significant roles in my life, used the system to spread lies. They painted me as a thug, a woman beater, a drug user. Selena even accused me of kidnapping our children, a lie that clung to me like a shadow. The impact of these accusations would follow me for years, but it was Ayanna's part in it that hurt the most.

Ayanna and I had spent hours talking about our lives—my past, my struggles, and the never ending drama that seemed to follow me. She seemed to care. She listened as I opened up about the altercation with Francine, my failed marriage to Selena, and the baby mama drama with Robin back in St. Louis. I was trying to be transparent, to create a fresh start, and I even shared my Uber driving career opportunity in Kansas City, Missouri.

Nevertheless, Ayanna's curiosity centered on Francine. She had this idea that Francine was white. I could see her mind working—*How could I, a Black nationalist, be with a white woman?* I told her Francine was Black, but she couldn't let it go. Something about that name sparked doubt.

While I dropped Ayanna and her friend Shady off at the Power & Light District that night, she began digging into my life, searching for Francine on Google and Facebook. And then it began.

That night, she continued to search for Francine online, but that wasn't enough. Her curiosity led her to look up Selena on Facebook too. Later that night, after we had talked several times, Ayanna sent me a text: *"You don't even like Black girls."* Her insecurities were consuming her, fed by her assumption that Francine was White.

I didn't argue. I couldn't. I had already cheated on Ayanna with Anita, and I feared that saying the wrong thing might expose me even further. Ayanna said she had forgiven me. I tried to play it cool. We met later, had sex for the first time, and everything seemed fine. But beneath the surface, Ayanna's doubts festered.

Yahkhahnahn Ammi

That's when things took a darker turn. At some point, Ayanna reached out to Francine and Selena through Facebook, and what started as curiosity morphed into something far more dangerous.

Francine, angry and vengeful, fed Ayanna every lie she could think of. She told her I was a woman beater, a drug user, and a gun toting thug. None of it was true, but it was believable enough to plant seeds of doubt in Ayanna's mind.

Selena, my ex-wife, joined in too, adding fuel to the fire. She told Ayanna I had kidnapped our two children. Another blatant lie. This information enraged Ayanna, and feeling betrayed and deceived again, she decided to get even.

Ayanna was no longer the woman I thought I knew. She became part of a conspiracy to destroy me. Driven by greed, fear, revenge that I had cheated on her and the threat that I might expose her past sexual history—which included contracting a sexually transmitted disease—she made her move.

I couldn't understand why she would go this far. Even as I tried to rationalize her actions—maybe she was scared, maybe she felt trapped—nothing could explain her choice to accuse me of rape, especially when we had consensual sex.

Ayanna went to the sheriff's department almost 1 week later and claimed I had raped her. Her accusation flipped my world upside down. Despite the sheriff's refusal to press criminal charges—due to a lack of evidence—the damage was done. Ayanna handed over her phone with our call, text, and photo history. The evidence didn't add up, but her lie set off a chain of events that led to an $8.2 million civil judgment against me. She decided to file a civil law suit against me since she and her co-conspirators could not get criminal charges filed. I am not sure what loopholes helped her fraudulently win that case, because none of my evidence was presented. I did attend the deposition, but I never appeared in court.

It wasn't just about Ayanna's lies—it was about how the law responded to them. The justice system, already biased against so-called Black or Melanated men like me, was quick to paint me as the villain. With a past criminal record, my story wasn't one the public was willing to believe.

My past—a 16-year prison sentence handed down when I was 14—was always there, looming over me like a dark cloud. I had served my time, and paid my debts to society but to them, I would always be a criminal. The civil courts were no different. The false accusations followed me wherever I went, leaving me with a mark I would never escape.

And then, Robin—my baby mama—piled on. She saw an opportunity in the chaos to make money, threatening to put me on child support despite my efforts to be involved in our son's life. "*I might as well get paid too,*" she told me, twisting the knife deeper.

I was left as the sacrificial lamb in their pursuit of money and revenge. My passion for writing and activism began to fade under the weight of these lies. My once strong voice was silenced, not by guilt, but by the systemic biases that crushed the presumption of innocence.

Alicia, an old friend and sister, called me one day to warn me that Ayanna had been reaching out to Francine and Selena. As she spoke, Ayanna's name flashed on my other line. I quickly hung up and called her back.

On any other day, hearing her voice would have been a life line, but now, her words felt like knives.

Ayanna: *"Hello."*

Yah: "Hey, what's up? What are you up to?"

Ayanna: *"I fell back to sleep."*

Yah: (laughing) "Straight up?"

Ayanna: *"Yeah."*

Yah: "That's how you feel, huh?"

Ayanna: *"It's been a long week."*

Yah: "Has it?"

Ayanna: *"Uh huh."*

Yah: "Poor baby."

Ayanna: *"Whatever, man."*

Yah: "Um, poor baby. Are you tired?"

Ayanna: *"Yeah, I actually am."*

Yah: "Oh, you sound good. Do I need to come back over there real quick?"

Ayanna: *"No, I'm good."*

Yah: "How does your body feel?"

Ayanna: *"It's okay."*

Yah: "Was the sex, okay?"

Ayanna: *"It was good."*

Yah: "It was good?"

Ayanna: *"Yeah."*

Yah: "That's it?"

Ayanna: *"Well, you asked."*

Yah: "So we're gonna have to make it great next time. How do we make it great?"

Ayanna: *"We'll see."*

Yah: "We'll see? Okay, um, don't you have labs to do today?"

Ayanna: *"Yeah, I know. I'm gonna go."*

Yah: "I don't want you out all night doing labs. I mean, I want to…"

Ayanna: *"I know, I mean."*

Yah: "Come by later on, maybe have dinner or something. Dinner would be nice, you know, a cooked meal, the Jamaican side of you. I don't know, do you cook Jamaican food?"

Yahkhahnahn Ammi

Ayanna: *"Uh, not really."*

Yah: "OK, so what do you cook, African food? I mean, Black food, Black folk food, American food."

Ayanna: *"Yeah, yeah. I have to go grocery shopping, but I probably won't go until tomorrow."*

Yah: "OK. But what are you preparing this evening for dinner?"

Ayanna: *"I have no idea. I haven't even thought about food yet."*

Yah: "Well, think about it. Let me know. I've been eating fast food since I've been here. So I'd like to have a home-cooked meal. You know what I mean? Show me some love."

Ayanna: *"I didn't say I was gonna cook; I didn't say I was gonna cook though."*

Yah: "Huh?"

Yah: *(laughs)* *"What did you say?"*

Ayanna: "I said, I didn't even say that I was cooking tonight."

Yah: *"Oh, okay, so you gonna make your man wait, huh?"*

Ayanna: *"I need... I need us to, like you said before, there's no rewinding or slowing down or whatever. But I need that, I need that, OK."*

Yah: "We'll work on it, we'll work on it."

Ayanna: *"Okay."*

Yah: "I'll try to give you a break."

Ayanna: *"Thank you."*

Yah: "But tomorrow dinner for sure. (laughter) I'll work on it. I appreciate you, I just wanna make sure you're okay."

Ayanna: *"Yeah, I'm fine. I'm just kind of planning in my head what I have to do."*

Yah: "Yeah, so at the labs, like explain that, how that looks."

Ayanna: *"What, the labs itself, or like?"*

Yah: "Like what you're gonna be doing, explain that."

Ayanna: *"I have a couple of different projects we're working on right now. So, uh, one of them is uh, it's really hard to explain. So, imagine like a mounted; like imagine I have a full fake mouth. Right. A full set of teeth, upper and lower, and they're like stone models of teeth. And there's this machine. It's kind of like an apparatus, I guess. Really, not really a machine, but like an apparatus that allows you to take those and mount them together. Like, you can open and close the mouth and it's positioned exactly on this apparatus, the way it is in the patient's mouth. It sounds like a lot of little exact measurements and stuff you have to take, and on the patient's head, in order to make sure that you know this. These, you know, upper and lower teeth that are on the apparatus exactly like that. So I have it mounted, I just have... Uh, I have one of the top mounts; now I have to do the bottom and make it pretty. That's due this week. I have, um, we're doing the working steps for making dentures. So it's like a lot of different steps in making, you* *know, taking impressions of the patient and recreating their mouth also. So, it's a lot harder to do that. Um, so you have."*

Yah: "So, like. I got Mercury put in my mouth like, um, years ago."

Ayanna: *"Amalgam, not mercury."*

Yah: "Well, you know it's still the same thing as mercury. I want that out of my teeth, and I want, I want it to be whatever white stuff it is they put on there instead. So I got… Huh?"

Ayanna: *"Composites."*

Yah: "Huh."

Ayanna: *"It's called composites, a composite."*

Yah: "So I need the mercury taken out, and I need a composite put in. I think I got them in two teeth like, my molar teeth or something. I need to like make that happen. But you won't even be able to get into that practice until what, three more years?"

Ayanna: *"Uh, a year and a half."*

Yah: "Damn, then you'll have your own little dental spot, huh?"

Ayanna: *"Um, no. I was saying, like a year and a half and then in school until I start seeing patients, but three and a half years until I graduate and decide what I'm doing after."*

Yah: "So how does that work? So, you're going to be in school somewhere seeing patients? How does that work? So, I just come up to your school?"

Ayanna: *"There is a school. At the dental school, there are multiple clinics inside the dental school. So, it's run like a humongous dental clinic like, you know, little small towns have their own little dental clinic. It's like that, but it's humongous. And so we have different clinics that are run by different, you know, um, sections, I guess you would say, and so we rotate through those clinics and see patients. So, I would be seeing patients, you know, and working on you know, restoring their teeth and stuff like that. So, it's a clinic, but it's in the school."*

Yah: "That's cool. I'm sure the teeth in the bottom have a lot of mercury in them."

Ayanna: *"Oh, no, no, no."*

Yah: "Well, not that many?"

Ayanna: *"No, no, no, no. I wouldn't say that many."*

Yah: "So, not that many."

Ayanna: *"I wouldn't say that many. I'm not like all on you like that."*

Yah: "OK, all right." (Ayanna laughs.)

Yah: Kind of like Barber colleges where you get to go in and you get whatever you want done for the low, like instead of $15 it's $8, so y'all got services like that too?

Ayanna: *Yeah. No, we have patients that come to his dental school and have been coming in for years, and they're taking new stuff. So yeah.*

Yahkhahnahn Ammi

Yah: Wow! I didn't know that.

Ayanna: *I can look and see if I have any friends, or I mean not social media friends, but they're there. They're actually accepting a lot of new patients right now. Yeah, if you're interested because the fourth year is about to have to take boards. So they can graduate. So they're screening for patients to do their board-type procedures on, yeah. So they're always looking for new patients. But yeah, it's considerably lower. The only thing is. UM, so you'll have a student. Working on you, so. Take the conversation a little bit longer because there are professors. That you know. Check off every little thing that they do and have to sign off on the thing, which is good for you because obviously. You don't want someone in there just doing whatever.*

Yah: Right, right, right. So what do I need? Do I just need to bring cash? Do I need insurance? I mean what?

Ayanna: *They take insurance; I believe they also take cash as well. I'm not sure. I don't really know exactly what it is, but like look up the dental school UMKC School of Dentistry, and there's a whole section on there. You know, being the patient and the information. You need to know.*

Yah: UMKC School of...

Ayanna: *Uh, are you really doing it? Thank you. Literally don't need to pay now.*

Yah: Yeah, I want this mercury out of my mouth, patient information. I mean, you said it. It's fresh on my mind. So yeah, I wanna, kind of.

Ayanna: *I thought you were like driving or something right now, that's all.*

Yah: Oh, no, no, no. I'm at the airport. I'm on my laptop. I'm on my hot, my hotspot. I'm waiting on a client now. We'll see a patient. I'm waiting on the client. General information. Rates and payment information. Let me go there. Oh, the exam is $41 bucks. They always going to throw in a damn exam anyway, right?

Ayanna: *Yeah, before you have anything done, you have to be screened. Yeah, there's like an initial appointment and stuff that you'll have, and the dental student will kind of decide where you're at.*

What you need as. Far as the treatment plan and take X-rays and stuff. To what you have going on.

Yah: Alright, so I see the Amalgam fillings are between $50 and $115 Composite filling is between $53 and $125. Now that's per tooth.

Ayanna: *I don't know. And yeah, I know nothing about prices. We don't know that stuff, yet.*

Yah: Right. So I had to figure out how to sign up for all of that. Alright, cool. Alright, I'll check that out later. I'll keep the page up and running. No, that's what's up. Yeah, I never Really looked at it like that. Never really thought about it.

Ayanna: *Yeah, but, you know, just going to the dental school is considerably less than going to actually going to a dental practice. It's just, you know, it may take a little bit longer time. May take a* *few more appointments than you originally was planning on. You know, just going in and getting everything done.*

Yah: Oh really? Oh, OK, I see what you're saying.

Ayanna: *Well, I mean, it's not like they're going to be half of it and half of it now in the same or. Take your first appointment will probably just...*

(Uber Notification Ping)

(Engine starts)

Yah: okay, I got a client to go pick up I got 10 minutes. Uh, No, I I hear you. Go ahead, I hear you go ahead.

Ayanna: *Alright, it's a good option, alright. I'm gonna have to...*

Yah: go get some rest, and I'll talk to you later.

Ayanna: *alright.*

Yah: Peace

The conversation left me stunned. Why was Ayanna involving herself in this deceitful scheme? As I pondered the implications, I realized the gravity of her betrayal. This wasn't just about her insecurities or curiosity anymore—it was something darker. She had aligned herself with people who wanted to destroy me, and I was their target.

However, I refuse to still be silent any longer. I took the advice of my attorney at the time, and that led to the courts putting a "GAG

Order" against me pending the outcome of the civil rape case against me.

This is my truth: I am not as bad a guy as they are portraying me to be, and I am certainly not the monster they painted. I am a man who was wronged by a justice system that is broken, biased, and indifferent. The lies they told won't define me anymore.

For seven years, I've sought legal counsel to press charges against Ayanna, Francine, Anita and Selena for making false police reports. Every lawyer I approached turned me away, unwilling to defend a so-called "woman beater" or "rapist." But my fight isn't over. I will continue the fight to clear my name, for me, for my children, and for anyone who has ever been falsely accused. It's been a long walk to freedom, but I will not give up. The truth is worth fighting for, no matter how treacherous the journey.

* * *

Personal Life Lesson Reflections

In this chapter, betrayal often comes from those you trust the most. I believed Ayanna was someone I could confide in, someone who would see beyond my past and accept me for who I was becoming.

However, trust is fragile, and outside influences can easily erode even the strongest relationships. The lesson here was painful but necessary: trust, once broken, is hard to rebuild, and I needed to be more careful about who I allowed into my life.

I stayed silent when I should have spoken up, thinking that ignoring Ayanna's insecurities or Francine and Selena's lies would make them disappear. But silence allowed these falsehoods to grow unchecked, and soon, I was left battling a mountain of lies. I learned that speaking up, even when it feels uncomfortable or risky, is essential to prevent misunderstandings from spiraling out of control.

The betrayal by Ayanna and the others nearly broke me. The justice system, which I had hoped would see the truth, was ready to believe the worst in me. But through that betrayal, I discovered resilience. I realized that no matter how deep the hurt or how unjust the system, I could survive and fight back.

Being falsely accused was one of the most soul crushing experiences of my life. It wasn't just about the lies themselves, but about the power those lies had to destroy everything I had worked for. I learned that once your reputation is damaged, it takes a monumental effort to repair it—and sometimes, the damage can never fully be undone.

In the aftermath of the false accusations, I felt abandoned by the justice system. But through that experience, I learned the importance of persistence. The system may be flawed, and it may be biased, but that doesn't mean you stop fighting. I realized that justice isn't just handed to you—you have to be prepared to pursue it, even if the odds are against you.

For a long time, I held onto anger and bitterness. It ate away at my peace, leaving me stuck in the past. But eventually, I realized that forgiveness wasn't about excusing what was done to me. It was about freeing myself from the weight of that anger so I could move forward. Letting go allowed me to begin healing.

For too long, I let others control the narrative of my life through lies and false accusations. But I came to understand that my story is my own, and reclaiming it gave me power. By speaking my truth and owning my journey, I regained control over how I was seen and, more importantly, how I saw myself.

Takeaways

Be Mindful of Whom You Trust

Trust is something that must be earned and protected. Not everyone who enters your life will have your best interests at heart. Evaluate carefully who you allow into your inner circle and be cautious of those who sow doubt or insecurity.

Speak Your Truth

Silence allows lies and falsehoods to grow. Don't be afraid to speak up when something is wrong or when you feel misunderstood. Address issues early on, rather than letting them fester. If you don't stand up for yourself, no one else will.

Stay Resilient in Tough Times

Life will test you, and sometimes the people you trust most will betray you. But resilience is about enduring hardship and refusing to let that hardship define you. Even in the darkest times, remember that you have the strength to rise above and rebuild.

Stand Against Falsehoods

False accusations can destroy lives. Don't take what you hear at face value, and don't be quick to judge others based on unverified claims. Seek the truth, and stand up for what's right, even when it's difficult or unpopular.

Keep Fighting for Justice

Justice is not always easy to come by, and sometimes the system will fail you. But that doesn't mean you should give up. Keep pushing for what's right, and understand that justice may be slow, but it is worth pursuing.

Let Go of Anger to Heal

Holding onto bitterness and anger will only weigh you down. Forgiveness doesn't mean forgetting or condoning wrong doings—it means allowing yourself to move forward. Free yourself from the past so you can create a better future.

Reclaim Your Story

Never let anyone else define your story. Your life is your own, and your truth is powerful. Speak it, own it, and don't be afraid to tell the world who you really are. Your journey can inspire and empower others, but it starts with taking control of your own narrative.

CHAPTER 22

The Conspiracy

"U Don't Know Me" - T.I.

A single false accusation, woven into a web of lies by women from my past, sparked a devastating conspiracy that destroyed my life—proving that even the truth can be buried beneath the weight of well-timed deceit.

A single false accusation from Ayanna, conspiring with women from my past, turned my world upside down and ignited a relentless battle for truth and justice. In a world where truth is supposed to be revered, I learned the hard way the devastating impact of a well timed lie. This is the story of how one accusation after another shattered my life and the uphill fight to rebuild from the wreckage.

As a child, I was taught the value of truth—how honesty could build character and trust. But no one ever told me how destructive a lie could be. A single statement from the right person at the wrong time can ruin everything, even when it's one person's word against another's. This is the story of how my world came crashing down.

Ayanna and I had been dating for about a month, and everything seemed perfect—no arguments, no drama. I was the perfect gentleman, careful to make her feel safe and respected. Our relationship felt like a breath of fresh air amid the chaos of my life. As a college student, she was bright and intellectually stimulating, and I thought she understood me in ways others hadn't. But little did I know, she was scheming behind my back.

I later discovered that Ayanna had contacted women from my past—Francine and my ex-wife Selena—through Facebook. Together, they conspired against me. To Ayanna, I wasn't a partner—I was a "mark," an opportunity for revenge and financial gain. Despite having little recent contact with these women, Ayanna manipulated our past relationships to suit her deceitful agenda.

At the same time, Anita—another woman I'd been involved with—reached out to Ayanna, revealing that I had cheated on her. This only added fuel to an already volatile situation. These women wove a web of lies that left me trapped.

When the civil courts got involved, during the deposition they coerced me into handing over my cell phone, claiming it would help prove my innocence. If I refused, they said, I'd never be able to use it in court. Desperate to clear my name, I handed it over. That phone held crucial evidence—texts, calls, pictures, videos— all of which could prove my innocence. But that decision was a grave mistake.

Ayanna went as far as accusing me of raping her during our relationship. With my past felony conviction, that charge could have sent me to prison for a long time. Fortunately, the evidence on my phone—her messages, pictures, and even an 11-minute audio recording where she confessed that everything was consensual—proved my innocence. Yet, the case wasn't dismissed. No one asked to forensically analyze Ayanna's phone. Why? Had they done so, the conspiracy would have been exposed, and those involved would have faced serious consequences. But that never happened.

Everything spiraled out of control after that. I started seeing a psychologist—yeah, I saw a damn shrink. I was prescribed medication for depression and anxiety, but it barely took the edge off. I couldn't sleep. I trusted no one. I felt like the entire world was out to get me. I was a living wreck, too overwhelmed to process why this was all happening.

Although I narrowly avoided prison for the false allegations, Ayanna wasn't finished. She filed a civil lawsuit against me for sexual assault, and it turned into a high profile case. The result was an $8.2 million judgment that went viral and destroyed my reputation. Even though I couldn't prove it, it felt like backdoor deals were being made to benefit everyone but me. I still don't understand how I was acquitted criminally but found guilty in civil court. They ignored the evidence—the texts, the police report, even the rape kit results. It was clear that something wasn't right.

Meanwhile, Francine and my ex-wife Selena filed fraudulent restraining orders against me, painting me as a violent abuser and even accusing me of kidnapping my own children. Selena, who had been absent for so long, was awarded full custody of our kids based on these lies.

That loss, combined with the political nature of my case due to my activism, cost me everything—my jobs, my career, and most painfully, my relationship with my children. I was left homeless, ostracized, and watching my life unravel while the world believed the lies.

No matter what I do, the label *rapist* follows me everywhere. No matter how many times I proclaim my innocence, it never fades. That word lingers in the minds of people who pass me on the street. It's what potential partners see when they Google my name before turning and walking away. It is what employers read on Missouri Case.net before they toss my CV in the trash. *Rapist*—a word that kills reputations, careers, and relationships.

Ayanna and her co-conspirators knew exactly what they were doing. Justice wasn't served—they turned their ears and eyes away from the truth.

However, as a young so-called Black or Melanated man in America, I had never been a stranger to unfair treatment or oppression. I've spent my life fighting for equity and equality, lessons I've passed down to my children.

I know I'm a good person with a good heart, someone who cares about standing up for those in need. But now I'm fighting a battle I never expected—the fight for my own truth. When Robin, the mother of my child, found out about everything, she turned on me too. That shattered whatever trust and respect I had left for her. She was controlling, manipulative, and when she couldn't control me anymore, she was done with me too.

People say if more than two people accuse you of something, it must be true. But it wasn't true. None of the accusations were. And it didn't matter that I had proof. This wasn't about guilt or innocence—it was political. I had upset powerful people within law enforcement, influential community leaders and the Black Lives Matter movement. Now, I had a target on my back.

What made it worse was the betrayal by the attorneys I trusted to stand for me. They knew what I was going through. I shared everything with them, even though I was on medication for anxiety. But that didn't stop them from taking my money. Case after case, I lost. They didn't fight for me—they just cashed the checks.

I believe what happened was the result of deals made behind closed doors, all with the intent to ruin me. My case was politically motivated—I'm certain of that. Everyone seemed to have their own agendas. It was the height of movements like #**MeToo**, #**Black Lives Matter**, #**Women's Liberation**, and #**Time's Up**, and I was cast as the villain—a womanizer, abuser, and rapist. In their eyes, I had to be taken down.

I can't prove a judicial conspiracy, but the outcome speaks for itself. The attorney I hired for the Ayanna civil case felt more like an adversary than an advocate. The $8.2 million dollar judgment against me felt like a predetermined outcome—proof that the system was stacked against me from the start.

Yahkhahnahn Ammi

Through all that, I continued to fight. I continued to tell my story, hoping that one day the truth would prevail. I fight to see my children again. I fight against the false claims. And, most importantly, I fight to rebuild the life that was torn apart around me.

* * *

Personal Life Lesson Reflections

In this chapter "The Conspiracy", reveals a time in my life when a single false accusation turned everything upside down. It was a brutal lesson in the destructive power of lies and the fragility of truth in a world where feelings can be manipulated so easily.

Growing up, I believed that truth and honesty would protect me, but I learned that a well timed lie could wreak havoc, casting long shadows over a person's life and reputation.

The false accusations against me, orchestrated by Ayanna and fueled by other women from my past, were devastating. They painted me as a villain, a rapist, and an abuser, labels that stuck despite my innocence.

The damage was swift and severe: I lost custody of my children, my career, and my standing in the community. My life became a nightmare of legal battles, public shaming, and emotional turmoil.

No matter how much evidence I had to prove my innocence, the mere accusation was enough to destroy everything I had worked for.

This chapter forced me to confront the harsh reality of how easily truth can be overshadowed by lies, especially in a society quick to judge without hearing both sides. It taught me the importance of resilience, the need to fight for my truth, and the reality that sometimes, the system is rigged against you. I also learned that trust is a fragile thing, easily shattered when those closest to you turn against you for their own gain. Despite the overwhelming challenges, I refused to let these lies define me. I sought therapy, faced my mental health struggles head on, and began the slow, painful process of rebuilding my life. This experience showed me that while lies can temporarily derail you, they cannot break your spirit unless you let them. I had to find strength within myself to keep fighting for my truth, for my children, and for the life I deserved.

Takeaways

The Destructive Power of Lies

A single lie can have devastating consequences, destroying reputations and lives. It's crucial to understand the impact words can have and to approach accusations with caution and fairness.

Resilience in the Face of Adversity

When false accusations are made, it's easy to feel overwhelmed and defeated. However, resilience and a steadfast commitment to the truth are essential for overcoming these challenges.

Yahkhahnahn Ammi

The Fragility of Trust

Trust is fragile and can be easily shattered by betrayal. It's important to be cautious about whom you place your trust in, especially during vulnerable times.

The emotional toll of false accusations can be severe. Seeking professional help and addressing mental health issues head on is crucial for recovery and for keeping the strength needed to fight back.

Never Stop Fighting for Your Truth

Even when the odds seem insurmountable, never stop fighting for your truth. Lies may cloud the truth temporarily, but persistence and integrity will eventually bring light to the darkness. This chapter serves as a reminder that while the world can be unjust, your response to adversity defines who you are. By staying true to yourself and continuing to fight for what's right, you can rebuild your life, even from the darkest of circumstances.

CHAPTER 23

Shadows of Custody

"Unsteady" - X Ambassadors

Walking into the courthouse felt like stepping back into a nightmare—each shadow cast by the halls was a reminder that in the fight for my children, I wasn't just battling for custody but survival.

In the heart of St. Louis, the City and County courts cast relentless shadows over my desperate fight for custody and justice. The legal battles I faced were marred by what appeared to be corruption and bias, tilting the scales against me from the start. This chapter delves into the depths of my suspicion and the exhausting struggle to prove myself as a father in a system designed to break me.

February 2017: Stepping into the courthouse, I couldn't shake the memory of being sentenced to 16 years in prison at just 14. Every echo of my footsteps reminded me of the injustice I had faced. Now, I was being pulled back into the court system—this time for the custody of my children.

Yahkhahnahn Ammi

My friend Alicia alerted me to another Facebook post from my ex-wife, Selena, who had filed a family court motion to gain full custody of our children. She used the alias "Angie Simms" and a fake address for me in St. Louis. Shocked, I confirmed it on Missouri Case.net. Once again, Selena had blindsided me. The anxiety was crushing. Despite my reluctance to drag my children through another court battle, I had no choice—I had to fight for them.

However, I was alone, without an attorney and unable to afford one. Each call to a lawyer ended in disappointment; they were either too expensive or unavailable. The four-hour trips from Kansas City to St. Louis for hearings felt like my life was spinning out of control.

Unbeknownst to me at the time, Selena and Francine had secretly written letters to the judges, assassinating my character—calling me a murderer, rapist, thug, and woman beater. I would later discover these letters, long after losing custody, from an attorney I eventually hired.

Despite the emotional and financial strain, I made the weekly drive from Kansas City to St. Louis with my children. I even asked Anita—a paralegal and, ironically, the same woman who betrayed me by revealing my infidelity to Ayanna—to accompany me to the courthouse. She had referred me to an attorney, Shystie, and I was hopeful for some help.

When I arrived, I saw Selena and Francine sitting side by side outside the courtroom. In that moment, everything became clear—they were lovers. I had been played for a fool. How could I have been so blind?

Inside the courtroom, I notified the bailiff that I was there for my custody hearing. Then, outside, while on the phone about my sister April—who was fighting for her life in the Siteman Cancer Center—I was ambushed. Out of nowhere, police officers rushed me. Francine and Selena had called 911, falsely claiming I was causing a disturbance. Before I could explain myself or speak to the judge, I was handcuffed. Before being escorted out of the building, I instructed Anita to post my bail. I was thrown into jail, leaving my children confused and waiting inside the courtroom.

As if that wasn't enough, I soon discovered Anita had betrayed me again. She and attorney Shystie had slept together, and Anita had cozied up to Selena and Francine after my arrest. She not only believed their lies, but she also stole thousands of dollars from my Regions Bank account while I was locked up. Her betrayal left me devastated.

I was taken to the police station and charged with domestic assault—an accusation that had already been cleared the year before. Why was the case reopened? Why was there a forged police report with different arriving officers' names? Where were the original officers? These questions haunted me as I was hauled off to the Workhouse Jail, where I spent two agonizing weeks waiting for a court hearing.

While in jail, I found out that Missouri authorities were delaying my release to see if Kansas City had enough evidence to indict me on Ayanna's rape allegations. Ultimately, no charges were brought, but the experience left me questioning the integrity of the justice system.

Yahkhahnahn Ammi

Being separated from my children tore me apart. In jail, I suffered from severe anxiety and depression. The female guards treated me like dirt, convinced I was a woman beater due to Francine's political connections. Her cousin, the Circuit Attorney for St. Louis City, had strong ties in the legal community. They wanted to make an example out of me, punishing me for my activism during the Ferguson protests.

Desperate to get out, I contacted Robin, my son's mother. I authorized her to withdraw money from my Regions Bank Account. She posted my bail, and after two long weeks, I was released. Reunited with my children, I drove back to Kansas City and prepared for the next court hearing. I cut ties with attorney Shystie and sought help from the Father's Support Center. After completing their six week program, I was assigned a pro bono attorney. But instead of representing me for free, she manipulated me and falsified legal documents and said that I retained her privately—something she knew I couldn't afford.

The tension in the courtroom was suffocating. Every time I entered it drained the life out of me. I had hired one attorney for the criminal domestic case involving Francine and another for the civil rape allegations filed by Ayanna. It felt like a game of legal whack-a-mole, and the stakes couldn't have been higher.

Every time I walked into court, it was like stepping into a ring surrounded by an audience that wanted to see me fall. The opposing attorneys' disdain hung thick in the air, and the judge, clearly influenced by defamatory letters Selena and Francine had sent to every judge involved, treated me with barely concealed contempt.

I wasn't just another case to them. I was a target, an activist fighting for his children, tossed between lawyers and judges like a hockey puck. The Guardian ad Litem, supposed to represent the best interests of my children, misrepresented them instead. Despite the blatant conflict of interest, he refused to step down. Selena's attorney, with her sneering remarks and smug arrogance, belittled me openly in front of the judge, feeding off the lies Selena, Francine, and Ayanna had so carefully constructed.

It wasn't enough that they were questioning my character—they went for my very identity. The judge, a Black man, was melanated like me. He looked at me with eyes clouded by something personal. He didn't just question my integrity; he questioned my faith. My Jewish faith. He insisted on confirmation from my Rabbi because he didn't believe I could possibly be Jewish. The message was clear: to him, I didn't belong.

Things only got worse from there. The Black male judge who had been overseeing our case was promoted and assigned to a different court, leaving our case in the hands of a White woman judge who seemed determined to make me suffer. She dragged out the case for over a year, making every step of the process a relentless ordeal.

Throughout the proceedings, opposing attorneys and the Guardian Ad Litem (GAL) complained that I hadn't paid the additional fees the court had ordered—despite the fact that I had already been granted a fee waiver due to my financial situation, a waiver that this very judge had signed. Yet, my inability to pay didn't matter. The judge ordered the GAL to file a motion to strike my pleadings, essentially stripping away my voice in court.

Yahkhahnahn Ammi

My attorney, a Black woman I had hired to represent me, stood by passively. She did nothing to contest the motion, making no effort to defend my rights. At that moment, I was powerless. As the judge brought down her gavel, my opportunity to be heard was erased, and with it, any hope I had left.

I lost. The court placed me on child support, granted temporary custody of my children to their mother, and left me financially shattered. My savings were drained. My bail had been paid. But my dignity—my sense of self—was gone, crushed beneath the weight of a system that had silenced me. And none of that seemed to matter in the eyes of the court.

The judges were relentless. They brought up my juvenile record, highlighted my activism, and vilified me for standing up during the Ferguson protests. It didn't matter that I was fighting for justice in a system that was broken. To them, I was the problem. The way they looked at me—jarring, judgmental, cold—spoke volumes. It felt like they were sentencing me not just for the accusations against me, but for my entire existence. I should have had a different judge. The one assigned to my case had just lost his father, and the personal grief he carried seemed to twist his perspective. I couldn't shake the feeling that my being a single, melanated father only added to his hostility. There was no way out—no one listened, no one cared.

Much of this outcome stemmed from the legal representation I had trusted. The attorney I hired—someone I believed would fight for my rights—ultimately failed me. She mishandled my case, neglecting to file a counterclaim when a motion was made to strike my pleadings due to my inability to pay the GAL (Guardian Ad Litem) fees. Her misrepresentation cost me dearly, leading to the loss of my custody battle and the right to meaningful time with my children.

Years later, the true extent of her betrayal came to light. Out of the blue, she emailed me a letter—one written by Francine and Selena—that had been sent to all the judges, including those presiding over my custody case at the time. It was a devastating revelation, confirming that my attorney had never had my best interests in mind.

I had placed my trust in the wrong people, and that mistake cost me everything.

The cases stacked up against me like a wall I couldn't scale. Ayanna's rape allegation had been dropped in the criminal courts, but now it loomed over me in the civil courts.

Francine's domestic assault claims simmered in the background. All the while, emergency restraining orders flooded in from every direction. It felt like a well coordinated attack. I was trapped, drowning in legal chaos, and to make matters worse, my Uber account—the only way I was earning money—was disabled. No income, no way to survive, and a system determined to keep me down. In the end, Selena won full custody of our children. My world collapsed. I was granted one-hour supervised visits every other week. No phone calls, no video chats—nothing. I became a stranger to my own children.

And it didn't stop there. The court wouldn't even consider re-evaluating visitation rights. It was as if I didn't exist in their eyes. My ex-wife systematically alienated me from my children, depriving them of a relationship with their youngest brother,

Yahkhahnahn Ammi

Prince, and my side of the family. They've seen Prince just three times in eight years. Three times. My parents, my siblings—they've all been cut off.

For seven long years, I fought relentlessly to regain full custody of my children. I poured everything I had into the battle—time, energy, and money—hiring attorney after attorney, hoping each one would finally help me break free from the cycle of loss. But in the end, they all drained me. They took my money, chipped away at my hope, and left me stranded in a world of sorrow and despair.

Seven years of fighting. Seven years of endless motions, appeals, and setbacks. And through it all, I watched my children grow up through the lens of court-supervised visits. I could only stand by helplessly as a broken legal system slowly tore my family apart, making the dream of being with my children feel more and more distant with each passing day.

And still, nothing has changed. My ex-wife dangles the possibility of ending supervised visitation like a carrot, but she never follows through. The DJO, biased and unyielding, sides with her every time. I've complained, filed requests for a new officer, but it's like screaming into the void. Their interactions, the way they cover for each other, have always felt suspicious, like something else was going on that I wasn't privy to.

In the end, I am left to wonder if the system is rigged—designed to divide families, not unite them. As I sit here, reflecting on this long, grueling journey, I realize just how much I've lost. Not just time, money, or opportunities. I've lost my children. But even in the face of this injustice, I refuse to give up. I will fight. For myself, for my children, for our future. This battle is far from over.

When Selena was granted temporary custody, everything began to unravel. Our son and daughter were plunged into a world of abuse—physical and emotional—inflicted not just by their mother, but by her male lovers, and possibly female lovers, too. My children, once so full of life and laughter, were silenced. Their vibrant spirits dulled by the weight of trauma they endured behind closed doors. But it wasn't just the abuse at home that haunted me. The real betrayal came in the courtroom, when Selena—my ex-wife—stood before the judge and lied under oath.

With shocking ease, she spun a web of lies, creating false accusations and fabricating stories about me all in pursuit of a favorable outcome. She had her co-conspirators, all aligned to ensure her victory, no matter the cost to our children.

The courts, blind to the truth, granted her full legal and sole custody. It was a crushing blow—a decision that would sever my bond with my children. In one fell swoop, Selena cut off their lifeline. She took away their cell phones, sold them even, and forbade any communication with me or my side of the family. Overnight, the calls and video chats we shared every day vanished, leaving a gaping hole in my heart. My children, trapped in her home, were now isolated in what felt like a mental prison, their world shrunk to four walls of silence and suffering.

Inside those walls, the abuse continued, unchecked. Prince Avatar, our eldest, bravely pointed out the neglect and cruelty happening to his siblings, but his voice—like mine—was ignored. Neither Selena nor the courts, who were made aware of the horrors unfolding in her home, lifted a finger to protect my children. The system failed them at every turn.

Yahkhahnahn Ammi

I brought these incidents to the court's attention time and again, hoping, pleading for someone to see the truth. Eventually, a new judge—a White woman—took over our case. I thought, maybe this time, someone would listen. But the silence remained deafening. My children were still left in their mother's care, exposed to strangers—both men and women—who behaved inappropriately in front of them, leaving them vulnerable and unprotected.

The inaction of the courts was staggering. Every time I warned them of the abuse, it was as though my words were spoken into a void. My concerns, my pleas for justice, were ignored. When I turned to Child Protective Services, hoping they would intervene, they labeled my claims as "unfounded" or simply chose not to investigate. I was left shouting into the wind, my children suffering while the system turned its back on them. Then there was Ms. Bias, the Deputy Juvenile Officer assigned to our case. From the start, she lived up to her name. After speaking with Selena privately on multiple occasions, she admitted her bias against me without hesitation. The best interests of my children were never her concern—her allegiance was clear, and it wasn't with me.

I had feared that Selena would not protect our children from the onset. And my concerns were confirmed after I received several calls from the biased Deputy Juvenile Officer (DJO) mediator assigned to the case late one night that confirmed recently that one of Selena's boyfriends had exposed himself to our underage daughter.

He masturbated in front of her numerous times, and had been doing so for over two years and on this occasion he attempted to sexually assault her while Selena was allegedly on her way to work during this incident.

The weight of injustice was unbearable. I watched, helpless, as the courts enabled the abuse, as the system I thought was designed to protect my children failed them. My fight to be heard was drowned out by a chorus of indifference. And as the days passed, the distance between me and my children grew wider, the pain of separation sharper.

When our children bravely confided in their mother about their fears, they were met with a wall of denial. Selena refused to acknowledge their concerns, turning a blind eye when they needed her most. I still remember the day our daughter escaped, terrified, while Selena chose to continue with her shift as if nothing had happened. The police were called, and the Department of Children and Family Services (DCFS) got involved. But even then, Selena's first instinct was to protect her lover.

She agreed—grudgingly—to let our daughter stay a few nights at her mother's house until the DCFS visit was over. But the reprieve was short lived. In just a few days, our daughter was back in the very place where the trauma had occurred. Selena took control, forbidding our children from having cell phones while she was away, isolating them even further.

As the investigation unfolded, I waited, expecting answers, expecting to be involved as their father. But DCFS never contacted me. Their findings, whatever they were, were shared only with the biased Deputy Juvenile Officer (DJO) assigned to our case. That same DJO, who had repeatedly sided with Selena, withheld the results from me. It was as though I didn't exist in this fight for my children's safety and well-being.

Yahkhahnahn Ammi

For seven long years, Selena didn't allow our children to speak to their Aunt April, who passed away from cancer in 2016, or their grandmother Jackie, who passed just recently. I fought tooth and nail with the DJO, pushing for my children to attend their grandmother's funeral. It felt like a battle just to grant them the right to grieve.

Finally, after endless back and forth, Selena relented, but the damage was already done. Seeing my children once or twice a month—if Selena didn't cancel at the last minute—was a far cry from the life I had envisioned. Every time the day of visitation came, my heart raced with the hope that I wouldn't receive that dreaded cancellation text. Each visit, I made sure they were well fed. I cooked meals with love, ordered catering, or bought food because their mother, so often, didn't even have enough for them at home. My concern was always their safety, their well-being, and their ability to just be kids.

What hurt the most, though, was Selena's persistent refusal to let me call or video chat with our children, who are now sixteen and seventeen. I wanted so badly to connect with them beyond our fleeting visits, to hear their voices and know they were okay. But she intimidated and alienated them for years, filling their heads with fear. They were too scared to call me, too scared to defy her.

This ordeal has been nothing short of heartbreaking. The weight of it, the sleepless nights, the unanswered texts—it has all taken its toll. I often found myself listening to the song *"Unsteady"* by X Ambassadors, its haunting lyrics capturing the uncertainty and pain that had come to define my life as a father. It played in the background of my thoughts as I navigated this storm, the constant waves of text messages, court orders, and emotional manipulation crashing down on me.

The following text exchange between Selena and I paints a vivid picture of our struggle—a father trying to stay connected to his children and a mother determined to keep us apart.

December 23, 2016, **Yah:** "Selena, when I brought the babies over for you to see, I did not like your aggressive behavior, especially around the children. Nor did my friend Alicia appreciate your tone with me. You were rude to her, and that was not cool. Again, you cannot dictate to our children or to me about visitation. It does not work like that! (Read the court order) You cannot pop up at my house like you did, demanding to see our children, especially when you do not consistently communicate with them/us! It was completely out of order for you to tell them they are coming over to your house for this weekend! I advised you we could meet at the temple, but, as usual, you declined. With your attitude and aggression, I will not allow your energy around us. Please take your medication and get it together. Until you do, I don't have to bring our children around you. It's unsafe and unhealthy for that. I am trying to work with you. Try calling consistently. We can always go back to court if you like. I'm okay with that. You are hot-headed, and I fear for my safety as well as that of our children around you. I will never be able to trust them alone in your presence. Now, I am trying, but you are making it difficult. You asked for my address, which I thought was strange considering you already know where I live and have visited our children and popped up unannounced. Please meet us at the Temple for the gift exchange on Saturday. My P.O. Box is 9998311 St. Louis, MO

Yahkhahnahn Ammi

1234—that's all I'm giving you due to your aggressive domestic behavior towards me in the past. Goodnight."

[I rub my temple, taking a deep breath before continuing.]

Selena: "Something is seriously wrong with you—you need Jesus!"

(Saturday)

Yah: Selena, we're at the temple. The kids are looking forward to the gifts you promised. They're asking for you—where are you?

Selena: "You said you didn't want me to come before, and now you do? Your games aren't going to work, Yah."

Selena: "From now on, I'm bringing someone with me whenever we meet. No telling what you might try."

Selena: "Please have the kids call me today or tomorrow. Thank you."

Selena: "I've been trying to reach you and the kids for weeks now. Why haven't you called me back? This is the third time you've disappeared without telling me where the kids are. You're wrong for this, and I'll fight it."

Selena: "Yah, what you did was very wrong. You didn't tell me where the kids were. I don't want to talk until we go to court. But my question remains—when will you let me see the kids again?"

Selena: "I need you to text me when you're bringing the kids. We have to follow the parenting plan. It's important."

Yah: We have court today at 9a. I am on my way there now with our children.

There were no more text messages between us. Our next interaction occurred in a courtroom hallway. I walked off the elevator with my children, followed by Anita. Selena and Francine are waiting, glaring at me. Tension fills the air. Moments later, police enter the hallway.

Police Officer: *"Sir, step back. We've received a report of a disturbance."*

Yah: What does that have to do with me?

Police Officer: *"What is your name?"*

Yah: Why do you need my name? It's Yah Ammi. I stand there, confused as the group of police officers bum rush me.

Police Officer: *"You have a wanted out for questioning, you are not under arrest."*

Yah: Then Why are you slapping handcuffs on me behind my back? This is an arrest against my will. Where are you taking me? My children are inside of the courtroom waiting on me, unaware of what's happening.

Police Officer: *"We are taking you down to the station."*

Yah: I am taken down the elevator into a hallway and placed inside the back seat of a police car. When the car stops, I am now at the St. Louis City Police Department in downtown. The Officer standing in front of me says, you are being charged for domestic assault on Francine Coldburn that occurred on **December 25th, 2016**. They placed me under arrest and sent me to the Workhouse medium security jail in St. Louis City.

Once I was processed and fingerprinted, I requested a phone call. I try to call Selena to speak to my children, but she refuses any of my calls. I did not communicate with my children for two weeks, and they had no idea what happened or where I was.

* * *

Personal Life Lesson Reflections

In this chapter "Shadows of Custody: St. Louis City & County Court," encapsulates one of the most challenging and emotionally draining periods of my life. My battle for custody in the St. Louis City and County courts were not just a legal struggle—it was a fight for my dignity, my children's safety, and my very existence as a father. The shadows cast by a biased and corrupt system loomed large, threatening to engulf everything I held dear.

The experience was a harsh reminder of the fragility of justice and how easily the scales can tip against those who are falsely accused. The courts, which should have been a place of fairness and resolution, became a battleground where lies, manipulation, and character assassination were the weapons used against me. Despite being innocent, I was treated like a criminal, with my reputation dragged through the mud and my relationship with my children jeopardized.

The psychological toll was immense. Each court hearing felt like a descent into a deeper layer of hell, where my voice was silenced, and my pleas for fairness were ignored. The system that was supposed to protect my rights as a father instead stripped them away, leaving me to navigate a legal nightmare without the support I desperately needed. Yet, through it all, I remained resolute. My love for my children and my determination to be a present father kept me fighting, even when the odds were stacked against me.

This chapter taught me the critical importance of perseverance and the need to advocate for oneself in the face of systemic injustice. It also reinforced the idea that support systems are vital during times of crisis. Without the unwavering belief and support of a few close family members and friends, I might not have found the strength to keep going.

Takeaways

The Importance of Perseverance

Even when the legal system feels rigged against you, persistence is key. Do not give up the fight for justice and the well-being of your children, no matter how difficult the journey becomes.

The Power of a Support System

During challenging times, the support of family and friends can be your lifeline. Surround yourself with those who believe in your innocence and are willing to stand by you through thick and thin.

Advocate for Yourself

When faced with systemic bias, it is crucial to be your own strongest advocate. Educate yourself about the legal system, seek out resources, and do not be afraid to demand fair treatment, even in the face of overwhelming adversity.

The Emotional Toll of Legal Battles

Custody battles and false accusations can take a severe emotional toll. It is essential to recognize this and seek help—whether through therapy, support groups, or other means—to navigate the mental strain.

Hope and Resilience

Even in the darkest of times, hold onto hope. The love you have for your children and your commitment to their well-being can serve as the guiding light that pulls you through the most challenging circumstances.

This chapter serves as a powerful reminder that while the road to justice may be long and fraught with obstacles, resilience and a steadfast belief in what is right can ultimately lead to a better future for you and your children.

CHAPTER 24

Devastating Fallout

"Scars" - I Am They

Scars fade, but the devastation of lies lingers—shaping a reality where words cut deeper than any wound, leaving a life shattered and forever altered.

"Sticks and stones may break my bones, but words will never hurt me." Growing up, I believed this phrase, clung to it as a shield. But in my case, those words were just another lie—one I had been fed since childhood. False accusations flipped my life upside down, proving that words can indeed be the most devastating weapons. Lies, once whispered, grow legs. They run, they spread, they consume everything in their path. And when those lies are aimed at your very soul, the damage they leave behind can be irreparable. I learned the hard way that words don't just hurt—they haunt you. They ruin your reputation, taint your name, and leave scars deeper than any physical wound. Defamation isn't just a moment of slander. It's a poison that seeps into your life and your livelihood, until all that's left is confusion, anger, and the aching question: How did this happen?

Yahkhahnahn Ammi

When the accusations first hit, I was completely lost, bewildered, and spinning in a whirlwind of confusion. I wanted to scream—to claw my way out of the storm that was swallowing me whole—but fear gripped me so tightly I could hardly breathe. Rape? Assault? Those words felt foreign to me, but there they were, tied to my name, branded into my identity. Panic surged through me as I struggled to find my next move. Never in my life had I been accused of such heinous acts, and suddenly, I was drowning in allegations that no one bothered to verify with me. The nerve of that woman—of all the women I had let into my life. Selena, Ayanna, Francine, Anita. One by one, they turned against me. My anger simmered beneath the surface as I watched my life unravel, fueled by the lies they had spread. It wasn't just the accusation of rape—it was the speed with which my world crumbled that left me reeling. Social media lit up like a wildfire. Tabloids ran with the story, each one more salacious than the last. I had gone from being a community anti-violence advocate to an accused rapist overnight. How could they label me this way? How could the world believe this without even hearing my side?

I hadn't raped Ayanna. But in the court of public opinion, it didn't matter. The damage was done. My reputation was left in ruins, and I felt betrayed by someone I had once trusted. Perhaps, on some level, Ayanna felt betrayed too—by the affair I had with Anita. But did that call for the destruction of my life? Anita had likely shared our text messages with Ayanna, pouring gasoline on a fire that was already raging out of control. I was numb. My thoughts raced endlessly, circling the same truths I knew in my heart but couldn't make anyone else see.

I had fought against domestic violence my entire life, raised by strong Christian women who taught me to honor and protect women. I had seen my mother, my siblings, suffer at the hands of abusive men, and I vowed never to be that man. So how could I be painted as one? How could the world believe I was capable of such evil? I needed something to stop the spiraling thoughts. I needed peace. But there was none. My name was plastered on every newspaper, my face splashed across police reports, and no matter how hard I tried, I couldn't escape the constant scrutiny. I reminded myself who I was—a man who protected women, who stood against violence. But in my darkest moments, as anger bubbled inside me, I could feel the resentment creeping in. I had fought to save women from abuse, and now, I wanted to strangle Ayanna for what she'd done to me. I had to remind myself, *"Don't be an abuser,"* over and over again. But the fear of jail, the fear of being falsely imprisoned, clung to me like a shadow.

I had slipped into a deep depression. For weeks, I stayed out of sight, locked away from the world, becoming an introvert in the blink of an eye. Every time I stepped outside, I feared that I would be arrested—that my children would be taken from me for a crime I didn't commit. Ayanna hadn't just accused me in whispers. She took her story to Francine's new radio show in St. Louis, Missouri, bashing me publicly and drumming up support from the so-called conscious community and the Black Lives Matter movement. They positioned her as the face of sexual assault victims, using my name to build her celebrity overnight. But Ayanna didn't stop there. She filed a civil lawsuit under the name "Jane Doe." If her accusations were true, if she was so sure of what had happened, why hide behind anonymity? Why not let me confront my accuser? It all felt like a twisted game.

Yahkhahnahn Ammi

So, I went into hiding. It was not because I had done anything wrong. The media circus turned my life into a spectacle, a freak show, where I was the main act. My family saw the headlines, heard the stories, and I felt their judgment, their uncertainty. Inside, I cried. My heart was heavy, weighed down by the fear that none of this would ever blow over. I prayed in silence, questioning God's existence, questioning the very fabric of who I was.

I was lonely, terrified of being alone in a world that seemed hell-bent on destroying me. I couldn't stop thinking about the possibility of losing my children, of the cops knocking down my door. It was a nightmare I couldn't wake from.

Before the accusations spiraled out of control, I hadn't lost custody of my children. I still had to take them back to St. Louis for weekend visits with their mother. But even as I held onto those fleeting moments, I could feel the ground shifting beneath me. The weight of what was happening pressed down on me like a storm I couldn't outrun.

Despite everything crumbling around me, the few people who remained in my life—my parents, my loving mother, my grandmother, and a handful of friends—never doubted me. Somehow, they knew to trust their intuition, to trust me. They stood strong while my world fell apart, believing that God's arms of protection would still shelter me from the worst.

I clung to that hope while hiding from the cops, lonely as hell, shaking with fear of losing the only people who truly mattered—the ones who would suffer the most if I got locked up for a crime I didn't commit. My children.

I still couldn't wrap my mind around it—why Ayanna would stoop so low as to accuse me of something so vile. The betrayal cut deep. My mother saw through it all, though. *"You have to be careful with these women. Your ex-wife has something to do with all this—she's evil,"* she told me, her voice unwavering. When I talked to mama (Jackie) about my problems, she took my hands and held them tightly, she whispered a prayer over me in the name of Jesus. *"Stop fighting. Turn it over to God. He will fight all your battles for you,"* she urged. But all I wanted in that moment was to clear my name, to claw my way out of the storm that was swallowing me whole.

I prayed for justice, but it felt like even God had turned His back on me—just like my ex-wife, just like the church, the synagogue, and even my so-called friends. So many doors closed in my face. Yet, my parents, my grandmother, my siblings, and a few close family members stood firm. They were my only sanctuary as I spiraled deeper into despair.

The depression hit hard. I mourned the life I once had, the closeness I shared with my children, and the future that seemed to slip further from my grasp each day. After two weeks in the Workhouse, I was released, but the world outside offered no refuge. I couldn't find work—anywhere. It got so bad that I couldn't even donate blood at the Interstate Blood Bank, a place I had frequented in desperate times before. But even they had shut me out.

I'll never forget the day I walked into the blood bank on Delmar Blvd, only to be treated like a stranger. The staff, people who knew me, looked at me differently. I asked why I was banned, why I couldn't give blood anymore. They didn't give me an answer at first, but I insisted on speaking to a supervisor. When one of the staff members finally showed me their computer screen, I was floored. There it was—my name, my photo, highlighted notes calling me a domestic abuser, a rapist. They had me blacklisted. The lies had followed me here, too. My reputation was smeared beyond recognition.

It didn't stop there. Social media censored me, categorizing me as a threat. Facebook seized my personal and business accounts, blocked me from creating new ones, and monitored my IP address. I had become an overnight pariah—a fallen celebrity in my own world, condemned by lies. My podcast? Silenced. My voice? Stripped away. I was cut off from everything and everyone I had built. It felt like the world had cast me into hell, and I was left to rot, alone. But even in this dark place, my family was there. My father's voice echoed in my mind: *"This too shall pass. Keep your faith in God."* My siblings rallied around me, saying we would get through it together. My uncles and aunts offered words of encouragement, but it was hard to believe in anything when my heart was so heavy with despair. The people I had once advocated for had closed their doors, abandoning me to wander in the wilderness for what felt like forty years.

I had carried this burden for over seven years—seven years of hurt, pain, rage, and betrayal. The lies that these women spread became a weight I couldn't shake. Nothing anyone said could wash away the stain they left on my name. It gnawed at me, deepening my isolation. I began to wonder if this was karma. Was this the price I paid for my mistakes? Was this what a Black woman's scorn looked and felt like? I didn't want to believe it, but I couldn't escape the thought.

At my lowest point, I even thought about drinking—anything to numb the pain. But I couldn't do it. I had seen what alcohol had done to my stepfather Goliath. I wasn't about to fall into that same trap. Instead, I sought professional help. Psychotropic medication became my crutch, something to dull the ache of depression and keep me afloat. The anger I had built up inside—the revenge, the rage—threatened to consume me. I had to hold on, had to find a way out of the wreckage of my life.

Ayanna, though, remained a looming presence. In my eyes, she became a black widow, a woman to be feared. She, along with the others who conspired against me, had woven a web of lies and deceit. Blackmail, fraud—it all piled up, suffocating me. They were dangerous, not just to me, but to anyone who crossed their path.

As I reflected on everything that had happened, I realized I had to take responsibility—not for the crimes I was accused of, but for the choices that had led me here. I had made mistakes, chosen the wrong relationships, allowed myself to be vulnerable in ways that had cost me everything. It was time to confront those choices and take back control of my life.

No matter how long it took, I had to fight my way out of this. I had to reclaim my life, my truth, and the future I wanted to leave for my children.

* * *

Yahkhahnahn Ammi

Personal Life Lesson Reflections

In this chapter "The Devastating Fallout", captures one of the darkest periods of my life—a time when false accusations and malicious rumors turned my world upside down. The saying "sticks and stones may break my bones, but words will never hurt me" was a cruel deception I had been taught to believe. In reality, words can cut deeper than any physical wound, and their impact can be long-lasting and life-altering.

The false accusations of rape and assault not only damaged my reputation but also shattered the very foundation of my life. The lies spread like wildfire, amplified by social media and sensationalized by the press. I went from being a respected advocate for non-violence to being demonized as a rapist, with no opportunity to defend myself. The betrayal from those I once trusted, combined with the isolation and fear of losing everything, pushed me to the brink of despair.

Throughout this ordeal, I wrestled with overwhelming feelings of anger, fear, and deep depression. The thought of being imprisoned for a crime I didn't commit haunted me daily, and the weight of public judgment felt unbearable.

Yet, in the midst of this chaos, I realized that I needed to find a way to heal and reclaim my life. I sought professional help for my mental health, understanding that I could not allow the lies and betrayal to destroy me completely.

Forgiveness played a critical role in my journey toward healing. I had to forgive not only those who wronged me but also myself for the choices I made that led to this point. Accepting responsibility

319

for the consequences of my actions—though not for the false accusations—was a necessary step toward reclaiming my power and moving forward.

This chapter taught me that even in the face of devastating lies and betrayal, it is possible to rebuild your life. It requires acknowledging the pain, seeking help, and finding the strength to forgive. Most importantly, it requires holding onto the belief that, no matter how deep the fall, you can rise again.

Takeaways

The Power of Words

Words can be more damaging than physical harm. False accusations and malicious rumors can ruin lives, so it's crucial to be mindful of the power our words carry.

The Importance of Mental Health

When facing overwhelming challenges, it's essential to seek professional help. Addressing mental health struggles head on is a vital step in the healing process.

Forgiveness as a Path to Healing

Forgiving those who wronged you, as well as forgiving yourself, is key to moving forward. It allows you to let go of the toxic emotions that can keep you trapped in pain.

Accountability and Growth

Even if you are falsely accused, it's important to take responsibility for your life and the decisions that led you to where you are. This accountability is the foundation for personal growth and rebuilding.

Resilience in the Face of Adversity

Life can be devastatingly unfair, but resilience is what will carry you through. No matter how deep the betrayal or how widespread the lies, you have the power to rise, heal, and reclaim your life.

This chapter serves as a reminder that while the fallout from lies and betrayal can be devastating, it is possible to overcome it with resilience, forgiveness, and a commitment to healing.

CHAPTER 25

Blackmail, Black Male

"The Kings Affirmation Acapella" – Iniko

In the darkest moments of betrayal, I found the strength to reclaim my soul, not through revenge, but by embracing the transformative power of forgiveness.

To My Exes,

You thought your manipulation could strip me of everything I cherished—my children, my home, my peace of mind.

You tarnished my name, dragged me through the mud, and watched as my reputation crumbled. But what you failed to realize is that no amount of lies, blackmail, or hatred could ever break my spirit. You conspired with bitter allies, tried to write me off, to end me. But through it all, God's hand was on me, and I was protected.

Yes, you succeeded in having me temporarily separated from my children. You thought using them as pawns in your war against me would finally bring me to my knees.

Yahkhahnahn Ammi

But your attempts to imprison me for crimes I did not commit failed. God had other plans.

You threatened to blackmail me, twisted the truth until it was unrecognizable, and preyed on my vulnerabilities. You struck when my world was already falling apart—when my sister was battling cancer, when she passed away at just 35 years old.

In the midst of my deepest grief, you pressed forward with your schemes, showing no mercy, no empathy. But I prayed. I called out to God and my ancestors, and their message was clear: "I am not finished with you yet." They stood between me and the prison gates, and I knew, despite everything, I would not be lost.

For years, I fought this battle in isolation. I confronted my mental health, faced my demons, and emerged stronger than before. I had to. In those moments of raw pain and suffering, I rediscovered who I was. The tears I had held back for so long finally broke through. Anger and bitterness consumed me, and in that rage, I found myself lost. Time passed, life moved on, but I stayed stuck in the trenches, haunted by betrayal. I hated you.

I hated you because, through your lies, I lost myself. Through your web of deception, my own children forgot who I was. *"Abba, I forgot what you looked like,"* they said after three months without seeing me. Your alienation tactics worked, and it broke me in ways I never thought possible. But as I sank deeper into that abyss, I realized that hatred wasn't the answer. Holding on to it would only destroy me.

Forgiveness became my lifeline. I knew I had to forgive you—not for your sake, but for my own. Forgiveness was my path to healing, my way to reclaim my power. The anger that festered inside me was a poison, a cancer that threatened to consume my body and soul. I couldn't let it win. I chose forgiveness because I had to. Without it, I would have lost everything that mattered.

Final Reflections

I write this letter not in pursuit of revenge, not with a thirst for retribution. Instead, I write to affirm my resilience, my unbroken spirit. I have learned that true strength doesn't lie in striking back, but in letting go. It lies in the ability to forgive and move forward with grace.

To those who are still in their own battles, struggling under the weight of lies and betrayal, I share my story to inspire you to find your own strength. I am living proof that even in the midst of the worst storms, you can survive. You can rise. Never lose hope.

As I move forward, I am committed to building a life filled with love, peace, and positivity. I am dedicated to being the best father I can be—showing my children what it means to live with integrity, to know their worth, and to understand the power of forgiveness. This journey hasn't been easy, but each trial has shaped me into the man I am today: strong, resilient, and unwavering in my faith.

This is my truth. And no one can take that away.

* * *

Yahkhahnahn Ammi

Personal Life Lesson Reflections

In this chapter, "Blackmail, Black Male: A Letter to My Exes", is a deeply personal and transformative chapter in my life. It reflects a period where I faced betrayal, manipulation, and attempts to break my spirit. The people I once loved and trusted turned against me, using our children as pawns in a cruel game to strip me of everything I cherished. My reputation was tarnished, and I was temporarily separated from my children. Yet, through it all, my faith and determination remained unshaken.

The pain I endured was overwhelming, but it also became a catalyst for profound self-discovery and growth. I confronted my mental health struggles head on, realizing that my anger and pain were not only destructive but were also preventing me from healing. I was caught in a web of bitterness that made me lose sight of myself, to the point where even my own children began to forget who I was. It was in these moments of despair that I learned the true power of forgiveness.

Forgiving those who wronged me was not an easy decision, but it was a necessary one. I understood that holding onto anger and resentment was like a cancer, eating away at my soul. By choosing to forgive, I reclaimed my power and began the process of healing. Forgiveness did not mean forgetting the pain or excusing the actions of those who hurt me, but it did mean freeing myself from the toxic grip of hatred. It allowed me to move forward with grace and to rebuild my life on a foundation of love, peace, and positivity.

This chapter taught me that true strength is not found in revenge but in the ability to rise above the pain and choose a path of healing and growth. It is through these challenges that I have become stronger, more resilient, and more determined to live a life of purpose and integrity. My journey has shaped me into a man who is unwavering in his faith and committed to being the best father and role model for my children.

Takeaways

The Power of Forgiveness

Holding onto anger and resentment can destroy you from within. Forgiveness is not about excusing the actions of others, but about freeing yourself from the burden of bitterness and reclaiming your peace.

Resilience in the Face of Betrayal

Even when those closest to you turn against you, your strength lies in your ability to rise above the pain and continue moving forward. Betrayal can be a catalyst for profound personal growth.

Faith as a Guiding Force

When everything else seems to be falling apart, faith can be your anchor. Trusting in a higher purpose and believing in your own resilience can help you navigate even the darkest times.

Healing Through Self-Discovery

Confronting your pain and mental health struggles is crucial to healing. It is through self-reflection and self-discovery that you can begin to rebuild your life and find true peace.

Yahkhahnahn Ammi

Commitment to positivity choosing to live a life filled with love, peace, and positivity, even after facing great adversity, is a testament to your inner strength. It is a powerful example to others, especially your children, of the transformative power of resilience and forgiveness.

This chapter serves as a reminder that no matter how deep the betrayal or how intense the pain, there is always a path to healing and redemption. By embracing forgiveness and focusing on personal growth, you can emerge from any challenge stronger and more resilient.

CHAPTER 26

Homelessness to Higher Education

"Letter to My Son"- Akon

From the harsh streets to the halls of higher education, my journey was forged through relentless adversity and unshakable faith, proving that even in the darkest times, hope and determination can light the path to greatness.

Homeless and desperate, I embarked on an educational journey that would transform my life and my children's futures. Navigating false allegations, homelessness, and systemic bias, I fought relentlessly to secure a better life for my family, proving that determination and faith can overcome even the darkest challenges. When I began my educational journey, I was homeless, living on the streets or wherever I could find a safe place to lay my head. The most hurtful part of this ordeal was that I had become homeless with my two children once again due to false allegations I faced. I had to make frequent trips to St. Louis for the court-ordered visitation exchanges with Selena. On one weekend exchange, I had to get the transmission on my SUV repaired. It sat in the shop for months until the mechanics were able to fix it. I could not get back to Kansas City, and I could not make it to any court hearings because of that. Meanwhile, things got worse; my children and I were going from shelter to shelter, struggling without transportation.

I was desperate and in need of support. I had to keep my children safe and maintain my sanity. Everything around me crumbled after losing our apartment and all of our possessions in Raytown, a small town outside of Kansas City, Missouri. I didn't know who I could trust. Being excommunicated from the synagogue that provided for my family spiritually was a deep blow, and being ostracized from a community I had put my life on the line for because of rumors and false allegations made it even more difficult. Not to mention the death threats from Francine and others from the Black Lives Matter movement. I had enemies on all sides, and I damn sure did not trust the police.

With limited options and only a few family and friends who were there for me, I was eternally grateful. When I lost custody of my children, I nearly lost my mind with everything that I had going on, but I never lost my faith in God. To improve my situation and self-worth, I completed a HI-SET educational program for adults and earned my high school diploma—a dream I had longed to achieve. Simultaneously, I attended seminary school, where I earned my certificate of credentials and was issued my license as an ordained minister. I was on a quest to earn my associates, bachelor's, master's, and PhD. It took time, but I successfully earned them even amidst the chaos surrounding me. The whirlwind I was caught up in motivated me. That's how I went from being homeless to earning a PhD. After losing my sister April and Mama Jackie, my passion for helping others continued to grow. It was therapy for me as a civil servant, and I enjoyed giving back to my community. I looked forward to entering college and enrolled in St. Louis Community College to earn my nursing credentials.

There I was, finally stepping into a dream I had held close for so long—continuing my education, a journey filled with both purpose and heartache. Losing my sister April to cancer was devastating, a wound that only deepened after losing mama, Jackie, several years later. Their absence weighed heavily on me, yet it also gave me clarity and purpose. I knew that I wanted to help others, to be a source of healing and support.

I decided to become a Doctor of Osteopathic Medicine, to honor their memories and fulfill a calling that had grown in my heart. However, before I could reach that goal, I would need to become a registered nurse. This first step was essential—a new beginning that would lead me down a path both challenging and deeply meaningful. I was taking my prerequisite classes at St. Louis Community College, hoping not only to achieve my own ambitions but also to show my children that it's never too late to chase their dreams, no matter the obstacles. It wasn't easy. Late nights blurred into early mornings, and I poured myself into my studies, often running on sheer willpower. I prayed through my worries, studied through my exhaustion, and held on through life's storms. Then, unexpectedly, Selena enrolled in the same school. I wasn't prepared for the challenges that would follow. The tension started quietly, almost unnoticeably, with subtle shifts in how staff and professors interacted with me. But one instructor, an English professor whose class I took online, soon made her disdain unmistakably clear. She accused me, wrongly, of using Otter.ai to transcribe a Teams meeting without permission. Despite clear evidence disproving her claim, she refused to back down. After I confronted her, and filed a complaint against her she began isolating me from the class. I was barred from group activities, directed to submit assignments via pre-recorded videos, and excluded from class links that were shared with other students. This meant I often missed assignment instructions or deadlines, putting me at a disadvantage through no fault of my own. This isolation grew even starker as the semester went on. I had no issues with any of my other courses; she was the only professor who treated me this way. When the time came for my final exam, she withheld the link to submit my final speech. Despite my perfect record in her class and the effort I had poured into my studies, she unfairly gave me a "C" instead of the "A" I had earned. The experience was devastating. My honor roll status and GPA were almost tarnished, a painful blow after all I had sacrificed. I took a semester off to appeal the injustice, expecting some support from the college, but they dismissed my complaints outright. Eventually, I was removed as a student without explanation or follow-up on my concerns. Heartbroken, I knew I needed a break, both for my mental health and to rebuild my strength. But I wasn't done. This was a fight I would take up again one day.

In the meantime, I was ready for the next phase of my life. The alarm was set for 3 AM, but my body didn't trust it. I couldn't risk oversleeping. There was too much at stake, too much riding on the next few hours. I slid under my black comforter, sinking into the plush red pillows that seemed to cradle me after such a long day. But the comfort I felt in that moment was more than physical—it was the feeling of being on the edge of something important, something that could change everything. I was lying on the precipice of success, yet facing a challenge greater than anything I had known.

As I stared up at the ceiling, the words of Eric Thomas echoed in my head like a mantra, "When you want to succeed as bad as you want to breathe, then you'll be successful." I had listened to him for years, his voice pushing me forward on days I wanted to give up. And now, on the cusp of a new beginning, those words circled my mind like an anthem. I couldn't shake them: "When you want to succeed as bad as you want to breathe…" It wasn't just a motivational quote anymore; it was a truth I lived. Success, at this moment, wasn't a distant dream or an abstract idea. It was a necessity. The hunger for it was as vital as oxygen.

However, before I could succeed, I had to make a choice—get up or stay in the comfort of my bed. It sounds simple, but the weight of that decision felt heavier than it should. I had been through a lot over the past years—facing the challenges of life during the pandemic, isolating from people, and questioning what came next. As the world slowly reopened, I wondered if I was ready to step back into it. The temptation to linger in the warmth of the bed was strong, and not just because of how cozy it was. That bed represented a safe space. In those moments, I was living inside of a tent and it was my sanctuary, where the fears of rejection, failure, and doubt couldn't touch me.

However, that day was different. I had a job interview with a private company to work as a cook at St. Louis Community College—my first since the false accusations arose in 2017, and then there was the pandemic, which turned everyone's life upside down. I imagined. It was my chance after the pandemic, a glimmer of hope in the aftermath of years spent isolated and unsure. The excitement of the opportunity warred with the nerves creeping in, reminding me that nothing was guaranteed. I was walking into the unknown, and part of me wasn't ready.

As I lay there, awake long before the alarm could go off, I couldn't help but ask myself: Am I really ready for this? Could I re-enter the world after so much time away? Could I face people again? The questions swirled in my mind, each one pushing me closer to staying in bed. It was comfortable here. I could stay hidden, shielded from failure, disappointment, and false accusations. But that voice, Eric Thomas's voice, echoed once more: "When you want to succeed as bad as you want to breathe…"

And just like that, I knew what I had to do.

I threw the covers off, the cool air of the early morning hitting me like a wake-up call. Comfort had its place, but it wouldn't get me where I needed to go. Not today. I had to push through the hesitation, the doubts, the lingering fears that whispered in the back of my mind. Success demanded action. It required me to face the discomfort head on, to step out of the warmth of what was easy and into the unknown of what was possible.

I got dressed in the stillness of the morning, my mind racing but my movements steady. This was a new beginning, a fresh start. It wasn't just about landing the job—it was about showing up for myself. Proving that no matter how hard the road had been, no matter how many times I'd been knocked down, I still had the strength to rise.

The interview came, and with it, a mix of anxiety and excitement. But what struck me most wasn't the outcome or even the nerves. It was the realization that I had support—people in my corner, lifting me up, whether they were physically there or not. I felt that encouragement in every step I took that day, from the moment I left my bed to the moment I walked into the interview room.

But it wasn't just people. It was that bed too, in a way. It sounds strange, but that bed had been my place of refuge, a space where I'd cried, doubted, and, yes, dreamed. It was where I'd found comfort on my hardest days. And now, stepping out of it, I realized it wasn't the bed itself I was leaving behind—it was the safety it represented. The safe space had served its purpose, but now I needed to move beyond it.

As I reflected on the journey that led me to that day, I realized something even more important: success isn't just about ambition. It's about the people who support you, the spaces that allow you to recharge, and the moments of quiet reflection when you decide to keep moving forward.

I had spent so long thinking that success was a solo journey, something I had to fight for on my own. But the truth was, I hadn't done it alone.

Even in my quietest, loneliest moments, I had support—whether it was from the words of a speaker like Eric Thomas, the silent comfort of my bed, or the friends and family who had stood by me, reminding me that I wasn't in this fight by myself. But it sure as hell felt like it.

There was a storm coming and I could feel it.

Yahkhahnahn Ammi

Amid homelessness and the destruction of my mother's home, I faced the hardest battle of all—fighting doubt and fear while stranded by a church that refused to help, despite preaching compassion.

Success wasn't just a goal anymore—it was a necessity, and the hardest part was deciding whether to leave the comfort of my bed or stay hidden from the world outside. The storm that uprooted trees in St. Louis felt like an omen of the upheaval in my life, as everything I knew was falling apart. The storm left my mother's house in ruins, with rainwater leaking through the roof and the power cut off. It wasn't just her home that was destroyed—it felt like the foundation of our lives had cracked.

In the midst of the chaos, my mother called me, her voice trembling. I was already struggling myself, homeless and trying to make it through nursing school. There wasn't much I could offer, but I knew I had to help. The church she had devoted her life to had turned a blind eye, leaving her without aid. I didn't have the luxury to linger in my own troubles—I had to step up, even though I had barely anything to give.

I scrambled together the last of my emergency funds and made plans to travel to Lansing, Michigan, where I became a member of APOC Ministries, and I hoped to find help. It was led by Eric Thomas. I had listened to him for years, his words driving me forward when I felt I had nothing left. He preached about helping the homeless, the fatherless, the widows—the very people we were. I booked a ticket and prayed for a miracle.

However, when I arrived in Lansing, that miracle never came.

The funds on my CashApp card froze, leaving me stranded at Amtrak station. I had no food, no money, and nowhere to go. Desperately, I reached out to a cousin and she sent me an Uber. I tried to reach the church, even camping on their property, hoping for a sign of help. But instead of compassion, one of the Pastors ordered the church staff to have me removed for trespassing. I was met with the coldness of the police, because the White security guard lied and said I had a weapon. Some of the church staff joined in by adding that I had a warrant for my arrest.

These were all lies, and I could not believe the hell I had been subjected to. I was asked to leave under threat of being arrested by the police for trespassing, the church that preached love and support turned me away. Luggage and tent in hand, I was forced to walk four hours back to the Amtrak train station in Lansing, Michigan from La Grange, Michigan.

I made it back just in time for my scheduled college tour at Michigan State University. While there, some local students invited me to attend a public speaking event by Eric Thomas, scheduled for that evening at 7:00 P.M. I saw it as the perfect opportunity to confront him about how his church had treated me when I desperately sought help.

When the event began, Eric Thomas didn't show up. Instead, the same pastor who had called the police on me was there in his place. He spotted me and immediately tried to criminalize me again, as if seeking help had been a crime.

I was left homeless and hungry in a city I didn't know, abandoned by the very people I had looked to for help. Nights were spent sleeping in a tent outside the station, washing up in public restrooms just to maintain some sense of dignity. The rejection from the church stung deeply. I had come for refuge, but instead, I found more closed doors.

Once again, I was met with silence. No help came. I returned home, crushed by the weight of repeated rejection. Returning to St. Louis felt like defeat, but I refused to give up. Back in St. Louis, my mother's situation grew more desperate. She was still without power, water, or any way to repair the damage. I had no funds to give her, but I reached out to my network, hoping someone could help. I connected her with contractors and eventually, we met with an insurance adjuster who had been holding her checks hostage. We met at a Chili's in North County, the tension so thick it felt suffocating. My mother and the adjuster clashed, but I kept them focused, mediating their disputes. After what seemed like hours, the adjuster finally agreed to release her money.

My mother had contractors lined up to give estimates for repairs on her house. As we were en route to her home, another contractor called—a referral from a friend I had reached out to for help. He was on his way over to begin the repairs. My little sister let him inside while my mother and I were still on the road. A contractor from Spire, the gas company, had also scheduled a visit to inspect the gas leak my mother had been complaining about for weeks.

When we finally arrived, the first contractor was already in the kitchen, getting to work. I decided to step into my youngest brother's bedroom to wait until the Spire contractor finished outside. A few minutes later, I met the gas contractor by the door and walked with him around the property as he checked the source of the leak. Afterward, I let him and my mother handle things inside while I returned to my brother's room. I decided to stay overnight.

Just as I thought we had turned a corner, something unthinkable happened. Sometime while I was asleep, at least one of the contractors wandered through the house. The next morning, as I prepared to leave, my mother sat down in the living room.

Her purse, which had been in plain view the night before, was still there—but the $3,000 in cash she had kept inside was gone. Her voice cracked with panic as she confided in me about the missing money. Tears filled her eyes, and she cried hysterically, overwhelmed by the loss. My Sister came to comfort her. Seeing her like that hurt deeply. I tried to comfort her, but she was inconsolable, refusing to calm down or accept my words.

The pain of seeing my mother in such distress was unbearable. I asked her to call me if the money turned up and left her alone with my sister to help our mother compose herself. I contacted my brothers and told them what had transpired.

Immediately, I reached out to the friend who had referred the contractor. I asked if his guy could have been responsible for taking the money. He didn't think so but said he'd try to ask subtly. The only other person who had been there was the Spire contractor. I felt lost, unsure of what to do next, so I called my brothers, hoping one of them had stopped by the house overnight. None of them had.

We searched every corner of the house, retracing my mother's footsteps, but the money was gone. With no leads and no answers, I left and caught the bus, my mind reeling.

Yahkhahnahn Ammi

Then, the accusation came. I was blindsided when I got a text from one of my brothers: "*Mom thinks you took the money, if you did, just return it.*" I wanted to snap, but instead I froze, my heart sinking. I had sacrificed everything to help her, given all I had, and now my own mother was accusing me of stealing from her? The shock cut deeper than anything I had ever experienced. This was the woman who had stood by me through so much—how could she believe this about me?

Four days later, she confronted me by phone through a text directly. Her words hit me like a hammer, shattering whatever was left of my strength. I fell to my knees and cried, overwhelmed by the betrayal. Our relationship had always been fragile, but I never thought it would come to this. I had prayed for healing, but all I found was pain.

Her accusations spiraled out of control. She didn't just think I'd taken the money—she believed I had stolen a fur coat, video games, and even a jar of coins. None of it made sense, but the weight of her words crushed me. I had fought for her, protected her, and now I was being painted as a thief.

In the end, I wrote her two letters. One was a plea, a reassurance that I had not stolen anything from her, that I still loved her despite the accusations. The other was a demand—a request that she stop defaming my name, stop accusing me of things I hadn't done. She never responded.

* * *

Personal Life Lesson Reflections

In this chapter of my life, it taught me that seeking help doesn't always yield the support you expect, but that doesn't mean you stop asking. There's a certain vulnerability in reaching out— trusting that others will see your pain and respond with compassion. When that trust is broken, as it was with the church, the disappointment cuts deep, especially when it comes from a place you believe in. I learned that sometimes, the people and institutions we look for guidance and aid may not deliver, and we have to be prepared for that reality.

In those moments, the temptation to lash out in anger or shut down completely is strong. But what I realized is that growth often comes from these disappointments. I had to confront the fact that not everyone who preaches compassion practices it. I had to stand firm in my own beliefs, knowing that my integrity would carry me through, even when I felt criminalized for simply needing help.

Perhaps the most important lesson was this: when you face rejection, the answer isn't to close yourself off, but to continue seeking the support you need, even if it comes from unexpected places. You can't let the actions of a few break your spirit or define your self-worth. My strength came from realizing that the only way forward was to keep moving, keep asking, and above all, keep believing that better days would come.

Yahkhahnahn Ammi

Takeaways

Rejection doesn't define your worth

When the people or institutions you trust turn their backs on you, it's easy to feel betrayed or even criminalized for your struggles. Remember, rejection reflects them, not you.

Compassion isn't always found where you expect

Sometimes the places we assume will offer support—like a church—don't live up to that promise. But help and kindness can come from unexpected sources. Stay open to it.

Confront adversity with grace, not bitterness

It is natural to want to respond to betrayal with anger, but there is power in choosing grace. Holding on to your integrity in the face of disappointment allows you to rise above the situation.

Keep seeking support

Just because one door closes doesn't mean others won't open. Don't give up on finding the help you need. Your persistence in seeking support is a testament to your strength.

Stand firm in your truth

When others try to diminish or misrepresent you, don't let their actions shake your confidence. Trust in who you are and let that guide you through adversity.

CHAPTER 27

Keep Ya Head Up

"A Change Is Gonna Come" – Sam Cooke

When life knocked me down, I learned that the true test of strength lies not in avoiding the fall, but in the relentless determination to rise again.

I could never forget the day I hit rock bottom. It was February 2017, the most devastating time of my life, when I lost custody of my children. I nearly gave up on life—I struggled to cope with the loss, the lies, and the allegations against me. It felt like I was in the ring with Mike Tyson, knocked down again and again, until I found myself lying there, staring at the sky, helpless.

I didn't know where to turn. The February air was heavy with despair, mirroring the weight in my chest as I sat alone in my small tent, the silence deafening after the judge's final gavel. The words echoed in my mind: "Custody lost." In that moment I was left staring at the ceiling, wondering how much more I could endure. Every day was a battle. My body betrayed me as I spiraled into depression, my once fit frame ballooning under the weight of sorrow and stress. At 230 pounds, each step was a reminder of how far I had fallen, not just physically, but in every aspect of my life.

Yahkhahnahn Ammi

I didn't recognize the man in the mirror—the one who struggled to breathe, who moved with a heaviness that wasn't just physical. The nights were the worst. I'd lie awake, the darkness pressing down on me, my thoughts spiraling into a pit of despair. How did it come to this? The church and the synagogue turned its back on me and offered no solace. I felt abandoned, not just by the institutions that were supposed to offer comfort, but by God Himself.

The judicial system forced me into EMASS, a domestic violence program for assaulting Francine—a crime I didn't commit. I had to catch buses, walk for miles to attend, and even hitchhike because I had no car. The system was relentless, and the program only deepened my trauma. I had to lie, to say I hurt her, when it was the other way around. It tore me apart, but I had no choice. I had not had any infractions with law enforcement in over 20 years, except for a traffic ticket. I was finally getting my life together until I ran into the crabs in the barrel, people that hated to see me or others succeed in life. I was homeless, jobless, and separated from my children—Prince Avatar and Princess Tiana, my heart and soul, were taken from me. The accusations, the lies—they crushed me, and I didn't know how to fight back. It was as if the world had conspired to break me, and I was powerless to stop it.. My health deteriorated. I was diagnosed with type 2 diabetes, despite being a vegan.

I sought a second opinion, learned about my pre-diabetic state, and realized my diet was part of the problem. But exercising was nearly impossible with my back injury, arthritis, and asthma. My body was failing me, just as everything else had. However, even as my body grew weaker, a fire sparked within me.

I started small, with the only thing I had left—my voice. I took to the streets, not with protests, but with podcasts. My voice, once silenced by fear and oppression, now reached ears across the world.

Each episode was a step, each word a breath of life into my weary soul. I talked about pain, about loss, about finding the strength to keep going when everything seemed lost. As I spoke to others, guiding them through their darkness, I found my own path illuminated.

The words of 2Pac played in my mind: "Keep Ya Head Up." And so, I did, not because the world demanded it, but because I finally believed I was worth the fight. My journey wasn't just about survival anymore; it was about finding purpose in the pain, about using my story to help others navigate their own struggles. I began to exercise, taking control of my life one step at a time. The weight began to drop, and with it, the fog in my mind started to lift. Writing became my sanctuary. I poured my thoughts and pain onto paper, finding a small measure of peace in the process. It wasn't much, but it was a start.

I had trust issues. Positive male role models were scarce, and those around me had their own battles to fight. Who would want to hear about my problems when they were drowning on their own? It felt like the world was telling me, "You got yourself into this mess, so get yourself out of it." As harsh as that sounded, it was the reality I faced. I dug myself deep into a hole, and it seemed there was no way out. Counseling sessions and psychotropic medication became a lifeline, though I resisted at first. But I knew if I didn't find a way to manage my anger, frustration, and despair, it would all spill out in the worst way possible. I started exercising more, eating less, and taking control of my life one step at a time. Lost and desperate, I found myself drawn to the quiet corners of a mosque, seeking peace in the rhythmic chants of prayers that echoed through the halls. The brothers welcomed me, offering a sense of community I hadn't felt in a long time. But it wasn't enough. The peace I sought eluded me, slipping through my fingers like sand. My mind was unraveling, and I sought refuge in food, each bite a temporary balm to the pain that gnawed at my soul. But I couldn't run forever.

The day came when I found myself sitting in a psychiatrist's office, the sterile walls closing in around me. I didn't want to be there, didn't want to admit that I needed help. But the alternative was unthinkable. I was on the edge, teetering between life and something far darker, and I knew that if I didn't reach out, I might never find my way back. "I feel like I'm drowning," I confessed, my voice barely a whisper. The psychiatrist nodded; her eyes filled with a kindness I hadn't seen in a long time.

"We're going to work through this together," she said, and for the first time in months, I felt a flicker of hope.

However, the system wasn't done with me yet. In America, there's a system that purports to protect the welfare of children but instead traps millions—both rich and poor—in a cycle of debt, despair, and powerlessness.

The child support system, as it stands today, is a revenue-generating machine that spares no one. From the courtroom to my own tent I had been reduced to because of these atrocities, this system ensnares families and forces them into an endless loop of punishment, stripping away dignity and freedom.

For ten years, I was a single father, raising my two children after my marriage ended. I devoted myself to providing for them, trying to navigate a life where I could be the best parent. But despite my efforts and love, the child support system found a way to entangle me in its web—a web that was not just about money but about control and punishment. One day, without warning, I was placed on child support. No child support court hearing, no assessment of my ability to pay, and no consideration for my youngest son from another relationship. The system didn't care that I was already struggling to make ends meet.

They didn't care that finding work was difficult, thanks to the conspiracies that tried to silence me and destroy my name. All that mattered was that I was now a name on their list—a source of revenue. When I tried to renew my CDL Class A drivers' license in Missouri, I was blindsided. The Illinois DMV had a child support division, and they placed a hold on my license due to unpaid child support. Without that license, I couldn't work, couldn't drive, and couldn't earn the money to pay for the very child support they demanded. But that wasn't the worst of it. My passport was also restricted, barring me from traveling outside the country. I had a job opportunity in Ghana and Nigeria, one that would have helped me pay off my arrears. But the system wouldn't allow it. The pandemic hit, and I found myself trapped—not just in my own country, but in a system that refused to let me work my way out of debt. It was a cruel irony: the child support system that was supposed to ensure the welfare of my children had effectively stripped me of my ability to support them. My story is not unique. It's part of a broader, more insidious crisis in America's legal system—a crisis of fines and fees that disproportionately impacts so-called Black, (Melanated) poor and marginalized communities.

Yahkhahnahn Ammi

Despite clear guidelines from the Department of Justice urging courts to assess an individual's ability to pay, many courts continue to impose excessive fines and fees, ignoring constitutional protections. These practices trap individuals in cycles of debt and incarceration, much like the child support system traps parents—particularly melanated fathers—in endless financial obligations.

When I read the Department of Justice's "Dear Colleague" letter, which called on courts to ensure they were not violating the rights of citizens, (people) I couldn't help but think of my own situation. The letter emphasized that individuals should not be jailed for non-payment of fines and fees without first determining their ability to pay.

But that's exactly what has happened to me—and continues to happen to thousands of others across the country. Courts fail to enforce laws designed to protect Americans, particularly those who are most vulnerable.

Instead, they use fines and fees as a way to generate revenue, prioritizing the financial health of municipalities over the well-being of families. This is not just an issue of injustice—it is a public health crisis that perpetuates poverty and destabilizes communities. And it's not just people like me who are caught in this system.

Celebrities like Nas, Tyrese Gibson, and Kelly Clarkson have also been ensnared in the child support trap. Despite their wealth, they too have been brought to their knees by a system that seems designed to extract as much money as possible, with little regard for fairness or the actual needs of the child. Tyrese famously broke down in tears on social media, expressing the emotional and financial toll that child support was taking on him. Nas battled child support orders that placed immense strain on him financially. Even A-Rod and Kelly Clarkson were ordered to pay staggering amounts—sums that would bankrupt the average American. These cases reveal a dark truth: whether rich or poor, the child support system extracts resources without concern for the people it claims to serve. The funds collected don't always go to the children. A significant portion is siphoned off to fund government agencies, leaving only a fraction of the money for the custodial parent and child. In cases involving public assistance, states recoup the cost of providing aid by taking a portion of the child support payments. What remains, after administrative fees and other deductions, is often a small amount that hardly reflects the exorbitant sums extracted, But the world wasn't done testing me.

When COVID hit, the isolation deepened. The courts shut down, and I was completely cut off from my children. There were no visits, no phone calls, no contact whatsoever. It was worse than prison. I was trapped, not only by the pandemic but by a system that seemed determined to keep me from my family. Desperate to escape, I decided to leave the country. I booked a flight to Ghana, for work and to rebuild my life. But even that plan was foiled when I was told my passport was damaged, and later, that I couldn't get a replacement because I owed child support. The airlines did not tell me, but the real truth of the matter was that the child support agency, and the U.S. Department of State Passport agency collectively restricted my passport, which meant that I could not travel. How was I supposed to make money to pay my debts if I couldn't travel for work? Every attempt to pull myself out of the pit was met with another blow, and it felt like the world was against me. And yet, through it all, I was told to "keep ya head up."

Yahkhahnahn Ammi

After almost eight years without a job, because of the lies, things began to turn around. I completed an application and got hired with St. Louis City. When I first took on the role as a lifeguard for St. Louis City, I approached it with the same enthusiasm and dedication I had for all my previous jobs. It was a position that required vigilance and responsibility—qualities I'd honed over the years in various roles. But what I hadn't anticipated was how quickly the job I loved would turn into a source of relentless stress and discomfort, all because of one supervisor's malicious intent. My troubles began subtly. My hours were mysteriously cut, and I was often called in to work only to be sent home upon arrival, or told not to come in to work at all. Other occasions my supervisor argued that I did not confirm my work schedule, but I had and offered to show the text history between her and I that I had communicated my availability but she refused to acknowledge it. These actions seemed more like attempts to undermine my confidence than legitimate work adjustments. Then came the probing questions—ones that had no bearing on my ability to perform my duties.

"Were you an Uber driver before?" my supervisor asked me one day, her tone dripping with condescension. When I inquired why it mattered, she simply walked away, leaving the question hanging in the air like a cloud of suspicion.

The situation escalated when she refused to give me a copy of my lifeguard certification, a document I requested and earned through the American Red Cross. Her reasoning was clear: she wanted to tether me to that job, to make it impossible for me to find work elsewhere. It was illegal for her to withhold that certification, but she didn't care. The power she wielded was enough to make my work life unbearable, and I was left to choose between staying in a hostile environment or leaving a job I once cherished. I chose to leave, and because I accepted another job working for the City of St. Louis.

It seems like for whatever reason, before things could get any better, they always got a little worse. When I resigned, I did so with the hope that a fresh start in another city department would be different, But it wasn't. It was not long before I found myself subjected to yet another round of unwarranted scrutiny. My new director at the job I accepted in my new role inside of the Neighborhood Stabilization Department seemed great except my director felt intimidated with my credentials and long history of being an activist and leader in the community. She had intentions of tearing me down and getting rid of me. I was made to undergo multiple background checks—an unprecedented demand for a simple departmental transfer.

No one else had been subjected to such invasive procedures. Why was I different? The answer became clearer with time: retaliation. I had raised safety concerns at work. I respectively made suggestions for change within my department that could prevent potential tragedies, new lawsuits against the city, and to protect my colleagues from dangerous conditions. Instead of acknowledging the validity of my concerns, my new director/supervisor retaliated with a campaign of harassment that culminated in my wrongful termination. She didn't even have the decency to tell me why I was being placed on forced leave. When she finally filed the termination papers, her claims were as false as they were shocking: I was accused of failing to use my legal name on my application and of having a criminal sexual assault in my background—both blatant lies.

It was at that moment, as I read the accusations against me, that I felt the weight of injustice pressing down on my shoulders. My name, my character, and my very identity were being smeared by those who were supposed to lead with integrity. But I refused to let their lies define me. I stood tall in the face of lies. Instead of succumbing to anger or despair, I focused on what I could control—my attitude and my response. I filed grievances, sent letters, and contacted Tishaura Jones, the Mayor of St. Louis City, who never responded. I pursued every legal avenue available to me. Although months went by and no one responded or contacted me after I filed the complaints. I knew that the truth was on my side, and I wasn't about to let their fabrications break me. Through it all, I held my head high, determined to maintain my dignity and integrity. The journey was grueling, filled with moments of doubt and frustration, but it was also a testament to my resilience.

In the end, I realized that while they could take my job, they couldn't take my spirit. The lies they spread only served to strengthen my resolve, reminding me that sometimes, the hardest battles are the ones that shape us the most. And though my time as a city employee ended in unfairness, it also marked the beginning of a new chapter—one where I would not be silenced, and where I would continue to stand tall, no matter the obstacles thrown my way.

My journey is far from over, but I've learned that strength doesn't lie in never falling—it lies in rising every time you do. I'm still standing, still fighting, and I'll keep my head up, not just for me, but for my children and everyone else who needs to see that it's possible to survive, to thrive, and be happy, even when the world seems determined to see you fail.

This chapter of my life taught me that true strength isn't just about pushing through the hard times; it's about acknowledging the hurt, the anger, and the despair, and choosing to keep moving forward anyway. I learned that I could be both strong and vulnerable, that asking for help didn't make me weak, and that sometimes the most powerful thing you can do is simply survive another day. But in my case, I had to 'Live or Die Tryin'.

There is no shame in falling down; the shame is in staying down. Life will throw its punches, and sometimes it will feel like you're being hit from all sides. But even in those moments, especially in those moments, you must dig deep and find the will to rise again.

My journey has been marked by setbacks and disappointments, but each one has made me more resilient, more determined to carve out a life for myself and my children that is defined not by our struggles, but by our triumphs over them. Life is relentless, and sometimes the challenges we face seem insurmountable. But no matter how dark it gets, there is always a light within you—a spark of resilience, of hope, of determination—that can guide you through the storm. Your circumstances do not define you; your response to them does.

So, I keep my head up—not because the world tells me to, but because I know that despite everything, I am stronger than I ever imagined.

* * *

Yahkhahnahn Ammi

Personal Life Lesson Reflections

In this chapter, looking back on this chapter of my life, I realize it was more than just a series of unfortunate events—it was a crucible that forged me into a person I never imagined I could become.

The pain, the injustice, the endless obstacles—they all served to strip away the layers of fear, doubt, and self-pity that had built up over the years. What was left was a raw, unfiltered version of myself, forced to confront my deepest vulnerabilities and find strength in the midst of overwhelming adversity. I had lost everything—I did not have anything left to lose, these experiences stripped away my fears and doubts.

One of the most profound lessons I learned is that resilience isn't about never falling—it's about rising every time you do. Life will knock you down, sometimes so hard that you're left gasping for air, unsure if you have the strength to stand again. *"When life knocks you down, try to land on your back. Because if you can look up, you can get up. Let your reason get you back up."* – Les Brown. But it's in those moments, when everything seems lost, that you discover the true depth of your inner strength. The key is to keep moving forward, no matter how small the steps, no matter how hopeless the situation might seem.

I also learned that asking for help is not a sign of weakness. Society often tells us that to be strong, we must face our battles alone, but that couldn't be further from the truth. It takes immense courage to admit when you're struggling and to reach out for support. In doing so, you open yourself up to healing, to growth, and to the possibility of finding a way through the darkness. The system that was designed to break me only taught me persistence and the importance of fighting for justice, even when the odds are stacked against you. It reminded me that the battle isn't just about surviving, but about changing the systems that oppress so many others. My story isn't over, and neither is yours. We are all still writing the pages of our lives, and within each of us is the power to turn our darkest moments into stories of triumph.

Takeaways

You are stronger than you think

No matter how hard life gets, remember that within you lies a reservoir of strength, resilience, and determination. When faced with adversity, it's okay to acknowledge your pain—but never lose sight of your power to rise above it.

Adversity can be a catalyst for growth

Hardship isn't just something to survive; it's something that can shape you into a better, stronger version of yourself. Use your struggles to fuel your growth and find purpose in your pain.

Seek help when you need it

Asking for help doesn't make you weak—it's a sign of strength. Sometimes, the bravest thing you can do is admit that you can't do it alone.

Keep your head up

Not because it's easy, but because you owe it to yourself to see just how far your strength can take you. Believe in your ability to overcome, to adapt, and to thrive, no matter how impossible the odds may seem. Your story, like mine, is still being written, and it holds the potential for greatness, no matter where you are right now.

If there's one message I want to impart to you, it's this….. You are stronger than you think. Life will throw challenges your way that seem insurmountable, but within you lies a reservoir of strength, resilience, and determination that you might not even realize exists.

When faced with adversity, remember that it's okay to feel broken, to acknowledge your pain—but never lose sight of your power to rise above it. The journey through hardship is not just about surviving; it's about using those experiences to grow, to become more than you were before.

It's about finding purpose in your pain and using that purpose to forge a path forward, not just for yourself, but for others who may be walking a similar road. Your struggles do not define you—your response to them does.

CHAPTER 28

9/11 Chaos and Heartache

"Don't Want to Miss a Thing"-Aerosmith

On the 23rd anniversary of 9/11, as the world mourned, my personal battle for my children's future reached a breaking point.

It was September 11, 2024—23 years after the day that changed the world. The country paused to remember, honoring those lost and the resilience that followed. But on that same day, I faced a crisis of my own, one that would forever alter my life.

A missed call and text from Ms. Bias, the Deputy Juvenile Officer who had managed my visitation for years, felt like another reminder of the barriers standing between me and my children. Ms. Bias was more than just a court official; she was a constant presence in the strained relationship between me and my kids. From the very start, she had supported Selena's agenda, subtly but steadily aligning herself against me and my rights as a father. This wasn't the first time I had been kept in the dark about important matters, but what I was about to learn cut deeper than I had imagined.

Yahkhahnahn Ammi

When I called her back, she told me that my son, Prince, had been hospitalized for four days. Four days of my son fighting an undiagnosed illness, and I hadn't been informed. Selena knew. Ms. Bias knew. Yet I, his father, had been left out. Prince was at Cardinal Glennon's Transitional Care Unit, struggling with a condition that even doctors couldn't diagnose. As her words sunk in, I felt an overwhelming sense of anger, hurt, and betrayal. How could they have kept this from me?

This wasn't an isolated event—it was part of a long-standing pattern. Selena had spent years using her influence over Ms. Bias and the family court system to keep me at a distance, controlling every detail of my relationship with my children. But what fueled this behavior was her own life's instability. Once again, she had been evicted, forced to move from one temporary living arrangement to another. My children were being dragged from hotel to hotel, sometimes left in the care of her mother, rather than with me—their father. Selena had promised me, and them, that they could stay with me. She said it was the best choice, considering her situation, but these were empty words. When it came time to follow through, she always found an excuse to break her promises.

Just days before, she had reluctantly agreed to let them stay with me. But when I arrived to pick up their things, Selena didn't meet me halfway. Instead, she sent down garbage bags of their belongings at her latest hotel. My daughter's clothes were crammed into the bags, unwashed, some smelling of mildew. My son's essentials were scattered, while my daughter, Princess Tiana, had more supplies for her emotional support cat than clothing. I was stunned. This was how she "prepared" for her children to stay with their father? It felt less like co-parenting and more like neglect. Yet, when I brought it up, Selena remained silent, focused only on what she could control.

The next morning, I took my daughter to school, determined to establish some normalcy in her life. We shared breakfast in the kitchen, and she even made sack lunches for herself, for me, and for her brother. I wanted her to feel stability, if only for a moment. After dropping her off, I spoke with the school staff—the social worker, the principal, and the counselor—explaining that I was her father and had a right to be part of their education. For years, Selena had kept me in the dark, going so far as to keep me off the school's registry, citing her own "concerns" and insisting on complete control. But I wasn't there to argue. I was there to advocate for my kids.

I arranged transportation with the Students In Transition department and conferenced Ms. Bias on the line with the school's administration. I thought it was a successful meeting. The school staff understood my situation, acknowledging the years of withheld information and Selena's efforts to alienate me from my children's lives. They added me to the registrar and agreed to inform me of anything related to my children's needs and accomplishments. It felt like a small victory—a crack in the wall Selena had built between me and my children.

Ms. Bias called Selena to inform her and even that small progress set her off. Selena, furious at my involvement, claimed I was trying to withdraw our children from school, going so far as to accuse me of "violating the court order." She spread these lies to Ms. Bias, and to the school administration, casting doubt and stirring suspicion, just as she'd done time and time again. All along it was

Yahkhahnahn Ammi

Selena who had tried to transfer them to another district—specifically **Hazelwood High School**, her alma mater without informing them or me. I had the documents from the school administration to prove it. And that wasn't the end of it. Selena went to the hospital, telling staff there were court orders barring Prince from being discharged to my care, a blatant fabrication. The nurses wouldn't share any information with me, leaving me to piece together whatever details I could about his condition. I had hoped to be there for him, to comfort him and support him. But once again, Selena's control had built a wall.

And all the while, she kept her focus on what she could gain financially. Although she received military benefits, government assistance, and child support, she continually claimed she didn't have enough to care for the children. Despite this, she refused my help. During visitations, I wasn't even allowed to provide them with food. She would often go through Ms. Bias, ordering her to enforce restrictions, leaving me helpless to provide the basics. This time, her manipulation came at the cost of our son's health, and I couldn't stand by any longer.

The final blow came when Selena tried to weaponize her latest lie: she insisted that Prince be released only to her, and when the hospital staff complied, I was left standing there, helpless. After hours of waiting, the truth began to unravel. She hadn't prioritized his well-being; she had once again prioritized control. And this time, the stakes were higher than they had ever been.

As I drove home, frustration boiled over. How many more obstacles would I face just to be a father to my children? How long would I be forced to fight for the smallest moments with them? Every time I made progress, Selena found a way to pull me back, leaving me questioning just how much longer this could go on. Yet one thing remained clear: I wasn't giving up.

No matter how many lies, manipulations, or roadblocks, I would be there for my children.

As I reflect on this journey, it tears at my heart to know that Selena continues to escape accountability for her actions. In previous chapters, I shared that she has three other children, two of whom live primarily with their father. Yet, for reasons that remain a mystery, she denies me the right to fully parent our children, Prince Avatar and Princess Tiana, using every legal and emotional barrier within her grasp. Recently, she allowed unsupervised weekend visits with our children—glimpses of normalcy that brought joy and connection. But just as suddenly, she stopped those visits without explanation, leaving our children, now seventeen and sixteen, hurt and confused.

I watched helplessly as Selena's manipulation and intimidation tactics took their toll. My children have grown up under her threats and her punishments, conditioned to believe that reaching out to me could lead to my arrest, fearing consequences that should never rest on their young shoulders. In truth, they don't realize the rights they hold. In Missouri, they are old enough to make certain choices independently: they could even take a job or, if they wanted, visit me freely. But Selena's power to instill fear runs deep, a tactic honed by her years in the military, used to isolate them from my family and from the experiences they deserve.

Selena's motivations, whatever they may be, have long been supported by our Deputy Juvenile Officer, Ms. Bias. Together, they present a united front in court, constructing a carefully

Yahkhahnahn Ammi

managed appearance when it serves them, allowing just enough contact to avoid scrutiny. But the truth remains: the very actions that keep me apart from my children are what bring them the most harm. It is our children who suffer the most under these tactics, manipulated to believe they have no voice, no right to choose, and no say in their relationships.

So to my children, and to others who may feel trapped by similar circumstances, I want you to know this: **you have rights.** As young adults, you are stepping into your own autonomy, your own ability to make choices and decide what you value in your life. You have the right to reach out, to speak up, and to be heard. Speak to your school counselors, to social workers, to adults who can listen and advocate for you. Let them know how you feel, and remember that your voice has power. You deserve to know your family on both sides and to experience the love that is waiting for you.

To Prince Avatar and Princess Tiana: no matter how far the distance, or how long this struggle continues, I will always be here. I will always fight for you, even when the odds seem insurmountable. I am proud of you both, and I know that as you grow, you'll find your way and your strength. Selena's tactics may keep us apart today, but the bond we share is something she can never sever. You are stronger than you know, and you are loved more than words can say.

And if there is one truth that I have learned from this journey, it is that love, even when tested, remains unbreakable. I know that one day, when the time is right, we will find our way back to each other.

* * *

Personal Life Lesson Reflections

In this chapter, as I look back on this chapter of my life, it's clear that love isn't always enough to bridge the distance created by manipulation, falsehoods, or the failures of an imperfect system. Despite my efforts, I learned that the road to reclaiming my place in my children's lives would be full of obstacles, many of which would test the very core of who I am. Yet, amid the battles and heartbreak, I also discovered the depth of my resilience and the lengths a parent will go to remain present in their children's lives.

One of the hardest lessons I had to learn was that love, when tested, often requires relentless persistence. Being there for my children meant showing up despite repeated rejections and false accusations. This journey showed me that, sometimes, being a parent isn't just about being there for the joyful moments; it's about staying committed in the darkest times, when everything seems stacked against you. Persistence became my strength, the fuel that kept me going when the walls around me felt insurmountable.

Navigating family courts and other institutional systems was eye-opening, particularly as a father fighting for equal involvement. It's easy to feel powerless in the face of systems that seem biased or inflexible, but that's precisely when I learned the importance of self-advocacy. Speaking up, documenting everything, and ensuring my presence at every critical moment became essential to reclaiming my voice. For any parent caught in a similar situation, know this: even when you feel unheard, don't allow the system to silence you. Your persistence can, and will, make a difference over time.

Yahkhahnahn Ammi

Family alienation is painful beyond words, especially when your children are the ones feeling its impact. Throughout these years, I saw the ways in which the tension between their mother and me left scars on them. I learned that, sometimes, the best way to fight alienation is to model love and consistency for my children. I had to learn to let go of certain expectations and focus on rebuilding trust and connection through small moments, like cooking breakfast together, dropping them off at school, or simply being there to listen. These little acts of love, though small, reminded them—and me—that our bond could withstand strain.

For years, I wrestled with frustration over things beyond my control: false accusations, withheld information, and broken promises. It's a hard pill to swallow, but I realized that trying to control what others do or don't do only drains energy better spent on what I *can* control—showing up, being consistent, and focusing on my relationship with my children. Accepting this doesn't make the situation easier, but it brings a sense of peace. It reminded me that true strength comes from resilience, not resistance.

Takeaways

This chapter of my life may seem like one father's struggle, but the lessons extend beyond me, and I hope they resonate with anyone fighting for justice, respect, or simply a place in the lives of those they love. If you find yourself up against a system or circumstance that feels immovable, remember these lessons:

Never underestimate the power of consistency. Even when it feels like nothing is changing, showing up again and again—without bitterness or resentment—is a powerful testament to love and commitment.

Stay true to your values. In battles where everything feels unfair, it's easy to get lost in anger or frustration. Instead, focus on staying true to your values and what matters most.

Don't give up on hope. Alienation and separation are painful, but hope, however fragile, is often the bridge that allows healing to begin. Hold on to it, even if it's just a small thread.

This chapter reminded me that the road may be long and filled with struggles, but the fight for family, for connection, and for justice is always worth it. If anything, it taught me that in the end, the love we give is what shapes us—and that is something no one can ever take away.

EPILOGUE

As I close this chapter of my life, I reflect on the journey that has brought me to this moment. Writing "Live or Die Tryin'" has been a cathartic experience, allowing me to revisit the highs and lows of my life with a newfound perspective.

Nothing could have prepared me for the events that followed. After all of that past drama, both Francine and Selena conjured another plan to seal my fate by writing letters to the judges prior to my actual court dates:

January 25th, 2017

Dear Honorable Judge Thomas C. Clark/ Honorable Judge Robert A. Ward,

I am writing in regards the children, Princess Tiana and Prince Avatar, and the Respondent, Yahkhahnahn Ammi, also known as Perrie Danielle Gibson, AKA Yah Ammi, in case #1522-FC00118. This violent con artist attacked me viciously in front of his two children on December 25, 2016! He tried to kill me with his fists. To this day, I suffer from multiple injuries: bruising and cuts on my head, bruising and pain in my face, legs, knees, back, and neck. He assaulted me as I screamed for help, begging him to stop.

His children were in the next room, awake but silent. This murderous con artist jumped on me fatally in front of his two children on Dec. 25, 2016!

I fear for the children's safety! Yah Ammi is psychotic! He jumped on me then calmly gathered his children and some of his belongings together to leave. He also stole my cell phone, my building's master keys, and some other personal items. Charges have been filed against Yah Ammi with the St. Louis City Metro P. D. the report number is CN# 16-064818. There is a warrant out for his arrest. He assaulted me after I gave his family shelter out of the snowy days of St. Louis's winter. Yah Ammi was living in his black Ford Explorer (Illinois license plates number Y000000) with Princess Tiana and Prince Avatar. He would sleep in parks with them in Tower Grove and other places along St. Louis. I witnessed the children's blankets and all of their belongings inside of his truck. Yah told me and showed how he laid the seats back; folded the blankets on top of the truck seats and lie down. I witnessed hair products, food and water inside of his truck that he lived in with his children. His family was guests in my home for 8 days. Every day he stayed; he became more and more verbally aggressive towards the children and me. I'd like you to know that he is armed with a felony according to his records in Illinois's Madison CO. Case #1995CF001623.

He and the children's behavior towards me were very peculiar. The children did not speak to me very much. I talked to them but got little responses from the children. When Yah assaulted me on Dec. 25th, 2016; the children did not respond to my cries for help. They did not cry or whimper or sound out at all! The children showed no signs of freight or fear while I cried out for help while their father beat me.

The children did not cry or ask their father to stop. I am not the first woman that Yahkhahnahn Ammi, AKA Perrie Gibson has assaulted me IN FRONT OF HIS CHILDREN.

They are desensitized to violence and think it is normal.

During their visit; I only saw him doing one educational activity with his children. He claims he is homeschooling them. He screamed and coerced them to draw one picture each as their logo. After he screamed at them to get the task done, Princess Tiana and Prince Avatar finally drew a picture. There were a few nights and mornings that the children were up very late at night and early in the morning unattended. Yah was sound asleep with the door closed. I questioned the children and their father. The children responded that this is a normal thing that they do. They are allowed to stay awake as long as they choose. And it's their choice if they sleep or not. Yah had no issues with them being awake in my home unattended as he slept. He provided no answers as to why he would sleep and leave his children unattended and awake. One day in particular, the children were awake while Yah slept on December 23rd, 2016 at 2 a.m. The Respondent, Yahkhahnahn Ammi AKA Perrie Gibson is the owner of this "home school" group "Freedom Home Scholar Academy" on Facebook and YouTube. The email is stlhomeschoolers@gmail.com. He has a corporation in Missouri, Black Lives Matter Inc, charter #0013-66335. This is not the type of person that should be leading homeschools or anything! This monster is twisted mentally and the children are endangered by their continued presence with Yahkhahnahn. The Respondent said he homeschooled his children. But I only saw him "teaching" or "educationally instructing" his children once.

He asked them to draw a logo with their colors and a sheet of paper. He screamed at them long enough until finally they colored one page apiece with a picture.

He was living in his truck with Princess Tiana and Prince Avatar since September 2016 when he was evicted with his case M-O-1622-AC03717. I allowed him to bring his family to my place; gave him keys to my place. As compensation, he brutally attacked me because I asked him to find new living arrangements!

Some days the Respondent and his children entered my home smelling horribly of marijuana. I do not know where they came from. They moved into my house on December 17th. During this time, he declared himself my tenant and property manager. Neither of which, I agreed upon or requested of him and I signed no binding contracts. I was helping a "friend" in need; so I thought. Since he did not have any money; he would help with any maintenance house issues. He asked to use my spot for temporary living. He told me that he could not afford his hotel weekly rates. And his grandmother was not allowing his children to stay with her anymore. I did not charge him to stay at my house. He charged me for two projects.

This man is a total opposite of the person that he portrays himself to be in deeds and words. I was quite fooled. But I was warned by a friend that he was a scammer. The Respondent preys on vulnerable women using his children as the scapegoat and prize. I wanted to help him because I thought he was taking care of his kids. After he revealed true diabolical self to me, I no longer wanted him in my space. He attacked me brutally when I asked him to move out!

Save Princess Tiana and Prince Avatar from their father, the Respondent! They are not safe. The children are numb and de-sensitized to his animalistic beatings. I am scared for them! HELP THEM!

Sincerely,

Francine Coldburn

* * *

Personal Life Lesson Reflections

In this chapter, in the midst of the chaos and turmoil that defined my relationship with Selena, there was one particularly deceitful act that stood out. It was a letter—a seemingly harmless piece of paper that carried with it a weight of betrayal and manipulation. This letter, crafted with cunning precision by both Francine, an actor with political ties and Selena, was a tool designed to deceive, to manipulate the truth, and to undermine my role as a father.

It all began when Selena and I were locked in a contentious battle over the custody and care of our children. The tension between the three of us had reached a boiling point, and it seemed that every interaction was fraught with anger and mistrust. Selena, desperate to gain the upper hand, devised a plan to paint me as an unfit father. She knew that the court system was often biased against fathers, and Francine wanted to paint me as a woman beater, they were determined to use that to their advantage.

The letter was their weapon. It was written in a tone that was both pleading and accusatory, designed to evoke sympathy and paint me as a villain. In it, Francine claimed that I was neglectful, abusive, and that I had no interest in the well-being of my children. With the help of Selena feeding Francine lies, and the full names of our children along with my full birth and spiritual name none of which Francine had previous knowledge of. Francine and Selena twisted the truth, turning my struggles as a single father into evidence of my supposed incompetence.

What made the letter truly insidious was that it wasn't just a simple statement. It was supported by fabricated evidence—false claims, distorted facts, and outright lies. Francine, was the true marijuana and cigarette chain smoker, but wanted to project that as my lifestyle. Especially since I never indulged in either.

Selena and Francine had gone to great lengths to create a narrative that would support their claims, and they were confident that the court would believe them over me. When I first read the letter they crafted, I noticed it was written two weeks after I publicly exposed Francine on Facebook for deliberately exposing men to sexually transmitted diseases, I was stunned. The words on the page were a stark contrast to the reality of my life. I had always done my best to be a good father, to provide for my children and protect them from harm. But here, in black and white, was a version of events that painted me as a monster.

I knew I couldn't let this stand. The stakes were too high, and the truth was too important. I gathered every piece of evidence I could find to counter both Francine and Selena's claims. I dug up old photographs, school records, and testimonies from friends, colleagues and family who knew the truth. I worked tirelessly to build a case that would expose the lies in their letter and show the court who I really was—a loving father who had been doing his best under incredibly difficult circumstances. But the battle was far from easy. Because, I didn't even know this letter existed until my trial was long over. While Selena was relentless in her pursuit of custody, and Francine hell bent on ruining my life out of revenge for exposing her dirty little secrets, and to keep her lover Teddy who no doubt found out about her dealings behind his back. The letter was just one of many tactics they employed. Each time we went to court, Francine was there.

I felt like I was fighting an uphill battle against a system that was stacked against me. The letter that I had no idea about at the time hung over every proceeding like a dark cloud, a constant reminder of the deceit I was up against. Despite the odds, I refused to give up. I knew that the truth was on my side, and I was determined to fight for my children. I stood my ground, challenging every falsehood and presenting my evidence with conviction. And slowly, as our children grew older the tide began to turn over the years. The court started to see through Selena's lies, and the truth began to emerge. Even though the damage of parental alienation and the abuse our children suffered in silence all of those bitter years, because they dared to speak or act out against the circumstances and lies they suffered while in their mother's care. It was evident when their grades in school began to fail.

In the end, the letter and all of the lies that were meant to destroy me became a testament and revelation to write this memoir. It was a reminder of the lengths to which people will go when they are desperate, but also of the strength that lies in standing up for the truth. The battle for my children was long and painful, but it taught me the importance of integrity, perseverance, and the power of truth. It had been a long walk to freedom, but the journey was well worth it. Since the publication of this memoir, I have continued on my path of healing and self-discovery. I have embraced the lessons learned from my past and used them to shape my future. I am grateful for the opportunity to share my story with the world, and I hope that it serves as a source of inspiration and empowerment for others. As I move forward, I carry with me the strength and resilience that have guided me through the darkest moments of my life.

I am committed to living authentically and passionately, knowing that each day is a gift and an opportunity to make a difference. To all those who have supported me on this journey, thank you. Your love, encouragement, and belief in me have been a beacon of light during the darkest of times. I am forever grateful for your presence in my life. As I turn the final page of this memoir, I do so with a sense of peace and purpose. My story continues to unfold, and I am excited to see where the next chapter will take me.

With love and gratitude,

Yahkhahnahn Ammi

RESOURCES and FURTHER READINGS

The journey shared in *Live or Die Tryin'* is one of overcoming obstacles, deep pain, and discovering resilience. Throughout this journey, I found valuable resources that helped me stay grounded and continue pushing forward. This guide provides support, insights, and context that were instrumental in my story. Whether you are seeking personal development tools, mental health support, or inspiration, these resources may serve as valuable tools for your path.

Books to Explore

Speaker's Edge co-written by Craig Valentine and various authors

The Elements of Rhetoric written by Ryan N.S. Topping

Perrie Daniell Gibson's work aligns with the core themes of this memoir—perseverance, survival, and the search for justice. His books explore personal and collective challenges within the context of a modern, unjust world.

Live or Die Tryin' Book 1: Unbreakable Spirit

Available by contacting: pdgpublishingcompany.com

Live or Die Tryin' Book 2: An UnAmerican Dream

Available by contacting: pdgpublishingcompany.com

Live or Die Tryin' Book 3: My Journey to Freedom Forgiveness and Healing

Available by contacting: pdgpublishingcompany.com

Influential Figures

Terrie Williams

Renowned author, public relations expert, and mental health advocate, Terrie Williams emphasizes the importance of mental health, particularly in communities of color. Her work resonates deeply with the themes of resilience and recovery in *Live or Die Tryin'*.

Black Pain: It Just Looks Like We're Not Hurting – A profound exploration of mental health struggles in the Black community.

Stay Strong: Simple Life Lessons for Teens – Inspirational advice for young people facing life's challenges.

Les Brown

World renowned motivational speaker and author, Les Brown is known for his powerful messages on overcoming obstacles and achieving greatness. His teachings align with the memoir's themes of perseverance and inner strength.

Yahkhahnahn Ammi

Live Your Dreams – A book encouraging readers to overcome fear and pursue their passions.

It's Not Over Until You Win – Personal stories and motivational strategies for success.

You've Got to Be Hungry – A focus on discovering inner drive and resilience.

Mental Health Organizations:

National Alliance on Mental Illness (NAMI) provides resources and support for those struggling with mental health issues. Available at: www.nami.org

The Loveland Foundation offers therapy support for Black women and girls.

Spiritual Centers:

Your Local Mosque, Synagogue, or Church: Emphasizing the importance of spiritual support in personal healing.

Online Communities:

Equal Justice Initiative is a platform dedicated to ending mass incarceration and excessive punishment in the United States. Available at: www.eji.org

Advocacy Organizations:

Fathers' Rights Movement advocates for fathers' rights and equitable treatment in custody cases.

Available at: www.fathersrightsmovement.us

ACLU of Missouri is dedicated to defending civil rights and liberties.

Available at: www.aclu-mo.org

MacArthur Justice Center - Missouri focuses on criminal justice reform and civil rights litigation.

Available at: www.macarthurjustice.org/missouri

Mental Health Resources:

PTSD Information - CCHR St. Louis provides information and support for those dealing with PTSD.

Available at: www.cchrstl.org/ptsd.shtml

The Drugging of Postpartum Depression - CCHR St. Louis offers resources on understanding and addressing postpartum depression.

Mental Health Declaration of Human Rights - CCHR St. Louis advocates for the protection of mental health rights. Available at: www.cchrstl.org/declaration.shtml

Practical Tools

Legal Resources:

LegalZoom provides access to legal documents and services. Available at: www.legalzoom.com

Yahkhahnahn Ammi

Rocket Lawyer Legal Services offers online legal help for various needs. Available at: www.rocketlawyer.com

Missouri Court Forms

Child Support Forgiveness Form

Filing a Motion for Contempt - STL County Courts Family Law Self-Help Center

Missouri Attorney Complaint Form Missouri Attorney General Complaint

Bankruptcy & Credit Counseling: Missouri Bankruptcy Court Forms Debtor Credit Counseling

Credit Repair through Credit Versio, a tool for repairing credit scores. Available at: www.creditversio.com

Pro Bono Legal Services:

Legal Aid Services - Eastern Missouri offers legal help for those in need. Available at: www.lsem.org

Volunteer Lawyers and Accountants for the Arts (VLAA) provides pro bono services for artists. Available at: www.vlaa.org

Missouri Pro Bono Services offers free legal help for low income residents. Available at: www.mobar.org

American Bar Association Free Legal Help provides access to free legal assistance. Available at: www.americanbar.org

Civil Rights & Social Justice:

ACLU of Missouri defends civil liberties and rights within Missouri. Available at: www.aclu-mo.org

MacArthur Justice Center - Missouri is committed to criminal justice reform and civil rights.

Available at: www.macarthurjustice.org/missouri

Catholic Charities Legal Assistance provides legal aid to those in need.

Available at: www.ccstl.org/services/legal-assistance

Newspaper Interviews and Media Features:

"Sandra Bland: White Supremacy and Yahkhahnahn Ammi's Perspective" - Press TV, July 30, 2015.

Available at: www.presstv.ir/Detail/2015/07/30/422495/Sandra-Bland-White-Supremacy-African-Americans-Yahkhahnahn-Ammi

"Harris-Stowe Forum Looks at Ferguson from Varying Black Perspectives" - St. Louis American, August 12, 2015.

Available at: www.stlamerican.com/news/local_news/harris-stowe-forum-looks-at-ferguson-from-varying-black-perspectives/article_7cb33518-3ef8-11e5

"National Guard Deployed to Ferguson" - First Coast News, August 17, 2015

Yahkhahnahn Ammi

"Live or Die Tryin': Yahkhahnahn Fighting Cancel Culture with His Memoir" - Nigerian Eye Newspaper

https://nigerianeyenewspaper.com/2024/08/24/live-or-die-tryin-yahkhahnahn-fighting-cancel-culture-with-his-memoir/

"Live or Die Tryin': Ammi's Gripping Account of Trauma" - Vanguard

https://www.vanguardngr.com/2024/08/live-or-die-tryin-ammis-gripping-account-of-trauma/

"Yahkhahnahn Ammi's 'Live or Die Tryin' Explores Trauma of Falsely Accused" - The Nation

https://thenationonlineng.net/yahkhahnahn-ammis-live-or-die-tryin-explores-trauma-of-falsely-accused/

"Yahkhahnahn Ammi's 'Live or Die Tryin' Explores the Trauma of the Falsely Accused" - Graphic Online

https://www.graphic.com.gh/entertainment/showbiz-news/yahkhahnahn-ammis-live-or-die-tryin-explores-the-trauma-of-the-falsely-accused.html

"4th July: Yahkhahnahn Ammi Raises Questions on US Human Rights System in 'Live or Die Tryin'" - City Scoop NG

https://cityscoopng.com/4th-july-yahkhahnahn-ammi-raises-questions-on-us-human-rights-system-in-live-or-die-tryin/

"A Call to Action: Join the Fight for Justice" - Change.org

https://www.change.org/p/join-the-fight-for-justice-sign-our-petition-to-protect-the-falsely-accused

"As USA Marks 4th July, Ammi is Waking Demons of Recent Past in 'Live or Die Tryin'" - AAMN Africa

https://aamn.africa/as-usa-marks-4thjuly-ammi-is-waking-demons-of-recent-past-in-live-or-die-tryin/

"Sandra Bland: White Supremacy and Yahkhahnahn Ammi's Perspective" - Press TV

https://www.presstv.ir/Detail/2015/07/30/422495/Sandra-Bland-White-Supremacy-African-Americans-Yahkhahnahn-Ammi

"Live or Die Tryin': Yahkhahnahn Ammi Fighting Cancel Culture" - Modern Ghana

https://www.modernghana.com/news/1336364/live-or-die-tryin-yahkhanahn-ammi-fighting-cancer.html

"Live or Die Tryin': Yahkhahnahn Ammi Fighting Cancel Culture with His Memoir" - Arise Afrika

https://ariseafrika.com/2024/08/live-or-die-tryin-yahkhanahn-ammi-fighting-cancel-culture-with-his-memoir.html

"Continue to Fight for Justice, Ammi Charges Activists" - Independent

https://independent.ng/continue-to-fight-for-justice-ammi-charges-activists/

"Lockdown Drills Can Harm Mental Health" - The Scene FP

Yahkhahnahn Ammi

https://thescenefp.com/2024/03/08/lockdown-drills-can-harm-mental-health/

"Harris-Stowe Forum Looks at Ferguson from Varying Black Perspectives" - St. Louis American

https://www.stlamerican.com/news/local_news/harris-stowe-forum-looks-at-ferguson-from-varying-black-perspectives/article_7cb33518-3ef8-11e5-be33-fbb74533ca2b.html

"National Guard Deployed to Ferguson" - First Coast News

https://www.firstcoastnews.com/article/news/nation/national-guard-deployed-to-ferguson/77-271040803

Follow me on Social Media:

Instagram: @drkingya @perriedaniellgibson

Tiktok: @drkingyaspeaks

Podcast:

KSN Network

Kingya Speaks

Live or Die Tryin

Read Speak and Grow Rich

Website Coming Soon:

liveordietryin.com, pdgpublishingcompany.com,
    yahkhahnahnammi.com, perriedaniellgibson.com

Pre-Order Live or Die Tryin' Paperback $25:

https://checkout.square.site/merchant/MLHDM10GJW5QC/chec
    kout/GSFAKJMJ43PVZQQILVQWBBTS

Live Or Die Tryin' Book 1: Unbreakable Spirit

Live Or Die Tryin' Book 2: An Unamerican Dream

Live Or Die Tryin' Book 3: My Journey to Freedom Forgiveness
and Healing

Closing Statement:

As you navigate your own journey, I hope these resources offer the support, insight, and guidance you may need along the way. Life's challenges can feel overwhelming but remember—you are never alone in this. If you have any questions, need further assistance, or simply want to connect, please feel free to reach out to me through my Instagram or social media. Your story is important, and I'm here to help in any way I can. Stay strong and keep moving forward.

Yahkhahnahn Ammi

Essential Reading

African American Fathers' Experiences of Alienation from Their Children due to Texas Family Code

This academic study explores the emotional and legal struggles faced by African American fathers who have been alienated from their children due to certain provisions in the Texas Family Code. It sheds light on systemic issues, cultural biases, and the impact of such alienation on fathers and their families.

Digital Companion:

Online Version: Visit the online companion to this resource page on my YouTube for updated resources and links, providing ongoing support.

QR Code: Scan the QR code in my memoir to sign the online petition page directly.

ABOUT THE AUTHOR

Dr. Yahkhahnahn Ammi, born Perrie (Par-ree) Daniell Gibson, is a dynamic figure with a multifaceted life story.

Born in Brooklyn, Illinois, Ammi's path has been shaped by resilience, advocacy, and an unwavering commitment to justice. His life took him down a path of profound transformation. A former television talk show host, Ammi later earned a doctoral degree in theology, adding to his diverse portfolio as an author, scholar, and advocate.

Yahkhahnahn Ammi is an author, activist, and youth advocate. His journey from prison to earning a Ph.D. has inspired readers around the world. Ammi is passionate about promoting literacy to youth and advocating for social justice. His memoir series, "Live or Die Tryin'," talks about A True Story of a Man Who Survived a 16-Year Prison Sentence and His Journey to Freedom, Forgiveness, and Healing.

He is of Moorish and African descent, with ancestral ties to the Choctaw and Blackfoot tribes, Ammi's heritage is as rich as his life's mission. His advocacy focuses on human rights, anti-domestic violence, and social justice reform. He views police violence, systemic racism, and false accusations of sexual assault as critical public health crises that disproportionately affect Black, Indigenous, and Hispanic communities. These issues, which impact both physical and mental health, fuel Ammi's fight for equality and justice.

At just 14 years old, Ammi was wrongfully incarcerated and sentenced to 16 years in prison for a crime he did not commit. Despite this monumental injustice, he emerged with a deep commitment to fighting racial discrimination and advocating for those who are marginalized. His personal experience with the legal system and his fight to regain custody of his children continue to inspire his life's work.

Ammi's compassion extends into community service. He supports his tutoring program, *Read, Speak, and Grow Rich*, by baking and selling desserts to fund essential supplies for the youth and the homeless. He also ministers to those in need, drawing on his personal experiences with trauma and healing to help others through his podcast, *Unbreakable Spirit*.

Ammi's advocacy is deeply personal. His campaign against domestic violence began at the age of six when he witnessed the abuse of his mother. These early experiences, combined with his more recent struggles, including eight years of homelessness, have only strengthened his resolve. During this time, he graduated high school, earned his PhD, and became certified as an ESL teacher, tutoring K-12 students in reading and English.

As the author of the three-part non-fiction series *Live or Die Tryin'*, Ammi uses his platform to bring awareness to social injustices and inspire change. His podcast, writings, and community work reflect his deep-seated belief in justice, ethics, and equality. He continues to fight for reform, guided by the conviction that perseverance, faith, and hard work can overcome even the most formidable challenges.

Yahkhahnahn Ammi

Dr. Yahkhahnahn Ammi's journey is a powerful testament to resilience, faith, and an unyielding commitment to creating a more just and compassionate world.

BOOK REVIEWS

Dr. Njeri Rahab, Historian, mother, scholar and community activist: https://www.translationale-berlin.net/en/rahab-njeri/

"Yahkhahnahn Ammi's *Live or Die Tryin*, is a raw, deeply personal narrative that serves as both a powerful indictment of systemic injustice and a testament to the resilience of Black men in the face of state-sanctioned trauma. From a social justice perspective, Ammi's story uncovers the insidious ways in which racialized systems of oppression target and dehumanize Black youth, particularly Black men. His wrongful imprisonment as a minor is not just a personal tragedy; it mirrors the collective experience of countless Black boys funneled into the carceral system, denied their humanity, and robbed of their potential.

The memoir serves as a critical analysis of how carceral systems disproportionately target specifically Black men, robbing them of their potential, dignity, and humanity. Ammi's wrongful imprisonment is emblematic of the institutionalized racism that continues to plague societies worldwide. His story highlights how young Black men are often perceived as inherently criminal, a destructive narrative that feeds into the school-to-prison pipeline and perpetuates trauma across generations.

Yet, *Live or Die Tryin'* is more than a recounting of trauma—it is also a powerful testament to resilience, empowerment, and hope. Ammi's story is one of resistance against systemic oppression and a refusal to be defined by the trauma inflicted upon him. His fight for justice, both personal and collective, speaks to the broader struggle for Black liberation and healing. His resilience is not only an act of personal defiance but also a broader call for Black men to reclaim their narratives, resist dehumanization, and transform their trauma into a force for collective healing.

Ammi's memoir also reflects the importance of reclaiming narratives. He writes from a place of vulnerability, providing a voice for the often silenced experiences of Black men and the trauma they endure. His critical perspective invites readers to understand the intersections of race, trauma, and justice while urging action. Ammi's account is a crucial addition to social justice literature, offering not only a critique of systemic racism but also a blueprint for empowerment and collective liberation."

—Dr. Njeri Rahab

* * *

Cookey Iwuoha, CEO, Bibiani Books & Co-founder, All Africa Media Network: http://www.nigerianeyenewspaper.com/

"Live or Die Tryin' " is a powerful testament to self-belief and resilience in the face of human frailty. Yah's unwavering struggle to remain true to himself, despite a life filled with tragedy and betrayal starting at the age of 14, is deeply humbling. What's most remarkable is that, even after enduring such pain, his faith in humanity survives. This is a story that inspires, reminding us that the conscience can remain intact even through the harshest of experiences."

—Cookey Iwuoha

* * *

Kenneth Obiakor, Program Director, Leadership Development
Foundation: https://www.linkedin.com/posts/kenneth-obiakor-u-
6b639b91_sustainability-socialresponsibility-governance-
activity-6867190917036576768-84UM/

"In Live or Die Tryin' 3, Yahkhahnahn Ammi presents a raw and
powerful narrative of transformation, examining the nature of
human resilience and redemption. His memoir critiques the U.S.
prison system, highlighting its role in shaping identities through
suffering while simultaneously pointing to the potential for
personal evolution within oppressive circumstances. Central to
Ammi's story is the power of education, which he portrays as a
means of transcending the limitations imposed by society. The
memoir touches on existential themes of freedom, forgiveness, and
self-actualization, suggesting that inner liberation often precedes
external freedom. Ammi's journey, culminating in a Ph.D., reflects
the philosophical belief that knowledge and self-awareness are key
to overcoming structural injustices and personal despair. This
work challenges readers to reconsider how we view justice,
punishment, and the human capacity for change."

—Kenneth Obiakor

***

Yahkhahnahn Ammi

BOOK BLURB

"Ammi gives a meaningful account of his incarceration for attempted first degree murder at the age of fourteen, his brutal but ultimately transformative experience in the U.S. prison system, and an uphill climb out of poverty after his release. He battles systemic racism and the inequities of the legal system while trying to create a foothold in society in order to raise his children and create a life for himself. An ordained minister, he earned a doctorate in theology after his release from prison and tried to advocate for others upon his release but met obstacle after obstacle including further run-ins with the police, housing insecurity, and hiring discrimination. Still, he bravely tells his story here and offers his troubling experience with the American justice system."

—Kimberly Hallemann, M.A.T. (she/her)

* 9 7 8 0 9 8 3 0 8 1 5 5 5 *